eLearning and Mobile Learning – Concept and Script

Daniela Modlinger

eLearning and Mobile Learning – Concept and Script

Handbook for Media Authors and Project Managers

Springer

Daniela Modlinger
Bamberg, Germany

ISBN 978-3-658-44694-9 ISBN 978-3-658-44695-6 (eBook)
https://doi.org/10.1007/978-3-658-44695-6

Translation from the German language edition: "eLearning und Mobile Learning – Konzept und Drehbuch" by Daniela Modlinger, © Springer Fachmedien Wiesbaden GmbH, ein Teil von Springer Nature 2020. Published by Springer Fachmedien Wiesbaden. All Rights Reserved.

This Springer imprint is published by the registered company Springer Fachmedien Wiesbaden GmbH, part of Springer Nature.
The registered company address is: Abraham-Lincoln-Str. 46, 65189 Wiesbaden, Germany

Paper in this product is recyclable.

Foreword

The pioneering days of eLearning are over. While just a few years ago, the creation of eLearning offerings was often a complex and unpredictable adventure, very different didactic concepts competed with each other, and entire conferences were spent identifying the appropriate portals, servers, and authoring tools, the eLearning landscape has now established itself. There are standards—technological, methodological, and didactic—and this has led to media authors and other creators of learning content now being able to focus on their actual task: to process the new internet-based and multimedia technologies in a learner-oriented, methodologically sensible, and topic-appropriate manner.

The present book describes in detail the process of scriptwriting for eLearning products. It provides its readers with all the necessary knowledge needed to write successful scripts. The reader can sense that this is written by a practitioner who understands her craft. Many tips and literature references complement the very vivid texts and illustrations, and an extensive appendix provides helpful checklists and further information.

Karlsruhe
in August 2004

Prof. Dr. Frank Thissen
Stuttgart Media University

Preface to the 3rd Edition

Almost 15 years have passed since the first edition of this book was published. In a technology-oriented industry like further education through the medium of eLearning, this is a long period of time, which has allowed for numerous changes. These changes are taken into account in the now third edition of "eLearning and Mobile Learning—Concept and Script".

The most comprehensive of the technical innovations in the past decade is associated with the rapid spread of smartphones. With their triumph across all generations and social strata, our everyday behavior and the cultural techniques of reading and writing, indeed of communicating in general, were virtually turned upside down and newly "invented". This reorientation of old cultural techniques naturally also influences our way of learning. From eLearning, which in principle also includes face-to-face training with electronic teaching and learning media, a second method has emerged: mobile learning or "Mobile Learning". Thus, eLearning has arrived where it has always been located, but in fact was not yet, namely learning at any place and at any time. The newly added 6th chapter "Mobile Learning—Concept and Script" deals with this groundbreaking development.

New developments are also emerging in the field of "Artificial Intelligence". "Text to Speech" is a relevant topic for the production of eLearning applications, about which you can learn more in Chap. 3.

Since the year 2018, the General Data Protection Regulation (GDPR) has been in effect across the EU, which is why a note was included in the book for the work as an eLearning author.

Important content, such as scriptwriting for educational videos, has been extensively supplemented. Bundled in one chapter, you will now learn more about fields of application, planning, scriptwriting, and project or production flow. This picks up on the trend of institutions and companies increasingly designing or enriching eLearning via educational videos.

Fundamental contents such as the individual phases in the process of an eLearning project or the job profiles of the participants have not changed. The didactic approaches and perceptual psychological findings have also remained the same. Regardless of how much the technology changes, the content related to scriptwriting itself will also fundamentally remain the same in its structure in the future: the creation of on-screen texts, visualizations, and tasks. Nevertheless, the entire text has been revised and partially restructured. The acquisition of new customers for media authors via social media also continues to be current.

All references, screenshots, examples, explanations for recommended user software related to eLearning, as well as technical terms and all internet addresses (hyperlinks), have been completely revised and updated. The chapter with extensive further information has been fully updated. The information on costs and fee calculations is based on current figures. Many illustrations have received a fresh look. The glossary and table of contents have been expanded, the checklists and tables have been reviewed and updated for their content and values. You can access the checklists online using the code printed in the book.

For reasons of better representation, this book uses the masculine form of language, for example, "he, *the* learner". However, all genders (m/f/d) are always meant in the sense of equal treatment. The shortened form of language is solely for editorial reasons and does not include any evaluation.

Enjoy reading and much success in developing innovative and vibrant eLearning or mobile applications!

Bamberg
in September 2019

Daniela Modlinger

Contents

About the Author

Daniela Modlinger, M.A. has been active in the publishing and multimedia industry since 1990. Since the year 2000, she has been working as a media author and consultant for eLearning applications in institutional and corporate education. Ms. Modlinger also offers in-house training on the topic of "Concept and scriptwriting for eLearning and mobile Learning". Her rich practical experience from numerous projects and her ongoing teaching activity have flowed into this book.

Further information and
Contact: danielamodlinger@gmail.com.

1 How Does the Script Go From Film to eLearning?

Abstract

A good movie needs "…three things: firstly a good script, secondly a good script, and thirdly a good script." At least that's how Alfred Hitchcock sees it, because the script already tells the entire film story. The script details where and when something happens, what the characters in a story say and do, and how the images follow each other.

The significance of a screenplay for a successful film is paramount: it initiates the production process and influences all subsequent steps. The screenplay serves as the central working basis, without which a film cannot succeed.

Similar to a film screenplay, an eLearning screenplay must also detail what happens, when and where, the spoken texts, and the sequence of screen pages. The screenplay forms the foundation for the entire production of an eLearning application, serving as a guide for software developers, graphic artists, animators, and screen designers. It provides project managers with a manual to specifically control and direct the production.

The task of writing screenplays for digital learning media is not widely known outside the eLearning community. When a media author mentions their profession and adds that they write "screenplays", they often receive a puzzled look, usually followed by the question: "Oh, how exciting! Are you in film?" Even within the industry, the professional image is somewhat blurred. Consequently, job titles vary: they range from "media author" to multimedia author, media developer, WBT author, screenplay writer for WBT, eLearning author, developer for interactive learning media, specialist for multimedia authoring, or courseware designer.

This book aims to clarify the professional image of the media author for eLearning by outlining the core areas of their work and distinguishing their role from other professions. The responsibilities of all project members involved in an eLearning production

D. Modlinger, *eLearning and Mobile Learning – Concept and Script*, https://doi.org/10.1007/978-3-658-44695-6_1

are precisely defined, and their range of activities is described in a way that clearly delineates who undertakes which tasks during the project.

Primarily, the following pages are intended to serve as a practical manual for media authors and project managers. The book's core topics are the development and writing of concepts and screenplays for eLearning. It is therefore targeted at all those involved in screenplay development: the clients in a company, the project managers of a multimedia agency, and the media authors. The development of rough and detailed concepts and the writing of screenplays are presented so comprehensively and in detail that even a beginner can make a good start in this profession after reading. For experienced media authors, numerous checklists are available as practical tools in Chap. 9. To begin with the book, a brief overview shows the central phases that characterize an eLearning project.

Who Takes a Stand in the Production of eLearning?

2

Abstract

The chapter provides an overview of the most important phases of eLearning production and the associated requirements in the first part. In the second part, all those project participants who take on significant tasks in creating an eLearning application are introduced.

The production of eLearning is a team effort involving many participants, each with distinct professional profiles. The logical software developer collaborates with the creative, sometimes playful, graphic designer, while the analytically oriented, number-focused insurance specialist works with a media author full of ideas, who often has a humanities background. The challenge for the project team is to harmonise these seemingly opposing natures so that each individual's unique abilities become part of the larger mechanism that continuously interlocks during an eLearning production. This challenge is typically managed by the project manager of a multimedia agency, who ensures that the process runs smoothly.

The diverse mix of skills and competencies among the project participants makes the eLearning world exciting, but also demanding. The project manager must harness the emerging forces to achieve the best results with minimal friction. A detailed project plan assists in monitoring and controlling the production. Creativity and order are not mutually exclusive; on the contrary, as Austrian journalist Georg S. Troller puts it, "Creativity means creating order out of chaos."

This book presents the individual phases of the production process step by step. It focuses on making the creation of a script for eLearning transparent by highlighting the production phases relevant to the script. The following chapter briefly presents the overall process with all phases for clarity. This is followed by an introduction to the

D. Modlinger, *eLearning and Mobile Learning – Concept and Script*,
https://doi.org/10.1007/978-3-658-44695-6_2

"creators" who contribute to the development of learner-friendly, learning objective-oriented, and entertaining eLearning. Readers can expect a small team to guide them through script development with numerous practical tips and hints.

2.1 Overview of Project Phases

In the following, you will learn more about the project phases of an eLearning production. Using a flowchart, you can always see where you are in the production process: The currently discussed box is thickly framed. The project phases relevant to the eLearning author are additionally highlighted in gray.

2.1.1 Project Initialization

The eLearning production process begins with the company's decision to support or even replace internal training and further education with a digital medium. With this decision, the budget for the project is also allocated, and the training objectives to be achieved with the new education concept are determined. This is the so-called "project initialization" (see Fig. 2.1), the starting signal for the project. An employee of this company takes responsibility for the project from start to finish: He is the project manager.

To distinguish him from the project manager of a multimedia agency, he will be referred to as the client in the following. The client creates an exposé that contains goals and conditions, as well as ideas and special problems related to the project. Based on

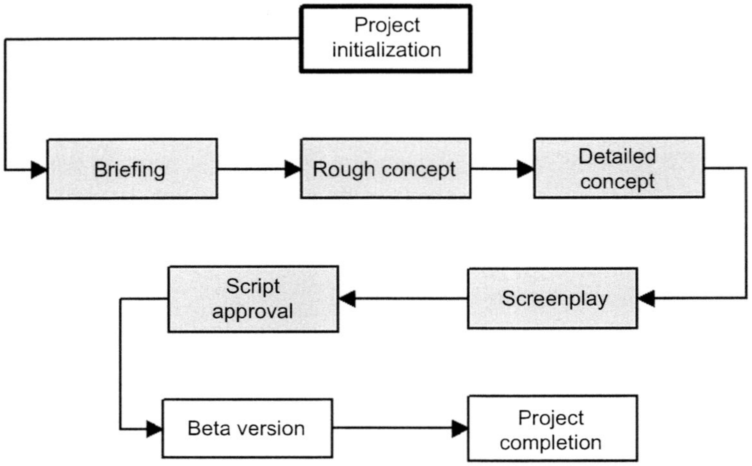

Fig. 2.1 Project phase "Initialization"

this exposé, he selects a suitable multimedia agency for the production of the eLearning application.

Tip!
To ensure the quality of eLearning, there is a reference model titled "PAS 1032" for the planning, development, implementation, and evaluation of the associated processes and offers, available at: http://www.beuth.de.

The choice of producer should be well considered, as this will be a close and important business partner for several months, sometimes even years. For larger productions, it is worth tendering the project and holding a so-called "pitching". Pitching is a competitive presentation to which at least two agencies are invited. They create a first draft of how they would transform the contents of the client's exposé into a learning program. This draft is then presented by the agency team (project and sales manager, art director) at the pitching. As a rule, pre-visualizations are presented, sometimes already animated. This is usually referred to as a "prototype". In this way, the client can get a relatively good picture of the compatibility of his expectations with the offer of the respective agency.

Tip!
For the selection of the producer, see Sect. 9.1.

As soon as the decision for a multimedia agency has been made, the responsible project manager determines which employees of his agency he will involve: media authors, graphic designers, screen designers, software developers, team assistants.

2.1.2 Briefing

The client is currently preparing the first major team meeting with internal and external participants, in the form of a "situation briefing". The client sets preliminary values for the duration and content of the learning application and invites all project participants. This first major meeting discusses technical possibilities, such as learning platforms, and design aspects, such as the integration of an existing corporate design. The multimedia agency assumes an advisory role at this stage. In professional practice, this initial project meeting is also known as a "kick-off meeting". The outcomes of this kick-off meeting are incorporated into a *Style Guide*, which serves as the foundation for the further development of the learning program.

Following the first meeting, which establishes the framework conditions, the actual briefing takes place. This primarily deals with the digital learning content to be created (see Fig. 2.2). For this, the client invites the media author, the project manager of the multimedia agency, and experts from his own company to form the core team of the production. In this meeting, which can last from two hours to two days, the core team coordinates all learning content to be included in the learning program. All members of the core team receive the minutes, which are binding for the next module—the conception.

2.1.3 Conception

The conception begins with the rough concept, which the media author creates based on the briefing minutes and the style guide. Depending on the project's progress, the rough concept can coincide in content with the exposé or the offer of the multimedia agency (for more on the "rough concept", see Sect. 4.1). Only when the rough concept has been approved by the client does the media author write the detailed concept, which then undergoes a first review: It is sent to the client and the experts there. Any corrections that come back are incorporated by the media author. Only when the detailed concept has been approved in writing, the script is developed in the next step (see Fig. 2.3, for more on the "detailed concept", see Sect. 4.2).

2.1.4 Script and Script Approval

Once the media author has finished writing the script, it is forwarded to the agency. The project manager and possibly an editor thoroughly proofread the script. It then goes

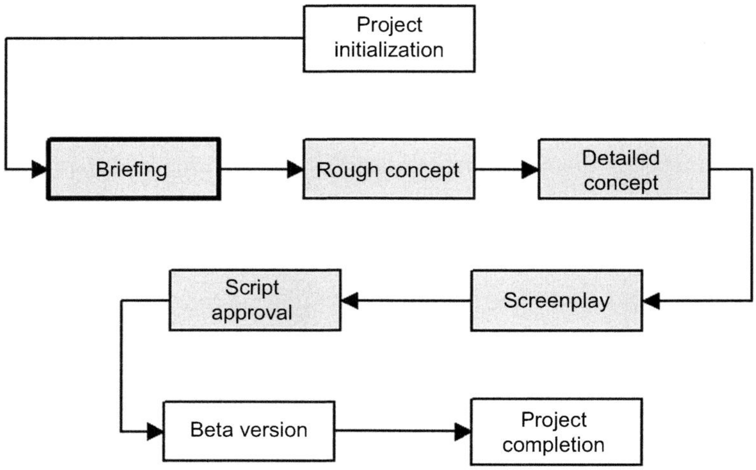

Fig. 2.2 Project phase "Briefing"

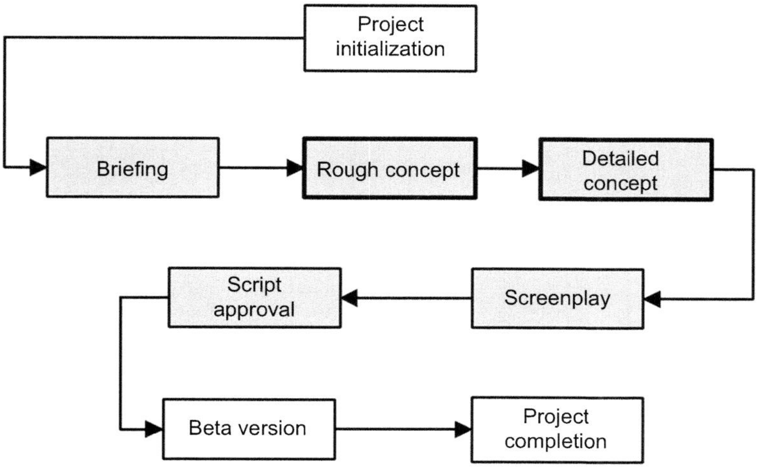

Fig. 2.3 Project phase "Conception"

through its first correction loop back to the media author. Only the script revised by the author and checked again in the agency is sent to the customer. There, the client and the experts check it for contentwise accuracy and whether the author has implemented the content as learning objective-oriented as the briefing and the detailed concept specify. Corrections, which are common at this stage, are sent simultaneously to the agency and to the media author (for more on "script writing", see Chap. 5).

Only when the script has been approved in writing by the client can the technical production of the learning program begin. Depending on the scope of the script, there can be interim approvals. A maximum of 100 pages is expected for a script approval. This saves further correction loops and thus time and money. It also accelerates production, as the agency can already start developing the software, reading in texts, and creating graphics while the media author is writing the next script chapters (see Fig. 2.4).

2.1.5 Beta Version and Project Completion

Once the complete script has been approved and the content technically implemented, the so-called "Beta Version" of the learning program is ready. This version is comparable to a prototype in car manufacturing and now undergoes an intensive testing phase. The project team and deliberately heterogeneously selected learners from the ultimate target group of the learning program act as testers. During this phase, the testers primarily focus on technical errors. However, content changes or new structuring in the Beta Acceptance also occur every now and then (see Fig. 2.5).

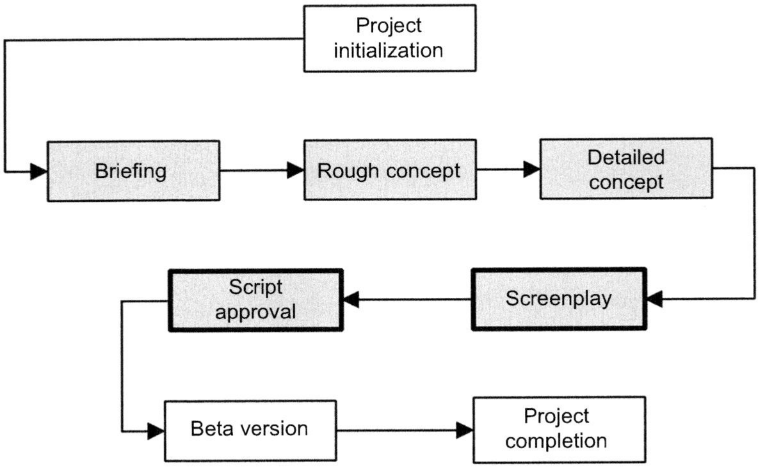

Fig. 2.4 Project phase "Script"

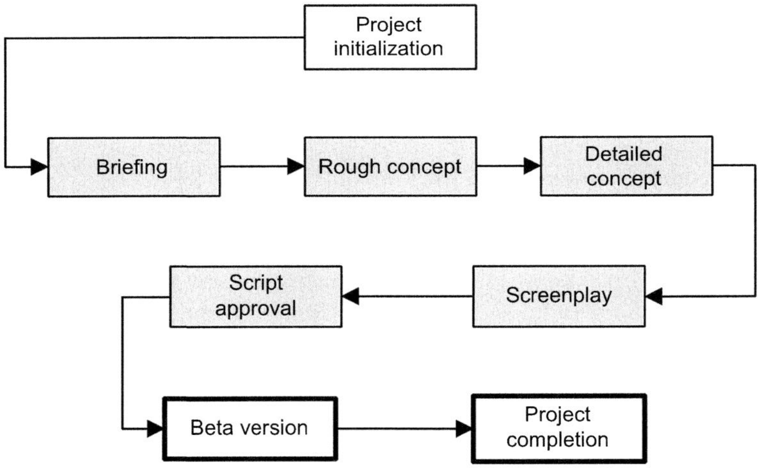

Fig. 2.5 Project phase "Completion"

After the customer has accepted the beta version, the final learning program is produced and delivered or set up in the Intranet/Internet. However, the project is not yet finished. A proper Project Completion includes an evaluative quality assurance of the production process and the transfer performance achieved with the new learning program by the learners.

Tip!
"Checklists for the evaluation of production progress and transfer performance", see Sect. 10.1 and 10.2

2.2 The "Makers" Introduce Themselves

2.2.1 Media Author

The Media Author is usually hired by multimedia agencies as a freelancer for a project. Together with the project team, they develop the concept and, based on this, create the final script for the eLearning production. In addition to their conceptual work, the media author also takes on a consulting role: At the beginning of the production, they are significantly involved in the decision-making process to select the optimal eLearning variant (see Table 4.1). The tasks and functions of the media author are a core topic of this book.

2.2.2 Project Manager of a Multimedia Agency

The Project Manager of an Agency is responsible for the entire handling of the eLearning production. Their main tasks are scheduling, team organization, and the creation of production plans. In addition, they coordinate and monitor the project process, and calculate and control the costs.

> "My business education supports me in the calculation and cost planning." Elke Kast, Senior Project Manager, M.I.T e-Solutions GmbH.

It is not uncommon for them to also develop the rough and detailed concept and only bring a media author into the team for the script. For meetings with the client, the project manager needs a quick grasp and a good general education, as the range of topics for the eLearning applications to be created covers a wide content spectrum. In addition, they must always be up to date with the latest developments in the digital sector and social media. Within the agency, they need comprehensive specialist knowledge about the many areas of multimedia production. Because they lead a team of multimedia specialists in such a way that a high-quality eLearning product is created in the end that meets the requirements and expectations of the customer. For this, a project manager must also bring analytical thinking and high consulting and leadership competence. Ultimately, like a theater director, they must perform the feat of combining creativity and economic thinking. The tasks and functions of the agency's project manager are core topics of this book.

2.2.3 Project Initiator

Before a company can initiate an eLearning project, it must assign an employee as the internal project manager, who will act as the "project initiator". The project initiator outlines the project at the start and conducts an environmental analysis (refer to Sect. 3.1.1 and 4.1.1). Only after this does the project initiator specify and establish the project goals. In the subsequent step, the project initiator defines the task to be pursued with the eLearning application to be developed. Finally, a detailed description of the desired project outcomes is provided, serving as a basis for the later evaluation of the finished product. Other responsibilities of the project initiator include forming the project team, i.e., selecting representatives from the specialist committees of the training content to be conveyed, and choosing the external service provider, i.e., a multimedia agency that produces the eLearning program.

> "Although we are a successful team in eLearning production, it was a leap into the deep end at the beginning. It would have been easier if we had been better prepared for the individual project phases of an eLearning production."—Timo Rettig, eLearning Project Manager, Versicherungskammer Bayern.

2.2.4 Software Developer

The software developer is typically an employee of an agency. They create a prototype according to the layout specifications by the screen designer and the framework data in the rough concept. Their primary activity is the implementation of conceptual specifications and process descriptions into computer programs. For this, the software developer must be proficient in the common programming languages. Standard software is usually not sufficient for larger eLearning productions. In such cases, highly qualified software developers develop custom solutions for the customer.

> "It is always advantageous if I can discuss with the media author what is technically feasible and what is not; and that before he starts the conception. This saves many detours in the hot, always time-critical production phase."—Güner Sakinc, Software Developer at M.I.T e-Solutions GmbH.

2.2.5 Screen Designer

Depending on the size of the multimedia agency, the screen designer is either a freelancer or a permanent employee. They design a learner-friendly screen interface using colours, shapes, fonts, layout, images, sounds, texts, videos, and animations. For this, they bring graphic know-how as well as in-depth knowledge in the navigation of multimedia applications. The screen designer is familiar with the common graphic and visualisation software and knows how to use it effectively. Their core skill is mastering the aesthetic and functional criteria of the individual design elements in order to connect them effectively. It is not uncommon for the same person to perform the activities of the screen designer and the graphic designer (refer to Sect. 2.2.6).

2.2.6 Graphic Designer

Similar to the screen designer, the graphic designer also works on a project basis as a freelancer or in large agencies as an employee. Their task is to develop visualisation concepts. For this, they coordinate with the media author, who visualises the technical content in the form of scribbles and delivers it to the graphic designer ("Scribbles" refer to Sect. 5.2.3.1).

> "Authors make too much work for themselves by creating elaborate graphics. Simple, hand-drawn scribbles are enough for a professional graphic designer; this saves time and everyone focuses on what they do best."—Christian Ertl, bildersprache.

For creating the required graphics, the graphic designer uses various tools, such as Photoshop, Painter, Illustrator, PowerPoint, as well as HTML or XML tools. In addition to their creative activity, they actively communicate with the media author, the software developer, and the screen designer to ensure high quality and timely completion of the material. In smaller agencies, the function of the graphic designer can coincide with that of the screen designer (refer to Sect. 2.2.5).

2.2.7 Animator

For modern, interactive learning media, the animator is very important. They evaluate rough and detailed concepts as well as scripts to create sound montages and image effects for computer-capable video films or animations. Possible applications are lead characters or trailers for eLearning applications as well as simulations to illustrate complicated learning content (refer to Sect. 5.3.3, 5.2.2.5 and 5.4.1.7).

References

PAS 1032-1, -2 (2004). Aus- und Weiterbildung unter besonderer Berücksichtigung von e-Learning – Teil 1: Referenzmodell für Qualitätsmanagement und Qualitätssicherung – Planung, Entwicklung, Durchführung und Evaluation von Bildungsprozessen und Bildungsangeboten Teil 2: Didaktisches Objektmodell; Modellierung und Beschreibung didaktischer Szenarien, siehe: http://www.beuth.de.

Briefing: What Content should Go into the Script? 3

Abstract

Chapter 3 on the topic of "Briefing" focuses on the teamwork of an eLearning production. The requirements that the participants of a briefing or script approval session are confronted with are explained in detail. Another focus is the consultation of the client regarding the selection of the eLearning variant suitable for his company as well as regarding the didactically sensible implementation of learning content. The chapter is enriched with many practical tips, examples for cost calculation, and forms for secure project management.

The briefing is an informational meeting from which all participants depart with a work order.

The briefing serves as the pivot point for subsequent script creation, as it determines the content that the learner will later engage with in the eLearning application. Essentially, the briefing is the craft knowledge; it facilitates the exchange of information between project participants and solidifies the task. It should provide a platform for the client to communicate their goals and learning content. The outcome of the briefing is a precise task description and assignment for each team member. Therefore, the binding nature of the statements is of crucial importance. The client should take a clear position and ideally maintain this throughout the project. This refers, for example, to the responsibilities in the project: The project leaders of the client should have decision-making authority. For a successful briefing, the client brings their profound expertise and the contractor,

D. Modlinger, *eLearning and Mobile Learning – Concept and Script*,
https://doi.org/10.1007/978-3-658-44695-6_3

i.e., the agency, brings good market and implementation knowledge. Loyalty and trust are added to this, both within the respective company and among each other in the project team. Changes of direction during the project (change of responsibilities, change of the chosen eLearning variant or similar) should be avoided as much as possible, as they are usually associated with very high effort.

No briefing takes place without an agenda. It is therefore important that all participants are well prepared, because the briefing, just like the multimedia production as a whole, is teamwork. The media author and the employees of the multimedia agency have equally advisory functions. At the end of this chapter, you will learn how script acceptance meetings are conducted. These are assigned to the briefing, as in large projects the partial acceptance of a script and the further steering of briefing content can coincide.

3.1 Preparations

Thorough preparation for the briefing by all participants saves time and thus money. Two core thoughts guide the preparation: *learning objectives* and the *focus on the essentials.* Especially the client should be aware at this point that they must get intensively involved in the preparation phase in order to receive a high-quality eLearning program in the end. The preparation phase is characterized by extensive analyses, the results of which are presented in the briefing. The briefing therefore includes not only the date of the meeting itself, but especially the preparation and follow-up. This has a corresponding effect on the author's proposal creation, who must include the preparation and follow-up times in his daily fee (see Sect. 7.1.1).

3.1.1 The Client Prepares

The most important actor in the preparation phase is the client. Even before the briefing, they hold an internal decision conference in which they decide to produce a learning program. A project leader (or several) is appointed and the budget is set. The project leader named in the decision conference takes all the information from the meeting. This forms the basis of their preparation for the briefing, which is held with the agency that emerged from a pitching. The conference also serves to set the target of the learning project and to identify the people who are to be trained or further educated with the learning program, i.e., to define the target group. Before the meeting as a project team and the project start, numerous pieces of information must be collected and bundled to prevent misinvestments and delays in the later course of the project. In addition to presenting the results from the following preparation steps, the client should create a brief presentation of the company for all project participants. Important here are information about the company's own positioning in the market, the communication channels to the outside and overarching corporate strategies. Attached to the brief presentation is a list of project members from the client's own company with name, function and contact details. The briefing itself is then the best time for the client to express special design wishes, because the production has not yet started and all ideas, peculiarities and wishes can be given appropriate space here.

3.1.1.1 Identifying the Initial Situation and Problem

The first step in preparation is to identify the initial situation. The client explains why they have chosen to produce an interactive learning program. What is the problem? What goal should the eLearning application pursue?

To identify this problem, the client must conduct an internal **problem analysis** that answers the following questions:

- What problem is to be solved with eLearning?
- Is it truly a problem based on educational deficits?

Only with an accurate definition of the problem can we ensure that the further training measure will be the right method for solving it. Simultaneously, the definition of the problem to be solved already indicates the target of the learning application, as it will be developed later (see Sects. 4.1.1.4 and 3.2.3). The identification of educational deficits already contains hints for the target group to be defined later (see Sect. 4.1.1.3).

The counter-question as a test for a logical definition of the problem is:

- Or is it a problem in technology, management, or similar?

If the counter-test reveals that the problem points to technical inadequacies or difficulties in management, then a further training measure and an associated eLearning application are misplaced.

3.1.1.2 Creating a Requirement Profile and Target Objective

The requirement profile should indicate which target groups need to build competencies and in which field a specific educational and training need via eLearning exists, for example …

- … for specific tasks?
- … related to financial consequences, occupational safety, smooth work processes?
- … as part of a company-wide training measure to be introduced?
- … as a data provider for later (comprehensive) training measures?

To answer these questions, questionnaires can be used, or personal or telephone interviews can be conducted. An online survey is also an option. Depending on the result of

Table 3.1 Categories of Needs Analysis

Normative Need	The educational goal is to achieve a national or international qualification standard in the target group.
Subjective Need	There is a desire for further education on the part of the employees; the subjective need is debatable.
Demonstrated Need	Employees show strong interest in seminars or similar; indicators: for example, waiting lists or pre-orders for specialist books.
Future Need	For example, there is a future need for further training for the introduction of new software (high analysis effort).
Event-oriented Need	Employees are not adequately prepared for crises or critical events; trigger: often a critical incident in the company.

the problem analysis, a sample of the target group of the learning program or managers should be surveyed.

Helpful for creating the requirement profile based on questionnaires or similar is the targeted narrowing down of the type and manner of the training need in the company. According to Niegemann et al. (2008), various need categories can be distinguished for this purpose, as listed in Table 3.1.

Ideally, the internal survey using the categories from Table 3.1 provides further information on the required learning objectives and the manner and circumstances in which the knowledge to be acquired should be applied. From the requirement profile, the target objective can now be formulated (for the formulation of learning objectives, see Sect. 4.1.1.4).

3.1.1.3 Describing the Target Group

Ideally, the client should conduct a target group analysis *before* the briefing, as described in Sect. 4.1.1.4. However, in many projects, this analysis is only conducted after the first briefing and with the support of the commissioned multimedia agency.

3.1.1.4 Analyzing and Bundling Learning Content

Narrowing down and bundling the teaching material to be conveyed requires a careful content analysis. A common pitfall is to collect existing content material from various sources and then try to filter out the most important content. This approach is seldom successful, as the preparation of the learning material must adapt to the entire content offer in this way. Therefore, the question is not "Which existing learning material do we use?", but rather a meaningful content analysis answers the following questions:

- What *knowledge level* do the learners have?
- Which *skills* and what *knowledge* do we aim to build *and how*?
- Which *contents* do we aim to convey *and how*?
- Which *materials* are *available* for this?

The materials collected in this way provide the basic learning content that should be prepared interactively. In multimedia jargon, they are therefore also referred to as "basal-text".

3.1.1.5 Compiling Resources

The compilation of resources can only provide a rough guideline in the briefing phase, as the duration, costs, technical requirements, and personnel effort of the production can only be concretized in the conception phase. The most important resource information for the briefing is shown in Table 3.2.

Tip!
Checklist "Preparation for the briefing by the client", see Sect. 10.5.

Table 3.2 Resource analysis of the client for the briefing

Company Team Members	For example, project manager, technical manager, specialist advisor, project assistant.
Company's Deadline Specifications	For example, definitive end or start date, periods with limited personnel resources.
Technical Equipment	For example, internet access and multimedia equipment at the learning workplaces; to be worked out in detail only at the level of the rough concept, see Sect. 4.1.
Place of Use	Name the learning location of the target group, for example at home, in the company, on the move/mobile, in the training center or mobile on the move. Name whether the use should be local, regional, national or international.
Budget	Pay attention to a coherent cost-benefit calculation, and have the agency explain the calculation bases in the briefing. Do not hesitate to ask about the underlying daily rates (see Sect. 3.3.6).
Available Material	**Examples of sources of didactic material:** • Existing visual material, possibly digital and free of license fees, • Previous training media (for example videos, PowerPoint presentations, textbooks and booklets, slide sets etc.), • Existing advertising material (for example print advertising) that can be incorporated into the content preparation, • Advertising jingles that can be integrated into the dubbing, • TV spots, • Information films or animations on the company's web presence, • Advertising with opinion leaders (testimonials), • Online marketing via social media, for example with Instagram stories and corresponding influencers.

3.1.2 Preparation by the Agency Project Manager

The preparation of the agency project manager for a briefing begins with the creation of the proposal, even before the order has been placed. The project manager has already familiarised himself with the company, as well as the content and learning objectives of the learning program to be created. Like the author, he understands the client's industry, the job titles and names of the project members, the hierarchies, and, if possible, responsibilities.

> **Tip!**
> Refer to the "Fact Sheet Client" checklist in Sect. 10.3.

A crucial part of the project manager's preparation is to create a rough project plan even before the briefing. Software programs, such as Microsoft Project, assist in this, as shown in Fig. 3.1. The project management software should have at least the following functions: time and resource planning, cost calculation, data exchange with other programs, plan creation with networked bar charts, and internet capability for virtual collaboration.

The scheduling is based on an estimate of the duration of the respective project phases, as described in Sect. 3.3.5. In general, buffer times should be planned for the delivery dates of individual project steps. The anticipated scheduling facilitates a rapid agreement on dates in the briefing and allows the project to start immediately. The media author can start writing the script immediately after the meeting and does not have to wait until further dates are announced by round mail to all meeting participants.

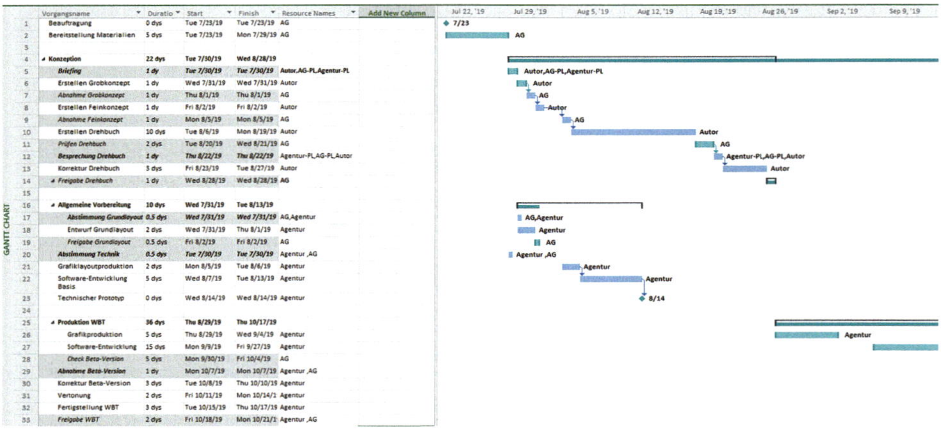

Fig. 3.1 Networked bar chart, created in Microsoft Project

> "I always plan a little buffer for the authors as well. This is the only way I can still meet the final deadline in case of delays." Elke Kast, Senior Project Manager, M.I.T e-Solutions GmbH.

Setting the cost framework is as important as scheduling. The project manager of an agency must prepare well here in order to be able to provide the customer with exact prices as well as exact dates at the end of the briefing. For clear statements about the costs, the project manager should compile a list that lists all possible technical implementations with advantages and disadvantages and assigns the respective costs.

Cost calculation also includes compiling an overview of correction costs. Here too, the project manager should be able to quote fixed prices, if this has not already been done in advance during the offer preparation. The specific details about correction costs are so important because they usually become a hotly debated agenda item again during the hot correction phase. This in turn delays the project unnecessarily and incurs further costs. One can say: The clearer the statements about costs, the smoother and thus more successful the project process (see Sect. 3.3.6).

Just like with the dates, buffers should also be planned for the cost calculation. This prevents a project manager from exceeding the cost frame in case of unforeseen work. For example, it is an unwritten law in the business that the software developer always uses exactly the budget he has.

Part of a project manager's preparation also includes developing ideas about how the eLearning to be created is to be technically implemented and coordinating this within his agency with graphics, screen design and especially software development. He brings an overview to the briefing of what is technically feasible and recommended. Ideally, a small prototype has already been developed that can then be presented. A briefing is expensive, all attendees use their paid working time for this. Therefore, it is all the more important that the project manager checks the technology needed for the presentation the day before or at least a few hours before it starts, in the rooms where the briefing will take place and with exactly the devices that are to be used.

It would be optimal if the project manager had a conversation with the media author the day before the briefing about how they both want to design the briefing together and how they want to distribute the roles among themselves. But in practice, there is usually no time for this. At the end of his preparations, the project manager sets up the agenda. That is, he writes down with time units and content information how the briefing appointment should proceed. Guiding questions could be:

- Which discussion points should be dealt with in which order?
- Which techniques and media will be used?
- Which presentation form is suitable?
- How much time is needed per agenda item?

The agenda is a kind of navigator that guides the project manager safely through the briefing, while he must also be aware that flexible deviations are sometimes necessary.

"If despite all preparation something doesn't work out, an experienced project manager must be able to improvise well." Elke Kast, Senior Project Manager M.I.T e-Solutions GmbH.

3.1.3 Preparation by the Media Author

The media author should allocate sufficient time to prepare for the briefing. He may encounter various initial situations: On one hand, he may know nothing about the learning program to be created. However, he usually receives preliminary information from the agency and can enter the briefing well equipped with concrete proposals.

3.1.3.1 Gathering Information about the Client

The first step is to research the commissioning company on the internet. The company's online presence provides information about its market position and corporate philosophy. These impressions must later be incorporated into the script when creating the navigation and specification sheet, and developing the graphic implementation. The website is also a good place to evaluate existing image material and convert it into a mini concept for the planned learning application.

Example

Suppose your client is the breakfast cereal specialist "mymuesli". A visit to the website reveals a colourful design with clear colours and structures. The product focus is also noticeable. The user mode is highly interactive: Upon entering the site, the customer is encouraged to mix their muesli with a click of a mouse via a central button. Each mixed muesli receives direct feedback, for example on nutritional values and taste, as well as further information, such as "lactose-free". A learning program for this customer should ideally be modular, just like the muesli ingredients, and allow the learner to put together their own "learning mix". It is also advisable to always give direct feedback on tasks for knowledge assurance. This should be of a differentiating nature, i.e., provide information on what the correct answer is and which modules the learner could still work on. The metaphor "healthy eating" can be incorporated into the learning modules. Here, for example, a "learning menu" is offered, and for "dessert" there are tests or competitions. The video-based stories about the company, product quality, etc. should also definitely be included.

A completely different orientation is presented by the internet presence of the German Volks- and Raiffeisenbanks. The company prefers a strongly personalised approach and is regionally located. The central message is: The focus is on people, and that locally. This is due to the specific business form of the VR banks as cooperative banks, which also allows every citizen to become a "shareholder" of the bank through membership. Personalisation also includes personal virtual contact via live chat. The product itself—"money"—takes a back seat here. Accordingly, a learning program for this customer would require strongly personalised learning elements, including a tutor with a real photo and the possibility to chat with them (possibly asynchronously). Networking the learners in an online community is also recommended. Social media could be used for this, for example.

In both examples, the customer will appreciate the concept ideas, as they see their corporate philosophy reflected in them. ◀

In addition to the web presence, the daily and trade press also provide insights into the client's business. For example, it can be determined whether the company intends to expand internationally in the near future. Then the author can already point out at the briefing that the content should be prepared in such a way that it will also be relevant for the new employees in the neighbouring country. The client will recognise their advantage of future cost savings in this and be grateful for the foresight. And for the agency and the author, this builds part of the foundation that is to serve a long-term cooperation.

Reading Tip!
Gabriele Fietz et al.: "eLearning for International Markets", Bertelsmann.

In addition, the author should be familiar with the client's industry and be well informed about job titles, hierarchies, responsibilities, and names of those present.

Tip!
Checklist "Fact Sheet Client", see Sect. 10.3.

3.1.3.2 Knowing and Communicating Analysis Methods

In addition to researching the company, the media author has another opportunity to professionally prepare for the briefing: He familiarises himself with the analyses that are part of the client's preparation (see Sect. 3.1.1). By asking specific questions related to the individual analysis elements, he can gain important information from the briefing and contribute to a successful process. As a supplement, the media author can prepare a slightly shorter list of questions that he can take to the briefing. If the client cannot immediately answer the questions, the author should always have copies of the questionnaire available to hand out for processing. This questionnaire later generates the didactic concept (see Sect. 3.3.1).

Tip!
Checklist "Questionnaire for the Client" and "Preparation for the Briefing by the Client", see Sect. 10.4 and 10.5.

3.1.3.3 Compiling Suggestions for the Rough Concept

If the media author already has information about the content to be implemented as eLearning, he can develop concrete suggestions for the rough concept in advance of the briefing. In addition to the analysis results of the client (see Sect. 3.1.1), the following guiding questions supports him:

- Which didactic concept is recommended (see Sect. 3.3.1)?
- Is a leading figure needed (see Sect. 5.2.2.5)?
- What tonality is advisable if the target group is already known (see Sect. 5.2.2.3)?
- Which types of tasks are best suited for securing learning success (see Sect. 5.4)?
- Which learning success control should be used (see Sect. 5.4.2)?
- Should illustrations be implemented artistically, photographically, cinematically or as an animation (see Sect. 5.3)?
- Which user guidance is suitable (see Sect. 4.1.1.7)?

3.1.3.4 Keeping Expertise Up to Date

Since questions will also come from the client and the agency project management to the media author, it is advisable to update one's own expertise before a briefing. Sources of information are trade journals, specialist portals on the Internet and the daily press (for further information, see Sect. 9.1).

3.1.3.5 Defining Capacities

An important preparatory step for the media author is to define their capacities:

- What times can they block for the upcoming project?
- How much time will they need to create a screen page?
- How many days will scriptwriting take in total (taking into account buffer times for vacation, illness and project delays)?

Although the agency's project management takes over a large part of the time planning, the author should also keep an overview when the schedule is discussed at the end of the briefing. This gives the client the assurance that the author can guarantee delivery reliability and that the project will proceed as planned.

3.2 The Briefing is Teamwork

> "eLearning projects are always time-critical, so there is hardly any time for buffers. Therefore, smooth teamwork is so important." Elke Kast, Senior Project Manager M.I.T e-Solutions GmbH.

The briefing is teamwork. The fact that the author and the representatives of the agency come to the customer and simply write down or file away what learning content is provided is not the purpose of a briefing. Rather, all participants must actively contribute to the briefing through solid preparation and high vigilance. It is better to ask one question too many than to signal understanding where there is none, just to pretend know-how. This insight was already followed by the philosopher and researcher Francis Bacon 400 years ago: "Being able to ask clever questions is half the wisdom." Therefore, one should think carefully about one's questions, but then not hesitate to ask them. The agencies and media authors are often not experts in the discussed field and handle eLearning projects for learning content for companies in various industries. Consequently, there is always a lot to question, also because each company designs its training and further education in a very individual way. But it is precisely the "non-expert" who is important for eLearning production, because their unobstructed view from the outside allows a didactically "clean" implementation, which is often not possible for experts.

The course of a briefing is usually according to the agenda prepared by the agency's project manager (see Sect. 3.1.2). It starts with the client explaining their concerns regarding the new learning program. This is followed by the agency's project manager presenting the possibilities of technical implementation, ideally using the demonstration of a small prototype. This is followed by the media author's advice on what kind of learning program they imagine with the information available so far.

Tip!
Refer to the checklist "Teamwork in the Briefing" in Sect. 10.6.

3.2.1 The Role of the Media Author in the Team

The media author, following thorough preparation, arrives well-equipped to the team. His contribution increases steadily with the duration of the briefing. Initially, he remains quiet, listens attentively, and mentally connects the client's knowledge and requirements with his potential suggestions, which he will present later. Once the client has shared his concerns, the project manager of the multimedia agency will intervene and provide suggestions for technical feasibility, including the most suitable learning platform and concept. He also provides a cost estimate. The media author continues to hold back, even if he has a constructive counterproposal for the technical implementation in mind. It is crucial that the author views himself as part of the agency team. This involves loyalty; he should not undermine the project manager to demonstrate superior knowledge. When he eventually presents a counterproposal in the final third of the briefing, he should proceed as follows: "I fully support the project manager's proposal. However, we had previously discussed an alternative, namely …, which would be very beneficial for this application because the problem orientation allows more identification opportunities for the learner, who is in sales every day." The media author brings technical and didactic competence to the briefing. He must also be familiar with the agency's offer concept and be prepared to present it if necessary. Ideally, the project manager and author should coordinate their preparations in advance to avoid surprises during the briefing. The process described above may not always be feasible due to time constraints. Sometimes, the author may have a sudden insight during the briefing that did not occur during the preparations. Regardless, he should share his valuable idea and maintain a loyal form of communication. Towards the end of the briefing, the media author presents his ideas for the didactic implementation of the content and seeks the client's approval. This approval forms the basis for the conception.

A significant task for the media author in the team is to guide the client through a consistent delineation of the learning content. Often, especially experts, want to include every minor detail. However, this affects the didactic implementation and ultimately the learner, who will later engage with the topic on the screen. The abundance of content can overwhelm him. The author should therefore be familiar with content analysis (see Sect. 3.1.1 and 4.1) and also be practiced and confident in editing. Editorial experience is certainly beneficial, as it teaches him to evaluate content and condense it to essential information daily. The media author may be overly zealous when editing, as the client's experts will fiercely defend every sentence and content detail. If the author visualizes this as a game, it helps him not to take these often heated discussions personally and to always focus on the matter, resulting in a good eLearning program. The media author should be particularly vigilant when numbers and statistics are presented for inclusion in the learning program. It is important to ascertain their importance in advance, as numbers and statistics are prone to change and can be costly in the long run. If they are not crucial (for example, product-related specifications), they should be ruthlessly edited. For instance, trends and developments can be generally described as "growing" or "falling". In general, the media author should possess high social competence, as he needs to understand, question, and often even sense wishes, then link them with his own expertise. Ideally, he guides the client to the point where he believes that the ideas and decisions for the optimal learning program originate from him.

Tip!
Ensure effective conversation management in the briefing using the checklist "Types of questions and techniques", see Sect. 10.7.

It is crucial that the media author provides concrete suggestions for the conception during the briefing. He should have prepared these in advance based on the guiding questions, as listed in the "Preparation of the client for the briefing" (see Sect. 3.1.1).

Tip!
As a media author, you will be well prepared for the briefing if you are familiar with the checklist "Preparation for the briefing by the client", see Sect. 10.5.

3.2.2 The Role of a Project Manager in a Multimedia Agency Team

In many respects, the project manager of a multimedia agency assumes the role of a moderator within the briefing team. He forms the interface between the production team (software development, graphics, author) on one side and the client on the other. Initially, the project manager should clarify the goal of the briefing and guide the meeting based on its agenda (see Sect. 3.1.2). Like the author, the project manager first listens to the client's ideas and their opinion on what content should be prepared for multimedia. This is followed by a brief discussion on how the agency envisions the implementation of the learning content from a technical perspective:

- Should it be a pure *Web Based Training* or rather a *Blended Learning* approach, for example, because the salespeople need to improve their sales behaviour in addition to pure knowledge building?
- Should a learning platform be used as a basis, because the company wants to continuously expand its training and further education with eLearning?
- Is it necessary to store learning status?

If these questions have already been addressed before the briefing, this is an opportunity to revisit these issues. For other, possibly newly added team members, these are important facts. The project manager of a multimedia agency should also ensure that the *tonality* is clarified in the briefing, as he must start selecting the speaker early. In all that the media author contributes, the project manager of a multimedia agency should behave loyally, even if it was not discussed beforehand. The author contributes his expertise and wants to use his knowledge together with the agency for the benefit of the client. Even if a suggestion from the author is not technically or financially feasible, it is advisable to use the suggestion as a basis for discussion, rather than dismissing it with a "cannot be done". It is important to the client that the agency and author appear as *one* team and stand loyally side by side. This has a positive effect on the entire project, especially in phases when negotiations with the customer become demanding or tension clouds the project progress. Due to his careful preparation, the project manager is able to provide accurate information about prices and deadlines (see Sect. 3.1.2). This leads to a clear conclusion of the briefing. All participants know what they have to do, by when, and when the next meeting will take place.

Tip!
As a project manager of an agency, you must inquire with the client up to the person responsible for the budget. You should not rely on vague promises, but *always insist on written commitments.*

During the briefing, the project manager takes extensive notes, ideally directly into a laptop. He documents the task distributions with deadlines and must subsequently ensure through queries that the team members also consider the deadlines to be realistic. This protocol is sent to all participants after the briefing. It serves a significant function: as soon as it is "approved" (i.e., marked with "ok") by the client, it serves as the basis for the concept together with the offer.

Tip!
Remind team members of the binding nature of the protocol and the deadlines listed in it.

A lot of time is saved by creating forms, into which the contents only need to be entered. Variants can be created here for each customer and each type of project. An example of a simple form protocol, created using a Word table, is shown in Fig. 3.2.

Project	WBT Sales training	Project no.	3NSWBTV01	Page 1 from 1	
Order donor	Insurance "Number safe"	Creator	Project Manager, MM2 Agency	Date	30.07.2019

Protocol:
WBT - Training for new health insurance tariff

MM2 AGENCY FOR NEW MEDIA

Participant / Name	Abbreviation	involved in function / from page
Bernd Bauer	BB	"Nummer Sicher", project management
Franka Förster	FF	"Nummer Sicher", project management
Mara Müller	MM	MM2" agency, project management
Paula Peters	PP	Agency "MM2", screenwriter
Stefan Siebert	SS	"Nummer Sicher", health insurance consultant

Topics

No.	Description / Comment / Info	To do
1	**WBT - Training for new health insurance tariff** Due to the legal changes, "Nummer Sicher" is introducing a new health insurance tariff. The sales representatives must be trained accordingly.	
2	Mr. Bauer presents the learning objective: "The sales representatives should know the new tariff well so that they can actively sell it." He distributes a fact sheet with the most important key data.	Bauer mails advertising material on the new tariff to Peters
3	Ms. Förster describes the target group of sales representatives according to company affiliation, level of education, gender and age group.	Förster emails further details to Peters
4	Ms. Müller presents the prototype for the technical implementation of the WBT, the team agrees on this version, but the colors should still be adapted to the corporate identity of the company.	Bauer emails the pdf file of the CI manual buchs to Müller
5	In the prototype, learners are addressed as "you"; this should be changed to "you" for a target group that is no longer quite young.	Peters observes reality in the script

Fig. 3.2 Example of a briefing protocol, created with Microsoft Word

Project order/project no.		
Client		
Date		
Duration	(from)	(to)
Project title		
Project outline		
Indicative objective of the project		
Project manager		

Schedule				
Milestone	Task(s)	Responsible	Duration (from...to)	Employee days

Schedule			
	Costs/EUR	Share in Total budget/%	Employee days
Internal employees			
External employees			
Material costs			
Investments			

Fig. 3.3 Example of a project order, created in Microsoft Word

For a detailed protocol with concrete resolutions and a schedule, the form of a *project order,* as shown in Fig. 3.3, serves as an alternative. However, this form is unnecessary if a project plan with time, dates, costs, and resources was created parallel to the protocol.

Reading Tip!

For tools of project management and project manager tasks, refer to: *Tomas Bohinc:* "Basics of Project Management", Gabal and *Gerold Patzak & Günter Rattay:* "Project Management", Linde.

3.2.3 The Role of the Client in the Team

The primary task of the client in the briefing team is to organise the event. Typically, the briefing takes place at the client's premises. Therefore, the client is responsible for booking the meeting room and ensuring that the necessary technology, such as a projector or an interactive whiteboard for the agency's presentation, is available.

During the briefing, the client often speaks extensively at the beginning, discussing their ideas that have been prepared in advance (see Sect. 3.1.1). This written preparation helps the client to remain concise in their verbal explanation. The client should identify which contents and learning objectives are particularly important for the emerging learning module during the briefing. They should reiterate their concerns and goals, emphasising their importance. Both the agency and the media author often find it challenging to balance the abundance of content and information when they return to their workplace after a one to two-day briefing.

Therefore, it is beneficial to develop a *guiding objective* and to prominently display it on each new flipchart sheet and use it as a header for the protocol. For instance, a guiding objective could be: "The field staff achieve a sales increase of 20 percent with the new tariff compared to the previous year." This signals to the media author that he must prepare the product specifications in a *sales-oriented* manner and avoid getting lost in pure information transfer. For such a guiding objective, they will also prepare learning content to promote sales and negotiation skills and link the product information accordingly. However, the media author will take a different approach if the client provides a guiding objective such as: "The field staff *pass the exam,* which entitles them to sell the new tariff." This objective is about implementing the examination catalogue in such a way that all possible questions in the examination can be answered one hundred percent. The resulting learning module will be *more information-heavy* than the one described before. Therefore, it is worthwhile to invest sufficient time in the preparation to develop a suitable guiding objective, which is then presented to the team members in the briefing. If everyone knows the direction, it is easier to work together.

In addition to presenting their own ideas, the client can use the briefing to clarify questions that have arisen during the preparation. Questions should also be asked about the structures within the agency, for example, who is responsible for which tasks, their contact details, etc. Often, the client is unclear about the role of an animator or the tools a software developer uses. A comprehensive understanding of the processes and tasks in the company of the respective team partner is important for smooth cooperation.

> "In the briefing, it is important to clarify responsibilities, i.e. to define the respective roles on the part of the agency's project management, the media author and in our company."—Georg Engelhard, eLearning Project Manager, Versicherungskammer Bayern.

Alongside the protocol, which is created by the project manager of the agency, the client should also take notes. The written word signals commitment and is often used as proof.

It is advisable to review both transcripts at the end of the briefing and coordinate them. This results in a binding protocol version, which is issued as a work order to all team members or made accessible in a jointly used cloud.

3.3 Aspects of Consultation

In addition to accurately capturing the learning content (see Sect. 3.1.1 and Chap. 4), which the client wants to implement as eLearning, the consultation is one of the main tasks of the media author and the project manager of the multimedia agency. If the client has not yet developed a guiding objective for the upcoming eLearning production, such an objective can be developed together at the beginning of the briefing. It prevents many potential problems if it is ensured right at the beginning of the team work that the client knows their direction. A possible technique for this is mind mapping, as developed by Tony Buzan (2013). It can be drawn by hand on the flipchart or created with a software and projected onto the wall with a projector. In Fig. 3.4, you can see an example of a mind map created with the software "MindManager". The advantage of a mind mapping session in plenary is that each team member can contribute their ideas. The guiding objectives of the learning application are visually in front of the eyes, so that the key terms only need to be underlined and formulated as a guiding objective. The creative part is exceptionally taken over by the client and not the media author or project manager, who should rather support and steer the mind mapping.

> **Tip!**
> Recommended mind map software: "MindManager" (http://www.mindjet.com/de) and "MindView" (http://www.matchware.com/de).

Optimal advice to the client necessitates knowledge of the most significant didactic approaches and eLearning formats. Additionally, one should be capable of arguing convincingly to persuade the boss or sceptical decision-makers about the development of an

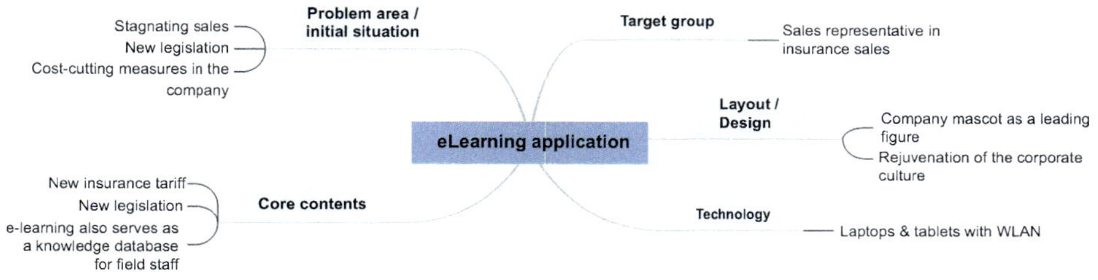

Fig. 3.4 Mind map for defining a guiding objective, created with the software MindManager

eLearning application. Last but not least, the client requires information and practical advice on how to maintain long-term motivation in their target group.

3.3.1 Didactic Approach

Didactics is the art of teaching, which electronic teaching media must also adhere to. The producers of an eLearning application can employ various approaches for this purpose and partly combine them. The choice of the appropriate didactic approach depends on the target group and the learning objectives that are to be achieved with the planned teaching medium. Broadly, the didactic approaches can be divided as follows:

- *Approach ofexternal control:* A tutor or a fixed navigation guides through the learning program. This approach is suitable for learning processes that should convey rather objective knowledge or orientation knowledge. Additionally, external control is recommended when there is limited teaching time available (also: "tutorial learning").
- *Approach ofself-control:* This refers to autodidactic information access when knowledge and skills are to be constructed independently. This approach is particularly suitable for complex learning processes that allow diverse answers. Fields of application are learning requirements where there is ample teaching time available and where, in addition to necessary, freely selectable orientation knowledge should also be conveyed (also: "self-directed learning").
- *Combination:* In practice, a combination of external and self-control is increasingly used. The learner is recommended a certain navigation, but they can alternatively decide for another learning path. This is particularly useful when the learner only wants to repeat certain chapters. The degree of external and self-control can vary depending on the eLearning concept.

When the decision is made to produce a new learning program, the focus is usually not on the mere transmission of facts. An important didactic claim is therefore to convey knowledge that can be used in concrete applications, i.e. *action knowledge*. This demand is largely met by the constructivist teaching method for multimedia teaching applications. This is also referred to as *"problem-oriented learning"* and embeds the learning content in situational contexts that have a reality reference for the learner. The aim is to actively involve the learner, rather than letting them passively receive information. Reinmann-Rothmeier and Mandl (2001) formulate four guidelines for the design of problem-oriented learning environments.

1. *Authentic problem situations:* The aim is to secure the application reference of what has been learned and to generate interest in the learner, for example a request conversation for a trip in the travel agency: Here the example of a customer should be taken who has already researched everything on the internet and knows "better" than

the agent behind the counter. The learner is familiar with this situation and therefore motivated to find out how they can design this conversation so that both are satisfied and they ideally also sell a trip.

2. *Multiple application situations:* They enable the learner to retrieve, implement and further develop the acquired knowledge in various problem situations; for example, a multimedia language learning program teaches greeting forms in the foreign language: The learner should be able to vary and practice these greetings in the most diverse everyday situations.
3. *Social networking:* Whenever possible, learners should work in groups, as communication increases learning motivation; problems can also be solved more quickly in small groups. Example: All learners of the eLearning offer have access to a forum where they can exchange knowledge among each other.
4. *Instructional support:* The learner can contact a tutor or lecturer if necessary; resources, suggestions and supports for learning are provided. Example: All learners have access to a forum where they can ask their questions to a tutor.

Tip!
Checklist "Selecting eLearning", see Sect. 10.9.

3.3.2 Comparison of eLearning Formats

3.3.2.1 Computer-Based Training (CBT) and Web-Based Training (WBT)

eLearning predominantly takes place as Web-Based Training (WBT), which requires internet access. Data storage and transport occur via this network access. As a result, the learner is no longer tied to a specific PC or location. However, for a long time, there were two equivalent basic methods for eLearning. In addition to WBTs, these were Computer-Based Trainings (CBTs). CBTs are based on a CD-ROM. This is an internet-independent data carrier and storage medium, but it requires a PC or a laptop with a CD-ROM drive. Nevertheless, CBTs without a CD-ROM are also in use, by pre-installing the learning program on the respective end devices. However, in this case, the storage of the user's data and their individual learning progress is tied to the respective hardware.

Although the mobile solution of WBT appears more advantageous, WBTs are still not necessarily the only right solution for all types of eLearning applications. The development of eLearning in the form of CBTs still has its justification. The comparison in Table 3.3 should facilitate decision-making. It vividly shows that the didactic approach must not focus solely on the chosen eLearning medium (e.g., WBT or CBT), but rather must take into account the entire conditions of the learning environment (Kerres 1999).

Before deciding which of the two variants is better suited for the eLearning module to be developed, information should be obtained about the average technical equipment of the target group. When querying the technology, it should be noted that of all the

Table 3.3 Comparison CBT vs. WBT

CBT	WBT
Medium: CD-ROM.	Medium: Browser (online and offline).
Learning alone: no possibility of communication with a tutor or other learners.	Learning alone and (virtually) in groups: Social media, chat rooms, forums, tutorial support; easy data exchange between different participants in a network.
Linear or modular content delivery possible.	Learner self-control through modular content delivery, also with tutorial support.
Fast data transfer: a lot of multimedia, 3D learning worlds or other large amounts of data possible, as high storage volume of approx. 700 MB available.	With a lot of multimedia, long loading times depending on network load and available mobile radio standard.
Can be used independently of location.	Can be used independently of location.
Can be used independently of networks, for example in regions with missing technical network infrastructure (see developing countries).	Requires connection to the internet, i.e., appropriate technical infrastructure.
Short and fast data transfer, as the PC accesses the data directly via the CD-ROM drive.	Sometimes waiting times for data transfer, depending on network load and available mobile radio standard.
Screen quality as intended by software development.	Often different or worse screen quality, sometimes missing image elements, depending on the chosen browser.
Contents must not be prone to changes, as the change process is complex (new pressing of the data CD).	Current and frequently changing contents can be easily, quickly, and without high costs adapted.
Storage of learner data (only) directly on CD possible.	Central management of learner data; easy adjustment of learning content according to the learning progress.

computers or mobile devices that are to be used for the learning application, those with the *lowest* performance are relevant.

> **Tip!**
> Checklist "Technical Facilities and Specifications", see Sect. 10.8.

3.3.2.2 Learning Platforms

If a company decides to implement a learning application as WBT within the framework of a learning platform, it has the following options:

- *The company operates its own learning platform.* For this, servers are required for the application, the stored database, the teaching materials, and the software that operates the database management. In addition, the company must provide personnel for the administration of the learning platform and the associated components. The advantage of possible individual adaptation at any time is offset by high ongoing costs and high organizational effort. A company's own learning platform is particularly suitable for the use of numerous applications with a large number of learners.
- *The company rents a learning platform.* Renting a learning platform is also referred to as "hosting". The company pays a regular rental fee to the operator of the learning platform, who ensures smooth operation in return. This cost-effective solution is offset by the limited individual adaptation to company wishes, for example to the corporate identity. Renting a learning platform is particularly suitable for small and medium-sized companies that want to get started with eLearning.

Literature tip!
Peter Baumgartner et al.: "Selection of Learning Platforms", Studien-Verlag and
Rolf Schulmeister: "Learning Platforms for Virtual Learning", Oldenbourg.

3.3.2.3 Comparison of the Most Important eLearning Methods

The overview in Table 3.4 compares the most common and important eLearning methods. It is a helpful consulting tool to select the optimal eLearning method together with the client.

3.3.3 How to Convince the Decision-Makers?

Although the decision to implement an eLearning program has been made, there may be reservations among decision-makers or other team members within the company. Sometimes, there are employees on the expert committee who were previously responsible for training their colleagues in face-to-face seminars and now fear a reduction in their tasks. However, the smooth operation of an eLearning program can only be ensured if all participants are on board and contribute constructively. A first step to dispel reservations is to ensure that all participants engage with eLearning themselves and have a successful experience. Decision-makers should be encouraged to try out interesting eLearning applications themselves, for example, during a presentation of the prototype in the briefing. Another possibility is for a small, heterogeneous target group of about five people to test the program and share their personal experiences with it. Further arguments for reducing reservations and prejudices against eLearning include:

Table 3.4 eLearning methods compared

Approach	Target Group	Learning Content	Short Description
Linear Structure: Linear Navigation or tutorial systems guide through the learning program (inform and test) = approach of **External Control.**	Homogeneous target group in terms of prior knowledge.	New knowledge, new technical content, new facts; often deepened later in face-to-face training (see method "Blended Learning").	Linear structure of the learning units, knowledge transfer and query with **commenting feedback,** eLearning takes on the role of the tutor, learning paths are partly predetermined.
Modular Structure: The learner chooses his own learning units and thus constructs knowledge and skills himself = approach of **Self-Control.**	Heterogeneous target group in terms of prior knowledge.	New or building knowledge is conveyed, knowledge is available for short-term refreshing; self-check of the current knowledge status.	Modular structure of the learning units, interactive tests with commenting feedback for self-control. Learning paths are recommended, but ultimately freely selectable.
Information Systems, Knowledge databases (Hypermedia Concept).	Learners with prior knowledge who want to independently retrieve information; learners in training.	Provide information accompanying learning and/or as a reference work.	Database systems with all types of media and with various navigation or search options, for example thematic, alphabetical, chronological; continuous networking via hyperlinks to further topics within the database; not suitable for acquiring new knowledge, as not didactically structured (risk of dispersion).
Information Nuggets, Learning on Demand	This approach is suitable for learners who wish to retrieve information and knowledge content on demand, such as professionals in everyday life, for example, at an information desk or in field service.	The learning content is available as a so-called "life situation concept" and can be retrieved as a self-contained information unit depending on the situation.	Possible methods of providing this include the intranet, a regularly updated weblog or podcast, or an "app" on a smartphone.

(continued)

Table 3.4 (continued)

Approach	Target Group	Learning Content	Short Description
Intelligent Tutorial Approach (ITS)	This approach is suitable for a heterogeneous target group in terms of prior knowledge.	It allows for the acquisition of new or supplementary knowledge, enabling the learner to generate their own knowledge model.	It offers a flexible response to the learner's current knowledge level, similar to an expert system, but it has high development costs.
Exercise Programs (Drill &Practice).	This approach is suitable for learners who want to test their acquired knowledge.	It allows for the repetition and practice of already learned content, knowledge control, and the imparting of factual knowledge.	It is a tutorial exercise system without annotated feedback, only "right" and "wrong", with no didactic preparation, and tasks are generated randomly from a larger pool.
Simulation	This approach is suitable for learners with prior knowledge; it is particularly useful for decision-making knowledge that has far-reaching consequences in reality.	It allows for the acquisition of operating, application, process, action, behaviour and decision-making knowledge as well as motor skills and intellectual abilities.	The program represents real processes in a model-like manner; the learner can intervene in various ways, only one of which is correct. Methods of representation include digital video or photo stories.
Virtual Reality (VR).	This approach is suitable for a heterogeneous target group in terms of prior knowledge.	It is particularly useful for complex, often "dangerous" knowledge (for example, medical operations, pilot training, virtual communication training).	The program runs by itself, and the learner interacts using special input devices, for example, a 3D mouse, a data glove or a flystick.
Virtual Reality- Environments in **Social Networks**	This approach is suitable for learners in education and further training.	It allows for direct communication in groups and between lecturer and learner, simulation of real work environments, virtual group work and seminars (synchronous learning is possible).	Features include a virtual team room, application sharing, an interactive whiteboard; communication in virtual classrooms, discussion forums, chat rooms or social media (see Sect. 8.3.2).

(continued)

Table 3.4 (continued)

Approach	Target Group	Learning Content	Short Description
Microworlds, Game-based Learning	This approach is suitable for students and university students.	It allows learners to use knowledge productively and creatively, independently work out solutions and strategies, and imparts intellectual abilities and motor skills.	It is similar to "Virtual Reality", but technically simpler: it is a discovery system with the possibility to experiment, without specific content and without predefined learning paths; it includes an introduction to operation.
Rapid eLearning.	Learners with varying levels of knowledge.	Information that needs to be disseminated to a large number of recipients in a short time, such as changes in laws affecting daily business, new sales strategies for the sales team, or the introduction of new products in the corporation.	Method of delivery: for instance, a presentation in Microsoft PowerPoint using an authoring tool like Adobe Captivate (see Sect. 5.6.3) as a learning program with simple navigation into the intranet.
Blended Learning.	Learners with varying levels of knowledge; the target group originates from a single educational institution or a company.	Learning content that should not be conveyed solely via eLearning, such as behaviour training, communication training, and professional interaction with people. Learning groups should be brought to a common level of knowledge to be able to work through eLearning. This is also for deepening the knowledge acquired via eLearning.	Combination of in-person training and eLearning application, for example, an in-person training of one or more days duration is preceded by an eLearning; this requires a fixed group of learners.

- *Flexibility:* Learning is independent of time and place.
- *Economy:* Travel costs to seminar centres are eliminated, as are fees for expensive (often external) seminar leaders and costs for seminar rooms.
- *Time saving:* Through individual learning, targeted information access and undisturbed work, the user reaches the educational goal faster.
- *Individuality:* Each participant can build knowledge at their own learning pace, repeat content as often as desired and set the focus according to their own interest; the "average" that a lecturer often has to maintain in a face-to-face seminar to be fair to everyone is eliminated.
- *Absences:* Location-independent learning reduces absences from work due to further training and thus the costs.
- *Synergies:* The workplace becomes a place of learning and vice versa, as professional competencies are continuously updated.
- *Self-responsibility:* Computer-assisted learning promotes independence in knowledge acquisition.
- *Incidental (casual) Learning:* In addition to the technical content to be memorized, users learn how to handle various electronic media and acquire (software) technical competence.
- *Knowledge society:* Conventional teaching methods are no longer able to cope with the amount of information that the individual has to deal with in everyday education and work; eLearning relieves face-to-face seminars of pure fact transmission and clears the way for the transmission of action-oriented specialist knowledge.
- *Teaching-/Learning materials:* Easy and cost-effective access to teaching and learning materials, for example in PDF or Word format or in the cloud.
- *Currentness:* Web-Based Trainings allow for a quick and cost-effective adaptation of learning content to current developments.
- *Motivation:* Media diversity, appealing design, individual feedback and successful experiences trigger high learning motivation in the user.
- *Internet:* Immediate access to portals and information sources on the Internet relevant for education and further training or work.
- *Overcoming inhibitions:* Unlike in face-to-face training, even learners who have little prior knowledge or are naturally shy can achieve the required educational goals without fear.
- *Directness:* In modern working life, situation-related knowledge updates are constantly required; eLearning meets this requirement due to its great temporal and spatial flexibility.

Due to the relatively high development costs, especially small and medium-sized companies shy away from eLearning measures. It should be understood that eLearning is a long-term investment tool that requires a certain amortization period. Therefore, costs cannot be the sole argument for or against the production of an eLearning application. Often, the solution is sought via a standard product available on the market. However, it is questionable whether this solution is more cost-effective in the long run. The project manager of an agency or the media author should make the client aware of possible follow-up costs of a standard eLearning product:

New laws or current facts would require a manual management of change lists, which must be given to the respective learner with the standard eLearning.

Also, technical errors must be documented separately and handed out to the learner.

A standard eLearning corresponds to the current development status of conventional computers. In no more than three years, the eLearning program will no longer be compatible with the technology that will be common by then.

3.3.4 How to Motivate the Target Group?

When a company introduces eLearning, it initially presents its employees with many new requirements. To prevent learners from being deterred by this, and instead, to encourage them to approach the new learning methods with motivation, it is the responsibility of the company or project management to provide motivating conditions.

3.3.4.1 Establishing a Solid Works Agreement

The introduction of eLearning in a company is preceded by a carefully thought-out coordination process. If a works council is present, it must agree to the introduction and application of eLearning. With a works agreement, employers and the works council send a clear signal to the workforce that the new training and further education concept is endorsed and supported by personnel management.

3.3.4.2 Creating a Vibrant Learning Culture

Executives play a key role in increasing and maintaining the motivation of the target group for applying eLearning. They are the ones who create a new learning culture by recognizing and actively addressing knowledge and education as a fourth factor of production. A positive learning climate should be promoted. Instead of dismissive comments like "There goes someone wasting his working time again", the colleague who is learning on the computer should be respected and supported. For example, by not interrupting them during learning time and not having loud conversations, or by the company management even setting up small office rooms as "learning islands".

Tip!
In practice, it has proven useful to include representatives of the target group in the briefing team.

Employees who feel connected to the company and the new learning culture are those whose bosses signal support for eLearning publicly through information events, publications in professional journals, contributions on online portals about proper learning and on social networks. The project manager of an agency and the media author create a win-win situation when they advise their client in this regard.

3.3.4.3 Engaging Learners through Appealing Design

A demanding film, with scanty equipment and poor quality, spoils the viewing pleasure to such an extent that the valuable contents are overlooked. An appealing design is essential to motivate learners for eLearning, for example through:

- an interesting, learning-promoting presentation,
- a theme-related design,
- high illustrativeness (include examples with practical relevance),
- simple and clear navigation,
- varied design,
- modernity,
- high-quality,
- vitality,
- quick successes,
- individualization,
- varied and challenging tasks,
- linking with social networks,
- rapid knowledge transfer and
- context-related help.

3.3.4.4 Attracting Learners with the Right Incentives

Incentive systems motivate the target group to learn, regardless of whether the knowledge is acquired through eLearning or in-person seminars. However, since eLearning often raises reservations, the project manager of the agency and the media author should explicitly discuss incentive systems in the briefing and guide their client in this direction, to offer something like this to their own employees for working on the planned eLearning program. Recommendable incentives are:

- Certificates,
- Premiums or similar financial incentives,
- Discounts,
- Career advantages,
- Promotion,
- Prospect of expanding the area of competence,
- Recognition of the measure as educational leave after successful certification,
- Time off, for example for successfully working through an eLearning application,
- Participation in regional, national or international competitions.

Experience has shown that the use of one or more of the incentive systems listed here has a positive effect on the acceptance, dissemination and learning success of eLearning. And the better the eLearning is accepted by the target group, the more likely the client feels (and is confirmed) to have made a worthwhile investment.

3.3.5 How Long Does the Production Take?

The scheduling of a project's production duration must primarily be realistic for all parties involved. (For more information on time management for scriptwriting, refer to Sect. 7.2.) This also involves informing the client during the briefing that sufficient time must be allocated internally for the project. The employees responsible should be largely available for the project, as they will be dealing with numerous tasks: information research, queries from the agency and media author, consultations with experts, meeting days and their preparation and follow-up, reading scripts, testing beta versions, launching target group surveys, and so on. This effort is often underestimated in practice, leading to significant project delays.

For the scheduling of an eLearning project, either forward or backward scheduling can be used as a foundation. Forward scheduling begins with the production start date and develops subsequent project phases with their respective end points up to the delivery of the eLearning program to the end user. In contrast, backward scheduling starts with the delivery date of the eLearning program and calculates backwards to the starting point. All necessary project phases, including time buffers, must fit within this time window. The following factors influencing project and working times should be considered when scheduling:

- The agency's working hours can be calculated relatively accurately in advance, and the project manager includes them in the initial project schedule during the briefing (these working hours also form the basis for his cost calculation in the offer).
- The project duration can usually be predicted by the agency based on the project's framework data, taking into account time for project follow-up.
- Documenting project times provides a solid foundation for scheduling future projects.
- The schedule includes an end date and numerous intermediate dates, which can be used to regularly check whether the project is still running within the planned timeframe.

The time parameters that underlie an eLearning production are shown in Table 3.5:

- 1 hour of learning duration,
- 1 media author, and
- 2 software developers.

Table 3.5 Time parameters for the production of one hour of eLearning

Project phase	Days
Briefing (meeting day)	1
Rough concept and acceptance	5
Detailed concept and acceptance	7
Create script	12
Check script	4
Discuss script (meeting day)	1
Correct script	4
Release script (meeting days)	1
Technical coordination, basic layout and prototype creation (parallel to script creation)	10
Software development	15
Voiceover	2
Graphics	5
Check beta version	5
Accept beta version (meeting day)	1
Beta version corrections	3
Release learning program	2
Total duration in days	**78**

The following data are used as a basis for writing the script of a one-hour eLearning application: an average of 45 minutes writing time per script page. This results in a time expenditure of 45 hours for 60 script pages. A maximum of five hours of pure work on the script is calculated per working day, resulting in nine working days of five hours each for a total of 45 hours of writing time. A buffer of three days is added, so that 12 days of work are listed in the table under "Create script". Figure 3.5 shows an example of the design and structure of a schedule for the production of a one-hour eLearning application, using a Sect. of the schedule created with Microsoft Project.

3.3.6 What costs are incurred?

Producing an eLearning module is an extensive project that requires at least three months to create just one hour of learning time, involving many participants. If the task is very clear, the production of a learning hour can be completed in six to eight weeks. Therefore, the cost calculation should be done carefully, taking into account all costs incurred. It is important to note that the cost development of an eLearning production is more akin to the creation of media, as seen in the film and advertising industry, rather than a classic, typical software development.

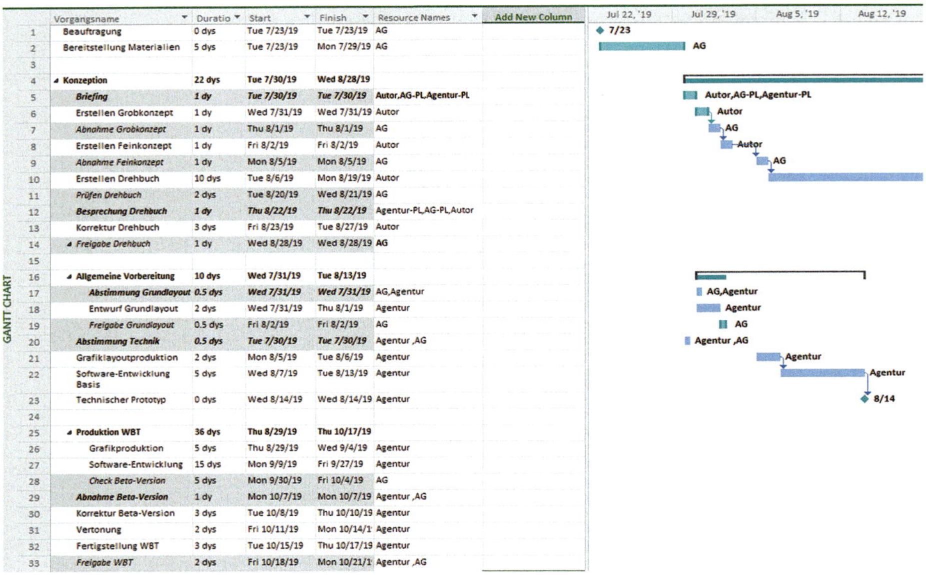

Figure 3.5 Schedule for the production of one hour of eLearning, created in Microsoft Project

As such, the production is high-priced. Simple eLearning applications, which are purely text-based or have a PowerPoint presentation with little interaction as a basis, start at 10,000 EUR. Highly interactive and complex eLearning projects, which require a high level of effort in terms of animations, videos, simulations, and technical research, often need a budget of 50,000 EUR and more. These costs are guidelines and can vary depending on the region, market, or industry. All amounts mentioned refer to fees in the middle range, as charged by multimedia agencies. Freelancers usually offer their services at a much lower cost. However, it is beneficial if the entire production process remains "in one hand", allowing the client to benefit from the high service quality and professionalism of the agency. A calculation in daily rates often comes cheaper than hourly fees. For example, the *concept* costs 760 EUR, if an *hourly fee* (= eight hours at 95 EUR) is used as a basis. However, a slightly cheaper, *flatdaily rate* is usually agreed, which ranges between 600 and 700 EUR per day for the concept. The costs for the *speaker* are much more detailed. Here, the calculation is made according to the guidelines of the Association of German Speakers e.V. per minute. For example, the speaker charges a 300 EUR basic fee for an eLearning production up to a maximum of five minutes of spoken text and 60 EUR for five additional minutes of spoken text.

For 60 minutes of spoken text, a speaker's fee of around 1000 EUR is therefore incurred.

Tip!
You can find fees for speakers of eLearning applications at: http://sprecherpreise.de/gagen-sonstiges-e-learning.html and https://www.sprecherverband.de.

In addition to these speakers who are freely available on the market, you can now also access brokerage portals on the Internet. These offer audio samples in over 70 languages and detailed expertise of the speakers, graded by beginners and professionals. For simple eLearning applications or the creation of prototypes, it is worth considering **automatic speakers**. These applications, referred to as "Text to Speech (TTS)", read PDF files or websites with different speaker types in different languages. This is possible for free using the standard speaker setting in the Windows browser *Microsoft Edge*. The *MWS Reader*, for example, works for a fee, but with a specific speaker selection. Depending on the range of functions, this software costs from 30 EUR upwards.

Tip!
If you are interested in a speaker, why not visit http://www.bodalgo.com or http://www.voicerebels.de and have sample texts read out and fee calculations output in seconds.

Table 3.6 provides further examples of common fees for eLearning productions, as outlined in the *iBusiness* Fee Guide. All mentioned values are net. The table clearly indicates that graphic work, especially the creation of 3D animations, is particularly costly. Customers considering a virtual, animated figurehead should be made aware of the associated costs by the project management. Often, a static figurehead that delivers witty comments can serve a similar purpose at a much lower cost. In addition to personnel costs, the company may also incur license costs for graphics and sound, which should be precisely itemized by the project manager. In general, all participants should be aware of the usage and exploitation rights of interactive productions (see Sect. 8.2).

Reading tip!
For a comprehensive list of all license costs associated with a multimedia production, refer to the *iBusiness* Fee Guide, published by Hightext Publishing (http://www.ibusiness.de).

An example calculation for the fee of a media author is shown in Fig. 3.6. This calculation is based on script writing for one hour of eLearning, which is typically equivalent to about 60 screen pages.

Table 3.6 Fee table for eLearning production

Area of responsibility	Cost/hour (EUR)
Project management	95
Pedagogical-didactic conception (Rough and detailed concept)	95
Script (based on video script fee)	95
Graphics (2D graphic illustration)	85
Graphics (3D graphics)	90
Graphics (2D animation)	85
Graphics (3D animation)	90
Graphics Screen-/Webdesign	90
Interface design (layout, usability design)	100
Software development C/C ++/#	100
Software development Java	100
Software development Python	98
Software development JavaScript	95
Video production: editorial support of the shooting team on site	97
Video editing	89

For a cost estimate, it is essential to include hidden costs in the planning. During the project, cost shifts can occur due to the need to add new learning content, consider new technologies on the market, or manage other unforeseen events. It is advisable to calculate in stages, adjust the cost planning at each stage, and re-coordinate with the client's decision-makers. This approach requires more effort, but it saves time and reduces unnecessary discussions about the invoice after the agency has completed the work. Examples of hidden costs include:

- Author corrections, i.e., customer change requests that deviate from the briefing or from an acceptance, or are introduced at a later date, for example, at the beta acceptance,
- Adjustments in the specification,
- Correction and test loops that exceed the normal level (i.e., more than two correction and test runs),
- Multiple decision levels until approval by the client,
- Intermediate versions for workshops, trade fair appearances, and similar events, and
- Additional meeting and presentation appointments.

If you, as a client, already know at the start of the project that your eLearning application should be updated soon and regularly thereafter, it is advisable to consider a Content

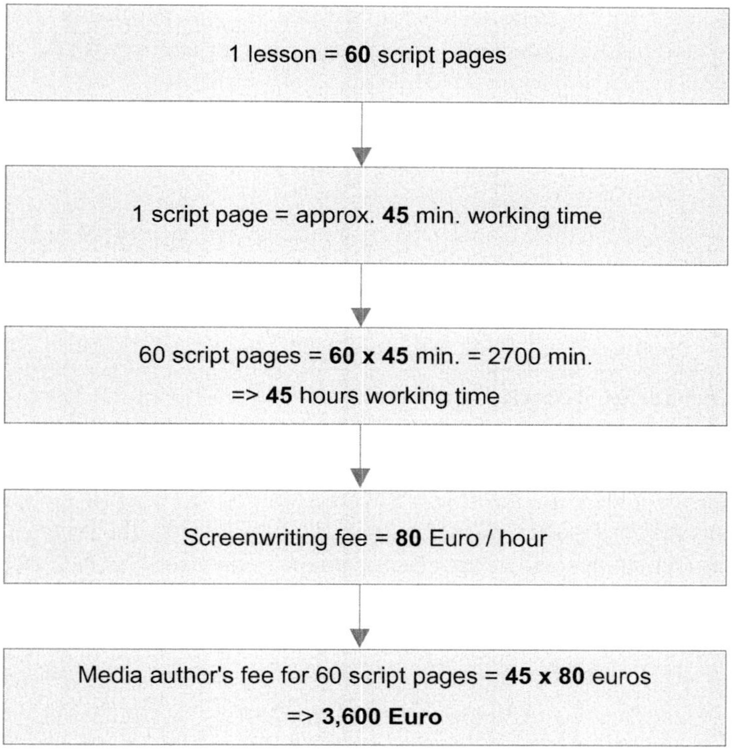

Fig. 3.6 Example of calculating the fee of a media author

Management System (CMS) with the multimedia agency. A CMS allows trained employees to carry out textual corrections and updates. This saves time and costs for commissioning the agency, even for minor changes.

Tip!
Pay attention to the runtime of the application! In small and medium-sized companies, a relaunch usually takes place after two to three years. In large companies, the first update often takes place after one or even half a year. In this case, follow-up costs for the eLearning project are incurred.

As soon as the cost calculation has been approved by the client and the order has been placed, a down payment of one third of the total fee is made. The agency receives another down payment upon submission of the script and the remaining fee after acceptance of the finished learning program. For larger multimedia projects with many learning hours, a monthly fee payment may occur. Just like the time expenditure, the cost trend should also be carefully documented to serve as a basis for future projects.

Reading tip!
Christoph von Dellingshausen: "dmmv calculation systematics", Hightext Verlag; a clear, easily understandable form work for the safe calculation of a multimedia project, supplemented by a well-understandable explanation of all items listed in the calculation forms.

3.4 The Script Acceptance

The script acceptance is a complex process. Ideally, the media author writes the script and then passes it on to the agency, which checks it to see whether the quantities and requirements match the offer; any corrections are forwarded by the agency to the media author. The revised version is then checked again in the agency for correctness before it is issued to the client for review. There should be an internal content discussion there before the changes and corrections to the script are discussed on the script acceptance day together with the agency and media author.

Tip!
A helpful tool for clients is the "Script Acceptance" checklist, see Sect. 10.10.

3.4.1 Technical Changes Contributions

When there are multiple representatives from the client side on the project team, which is typically the case, they should internally coordinate on technical changes and corrections before the script approval meeting. The costs of the project team for an approval day are high (see Sect. 3.3.6). Ideally, change requests and corrections should be presented to the agency and the media author as results. The ensuing discussions should focus on program-technical and didactic levels, rather than revolving around technical matters. However, it is crucial to provide the media author with a technical justification, especially when content has changed. In conclusion, the client should summarize the internal discussion on technical changes for the team, allowing the author to participate in the content development. The author should then consider this when didactically processing the changes and filtering out effects on other script parts. There are technical corrections that occur due to the author misunderstanding something in the briefing and then implementing it incorrectly. These are at the expense of the agency and the media author. However, there are also technical changes that have arisen on the client side since

Table 3.7 Decision matrix for changes by the client

Change request	Importance (School grades from 1 to 6)	Cost Concept/Script	Cost Design
Integrate 4 new product criteria	1	335 EUR	
Change color of Corporate Identity (CI) due to company merger	1		600 EUR
Always write "for example" instead of "about"	3	80 EUR	
Rephrase audio texts of the animation character (tonality should be funnier)	4	12 EUR(per audio text)	

the briefing. These exceed the scope of the offer and thus the cost calculation, which the project manager must clarify to the customer at this stage. Transparency is created by a decision matrix, which is projected onto the wall using a projector (see Table 3.7). This allows the customer to see at a glance how much each correction will cost. They can then make quicker decisions about the relevance of their planned changes. For an effective project process, the decision matrix is a powerful tool. The importance of content adjustments should always be considered in relation to the learning objective. The calculation that underlies the costs for the concept in the decision matrix is exemplified here:

- 4 new product criteria = 4 new screen pages
- Per screen page = 45 minutes of script writing
- 4 screen pages = 3 hours of script writing
- 3 hours of script writing at 80 EUR = 240 EUR
- Inserting into the didactic concept and checking for consistency = 1 hour of concept work at 95 EUR
  240 EUR + 95 EUR = *335 EURChange costs*

Additionally, it must be checked whether these new requirements fit into the calculated quantities of graphics, dubbing, and programming. Additional costs may arise for the coordination of all affected elements.

3.4.2 Correcting Spelling

In this delicate matter, it is especially important for all parties involved to remain objective. Clients who find a spelling mistake in the script should point it out objectively, refraining from comments such as, "Someone obviously hasn't learned the new spelling rules." While this may sound humorous, it will likely elicit a forced smile from the media author, who may have simply made a typing error. The risk is that project members may use the script approval process to demonstrate their knowledge, thereby unnecessarily worsening the project team's atmosphere. Conversely, the media author should also objectively confirm and note spelling corrections, avoiding both self-blame and arrogance. It is particularly detrimental if the media author blames the agency, saying, "Everything was correct in my script; the errors must have occurred during printing at the agency." This leaves the project manager in a difficult position and ruins the mood. The project manager should avoid ridiculing the author during spelling corrections, saying things like, "Such a thing should not happen!" While it is appropriate to discuss quality privately after script approval, loyalty between the project manager and the author is paramount within the project team. At this point, all parties involved in script approval are advised to use a uniform correction mode. In the publishing industry, the correction symbols listed in the Duden Correction Symbols are standard for proofreading texts. It's always worth a look.

3.4.3 Debating Over the Wording

A critical point in any script approval is debating over the right wording. The client side usually has a precise idea of how something should be worded. Often, team members have previously written the company's internal training materials themselves and now feel challenged to question or reject as many of the author's formulations in the script as possible. This habit can significantly hinder script development. A conflict arises between the media author's expertise in formulating screen texts and audios (see Sect. 5.2) and the client's desire to enforce a familiar style. The problem can only be resolved by the client stepping back and trusting the author, accepting formulations that may be unusual for them. During script approval, the client's focus regarding the correctness of the wording should be on the content and its comprehensibility for the target group. In addition, they should ensure that company-internal terminology has been considered in the formulations.

3.4.4 Documenting Changes with Change Request Lists

If the client expresses wishes for changes in content, timing, or financial aspects during script approval, this significantly influences the project order. This changes accordingly, unless the changes concern errors caused by the author or the agency. Extensive changes incur high costs, which should ideally be requested with a *Change Request Form* (= form for Change Requests).

All changes that occur on the day of the script approval meeting must be documented. Ideally, the project manager already has a change request list prepared on their laptop

1	Change-Request-Liste	Datum:							
2	Nr.	Kapitel/ Seite	Datum	Termin	Index	ToDo	wer?	Status	wann erled.
3	1	1/3	8.10.	10.10.	DB501	Korrigierte PDF-Datei zu Schadenfällen	GE	erl.	10.10.
4	2	1/8	8.10.	14.10.	DB501	Zusammenfassung Tarife	Autor	erl.	14.10.
5	3	1/9	8.10.	14.10.	DB602	Demoblatt zum Thema „Jugendtarif"	GE	erl.	14.10.
6	4	2/11	8.10.	16.10.	DB603	Nachvertonung Audio DB603a - 2.500 Euro ergänzen	Agentur	erl.	16.10.
7	5	2/11	8.10.	16.10.	DB722	Nachvertonung Audio DB722b=Sie wissen nun genau, welche Vorteile der Jugendtarif für Ihren Kunden parat hat. Aber nicht nur Ihr Kunde profitiert davon - auch für Sie und Ihre Kollegen schaut etwas dabei raus!	Agentur	erl.	16.10.
8	6	2/13	8.10.	20.10.	DB723	Audios anpassen und nachvertonen	Agentur		20.10.
9	7	2/20	8.10.	14.10.	DB815	Verwendung des Begriffs „Absicherung vom Feinsten"	Autor	erl.	
10	8	4/8	8.10.	14.10.	DB815	Rückmeldung zum Thema „elektronisches Berechnungstool"	TR	erl.	14.10.
11	9	4/10	8.10.	14.10.	DB815	Was leistet der Tarif? Zusammenstellung Leistungsbeispiele	TR		
16	14	4/13	8.10.	14.10.	DB911	Anpassung Demoblatt „Gliedertaxe"	Autor	erl.	16.10.
28									
29									

Fig. 3.7 Change Request List, created with Microsoft Excel

and only needs to enter the details. At the end of the script discussion, they then distribute the lists to all team members and project staff who have to implement the changes. A suitable tool for creating a Change Request List is the spreadsheet software Microsoft Excel, as the example in Fig. 3.7 shows. The advantage is that the list can be pre-configured, for example, by specifying different editor names or chapters. In addition, completed tasks can be easily hidden.

> **Tip!**
> For a checklist on "Change Request Form", see Sect. 10.11.

References

Baumgartner, Peter et al. (2002) Auswahl von Lernplattformen. Innsbruck: Studien-Verlag.

Bohinc, Tomas (2010) Grundlagen des Projektmanagements. Offenbach: Gabal.

Buzan, Tony (2013) Das Mind-Map-Buch. München: mvgverlag.

Dellingshausen, Christoph von (2004) dmmv-Kalkulationssystematik – Leitfaden zur Kalkulation von Multimedia-Projekten. München: Hightext Verlag.

Fietz, Gabriele et al. (2003) eLearning für internationale Märkte. Bielefeld: Bertelsmann Verlag.

Hightext Verlag (2015) iBusiness Honorarleitfaden. München: Hightext Verlag.

Kerres, Michael (1999) Didaktische Konzeption multimedialer und telemedialer Lernumgebungen. In: HMD Praxis der Wirtschaftsinformatik, Heft 205: Multimediale Bildungssysteme, Heidelberg, S. 9–21.

Kerres, Michael et al. (2002) E-Learning. Didaktische Konzepte für erfolgreiches Lernen. In: von Schwuchow, Karlheinz & Guttmann, Joachim (Hrsg.) Jahrbuch Personalentwicklung & Weiterbildung 2003. Köln: Luchterhand.

Kerres, Michael (2018) Mediendidaktik: Konzeption und Entwicklung digitaler Lernangebote. München: De Gruyter Oldenbourg Verlag, 5. vollständig überarbeitete Auflage.

Niegemann, Helmut et al. (2008) Kompendium multimediales Lernen. Heidelberg: Springer.

MindManager: http://www.mindjet.com.

MindView: http://www.matchware.com/de.

Patzak, Gerold & Günter Rattay (2017) Projektmanagement. Wien: Linde, 7. aktualisierte Auflage.

Reinmann-Rothmeier, Gabriele & Heinz Mandl (2001) Virtuelle Seminare in Hochschule und Weiterbildung. Bern: Huber.

Schulmeister, Rolf (2005) Lernplattformen für das virtuelle Lernen. München: Oldenbourg Verlag.

4 Conception: How is Structure Brought Into the Contents?

Abstract

Chapter 4 deals with the design of eLearning content. The focus is on the careful development of a rough concept as a basis for a smooth production process. The individual content elements of the rough and detailed concept are presented in detail, supplemented by numerous examples of navigation types. Special mention is made of the learning objectives, both in their taxonomy and function, as well as in the way they are aptly formulated.

The concept is based on the work orders taken from the briefing (see Chap. 3). The development of the script is later based on this concept. The more attention paid to the concept, the lower is the error rate in the script itself, the fewer correction loops are required, and the easier it is to adhere to the cost framework. This also fosters good teamwork, as all project members can focus more on their actual tasks and not on communication problems or discussions about costs. The concept usually includes a rough concept and a detailed concept in an eLearning production. However, it is not always clear what content belongs to the rough concept, what belongs to the detailed concept, and what exactly a specification sheet is. Depending on the project, there are very different views. The following chapters provide a structured assignment of the content to the individual concept phases.

4.1 The Rough Concept

The rough concept is the basis of the detailed concept, from which the script emerges. Starting from the rough concept, a specification sheet can be formulated (see Sect. 4.3). Sometimes the rough concept coincides with the agency's offer; then either the media

D. Modlinger, *eLearning and Mobile Learning – Concept and Script*,
https://doi.org/10.1007/978-3-658-44695-6_4

author is already involved in the project during the offer phase or he is only appointed when developing the detailed concept. If a media author develops the rough concept already in the offer phase, this has a disadvantage: The client no longer has a say and has to live with the author's writing style for the entire project duration, whether he likes it or not. As a result, entire productions have sailed into dangerous waters because this leads to an endless tail of formulation corrections for which no one wants to be responsible. It is clear: You can't turn a Benjamin Stuckrad-Barre into a Günther Grass—and that's not necessary. Both have exactly the right writing style for their target group. Therefore, it is advisable for an agency to include several text samples of the author in the offer, which allow conclusions about his possible writing styles. To a certain extent, a media author can also adapt his writing style to the company guidelines and the project. In addition, the agency checks the author's technical competence and whether he fits into the team in advance.

Whether the media author or a project manager with appropriate media didactic competence takes over the conception, their tools include a comprehensive knowledge of:

- Perception and learning psychology (see Sect. 5.7),
- Multimedia didactics (see Sect. 5.8),
- Standards for eLearning (see Sect. 10.12),
- Relevant learning concepts (see Sect. 4.1.1.5) and
- Authoring tools (see Sect. 5.6.3).

Tip!
Checklist "eLearning standards", see Sect. 10.12.

Only in the rarest cases does a company create a rough concept without an agency. This is justified, as the agency brings its full know-how into the concept phase, on which the entire subsequent production is based. Moreover, the agency usually draws on existing rough concepts from other productions, thereby increasing the degree of professionalism. The rough concept is a "soft" instrument, even though it is the basis for the detailed concept and the specification sheet. It can be largely modified in the acceptance discussion. This makes the phase of the rough concept a space for ideas and considerations that may also overshoot the mark. Together with other project management forms, the multimedia agency thus has a good template to deliver a decent job description with as little time expenditure as possible.

The rough concept structures the requirement contents for the multimedia processing of the selected learning contents.

4.1.1 Contents of the Rough Concept

4.1.1.1 Initial Situation

Table 4.1 clearly presents the various aspects of the initial situation. It is a helpful tool for the targeted development of the rough concept in the briefing.

Scribble: Example

The "example scenario" described at the end of Table 4.1 is an effective tool for creating awareness of the development of learning objectives. A rough concept comes to life when the scenarios are depicted in simple scribbles (see Sect. 5.2.3.1), as shown by the example scribble in Fig. 4.1.

Before the development of scenarios, a brief questionnaire can be sent to the target group to inquire about common problem situations in their daily lives. A beneficial side effect is that future learners feel valued and are subsequently more motivated to engage with this eLearning application, which is specifically tailored to their needs.

> **Tip!**
> For a checklist on "Questionnaire to the Target Group", see Sect. 10.13.

Leading Figures: Examples

For the VIP-S training of Versicherungskammer Bayern, the pre-existing mascot VIP-S-Punkt was utilised. This mascot was originally developed for a printed self-study program. The leading figure shown in Fig. 4.2 appeals to the target group (advisors of Sparkasse) as it was derived from the red Sparkasse point.

Figure 4.3 introduces the leading figure "Amanda". She was created by Beck et al. for Continental AG. Amanda guides the predominantly male target group with extensive knowledge and charm through the problem-oriented, English-language learning program to a new system for customer relationship management (CRM system).

As a leading figure, it is best to use a fictional representative of the target group or the pre-existing company mascot. This approach makes it easier for the learner to identify with the program. A knight serving as a leading figure for insurance advisors is interesting from a metaphorical perspective, but it is unlikely to motivate the target group to sell insurance seriously.

4.1.1.2 Learning Content

The rough concept lists all learning content that is to be didactically prepared for the eLearning application. This content is also referred to as "basal text". The learning content is selected in such a way that it aligns with the learning objective and is relevant for the target group. The following formula applies to the selection of learning content:

Table 4.1 Content elements of the rough concept

Content component	Example
Decision for an eLearning variant (based on the location of use and the variability of the learning content to be conveyed)	CBT, WBT or Mobile Learning
Chosen teaching approach (see Sect. 4.1.1.5)	**Examples:** • linear, • modular, • method mix of modular and linear, • cognitive information transfer, • constructivist or problem-oriented knowledge acquisition (see Sect. 3.3.1), • inductive (from the individual case to the general) or • deductive (from the general to the individual case).
Usage form of the eLearning program	• As a supplement to the seminar (Blended Learning), • standalone for self-study or • as a knowledge database or information medium.
Guiding objective of the eLearning program (see Sect. 3.2.3 and 4.1.1.4)	**Example:** "The salespeople in the laptop department learn to specifically win customers for an extended warranty contract when buying an Ultrabook." Further target fields can be: public relations, image, accessibility, use of existing media, modernity etc.
Ideas, preliminary considerations	**Examples of ideas:** • Intro by video, • Special features of the graphic implementation or • Patterns for later knowledge testing. **Example of preliminary considerations:** "The target group is already familiar with the information brochures on the services of the extended warranty contract and has learned with them so far. The employees will be given one hour per week to work with the eLearning application. The eLearning application should also serve as an information medium in customer consulting and enable the filling out and printing of warranty contracts."
Benchmarking	List or describe projects that the customer liked or did not like. **Example:** "The eLearning application should contain less theory than the eLearning of competitor XY, but should have more practical examples of real situations with questions from everyday customer consulting."

(continued)

Table 4.1 (continued)

Content component	Example
Framework data	• Amount of available budget, • Time frame for production, • Processing duration of the eLearning application, • Special requirements, for example: The eLearning application must be able to run on certain laptops, • Number of employees to be trained, • Cooperations that led to the initiation of the project, • Follow-up projects as well as • Predecessor projects that are being built upon.
Learning content	Basic text, training guide etc.
Intro	A trailer introduces the learner to the media that await him (for example, films from professional life), whether an animation figure will accompany him as a tutor, what skills he can acquire with the eLearning application, etc. The goal is to tune the learner into the learning unit, to sensitize him for the medium.
Example Scenarios	**Example:** "A customer enters an electronics store intending to buy an Ultrabook. During the conversation with the salesperson, it becomes clear that the customer travels frequently and requires a device that will not present any technical difficulties. This initiates a discussion about an extended warranty contract, which benefits the customer and earns the salesperson a commission."
Screen Design: Navigation and Design	**Examples:** • Programming a scenario as a template and presenting it as a screenshot in the rough concept, • Mentioning unique design ideas, such as comic style, Bauhaus style, eco design, etc.
Types of Tasks to be Used in this Learning Program	**Examples:** • Multiple-choice tasks, • Single-choice tasks, • Drag-and-drop tasks, or • Exercises with free input. For more on types of tasks and multimedia didactics, see Sect. 5.4 and 5.8.
Leading Figure	A rough sketch of a leading figure who guides learners through the eLearning application in a tutorial or commentary manner.
Media and Technology	A list of all available media that appear in the learning units, such as photos, videos, audios.
Addressing Problem Areas	**Examples:** • Missing audios, • Photos to be researched, • Clarification of copyrights.

Fig. 4.1 Rough Concept: Scribble of a Scenario

Fig. 4.2 Leading figure “VIP-S-Training”, Versicherungskammer Bayern

Fig. 4.3 Leading figure “Amanda”, Continental AG

As much as necessary for the learning objective, but as little as possible.

This approach reduces the learning content to the essentials. Verbosity may be interesting as a theoretical foundation, but it detracts from the purpose of the eLearning application, which is the direct progression towards the learning objective.

The basal text must be clearly designated in the rough concept:

- Title of the documents with the corresponding learning content,
- Author of the documents and contact details (for queries),
- Publication date of the documents,
- Delivery date of the documents to the agency or the media author,
- Indication of further sources of information on the contents (contact person, internet address etc.) as well as
- Emphases to be set in the basal text.

Examples of learning content that can serve as basal text

- Training guides,
- Manuals,
- Legal texts,
- Curricula,
- PowerPoint presentations,
- Textbooks, and
- Workplace guidelines. ◀

4.1.1.3 Target Group

The target audience for the eLearning program should be defined and delimited as precisely as possible. Often, the client already has a clear target group definition ready in the briefing. However, sometimes the target group is determined more precisely after the briefing. In any case, a target group analysis precedes, which should contain as many of the content elements listed in Table 4.2 as possible.

Tip!
Checklist "Target group analysis", see Sect. 10.14.

The target group analysis can be carried out in various ways, for example through questionnaires, observation, personal or telephone interviews, and research or based on job and task descriptions. The *target group definition* could read as follows:

Table 4.2 Possible content elements of a target group analysis

Size of the target group	How many users should be trained with the eLearning application?
Composition of the target group	Heterogeneous or homogeneous regarding: Age, gender, nationality etc.; especially in global use, consider other cultural circles and multilingualism.
Type of person addressed by the measures or position in the company	Managers, experts, users, clerks, trainees, craftsmen, customers, salespeople etc.
Relationships among each other	Hierarchies within the target group: superiors, team colleagues or similar.
Education level	Heterogeneous or homogeneous regarding: completed vocational training, type of school leaving certificate, university degree, further training measures etc.
Age group	Heterogeneous or homogeneous regarding: Proportion of 20- to 30-year-olds, 30- to 40-year-olds, 40- to 50-year-olds, 50- to 60-year-olds, over 60-year-olds.
Place of learning	Workplace, at home, learning center, at several places or on (business) trips.
Prior knowledge	The level of prior knowledge (low, medium, high) determines the design of the learning path.
Motivation	External or intrinsic motivation of the participants.
Special features	Special interests, characteristics, possibly disability (→ barrier-free eLearning).

"The eLearning application is aimed at 1000 electronics sales specialists in the nationwide branches of the electronics store.

The target group is relatively homogeneous, as they have the same training as retail salespeople; the employees are between 20 and 50 years old and predominantly male. The advisory and sales-oriented eLearning application builds on the job profile of a retail salesperson. The target group has a high user competence in dealing with electronic media, especially with computers; therefore, the processing of the eLearning application should largely be subject to self-control by the learner. This is facilitated by the structure with practical situation examples, which the user can call up problem-related. The eLearning application should be processed at home in exchange for time off. In addition, it should be available as an information medium for sales advice. The target group improves their advisory competence with the eLearning application and thus increases the number of sold netbook warranty contracts. This results in additional earnings for the sales specialist from the commissions granted for the conclusion of netbook warranty contracts."

If a target group is heterogeneous, it can be prioritised. For instance, the hairdressing industry may wish to release a learning application for hairstyling and hair advice. The highest priority within the target group are master hairdressers, who advise customers daily and need to be familiar with hair structures, hair dyes, head shapes, face types, and cutting techniques. The second highest priority are trainees, who can use the eLearning program alongside their training to reinforce their vocational school knowledge. Lastly, customers who are interested in the topic and wish to inform themselves before their upcoming hairdresser visit can utilise the eLearning application during their waiting time. Each of these three target groups must be described in the rough concept according to the procedures outlined above. This results in an eLearning application structure that caters to the heterogeneous user group of the eLearning program.

4.1.1.4 Learning Objectives

Learning objectives can be logically developed if they are categorised and certain formulation guidelines are followed.

Formulating Learning Objectives

The correct formulation of learning objectives in the rough concept paves the way for the meaningful structuring and didactic design of the learning content on the individual learning pages. Learning objectives specifically describe the behaviour, ability, or skill the learner should acquire. Learning objective sentences follow simple rules:

- A learning objective always begins with the subject that refers to the learner: It identifies the actor.
- The verb of the learning objective is meaningful and is always placed at the end of the sentence.
- Learning objective sentences are action-oriented; adjectives are omitted whenever possible, with verbs gaining importance instead.
- Learning objectives are formulated actively.
- The subjects and verbs accurately describe learning objectives.
- The rule also applies to learning objective sentences: "As much as necessary, as little as possible."

> "The clarity and power of language does not lie in the fact that nothing more can be added to a sentence, but in the fact that nothing more can be taken away from it." Isaac Babel, Russian writer, 20th century.

Examples of Introductions to Learning Objective Sentences

- The learner understands, ...
- The learner can ...
- The learner is capable of, ...
- The learner is able to, ...
- The learner knows, ... ◀

Examples of Verbs Suitable for Learning Objective Sentences

- understand, evaluate,
- realize, apply, recognize, explain, achieve,
- know, get to know,
- empathize, comprehend,
- (re-)activate,
- comprehend,
- understand, be familiar,
- reproduce, know. ◀

Tip!
Consider using a synonym dictionary (for example, from Duden) to find synonyms that better fit your learning objective; or go online at http://www.openthesaurus.de.

Examples of Formulated Learning Objectives

- The consultant is capable of recommending the appropriate product from the new tariff portfolio to the customer.
- The learner is able to apply the rules of the Harvard negotiation concept effectively in the sales conversation.
- The employee understands that different customs and practices await him at the Chinese branch.
- The user can understand the functioning of the database. ◀

Categories of Learning Objectives

The categorisation of learning objectives aids in the selection of appropriate teaching strategies. This varies depending on whether the learner should reproduce facts, understand complex terms, or is capable of transferring what they have learned to real or simulated situations (Kerres 2018). According to Bloom et al. (1976), learning objectives fall into three categories:

Cognitive Learning Objectives: Factual knowledge, concepts, rules, procedures, principles.

Affective Learning Objectives: Interests, attitudes and values, as well as the ability to form appropriate value judgements and align one's own behaviour accordingly.

Psychomotor Learning Objectives: Behaviours, mastering sequences of movements, for example, manual skills, operating machines.

Levels of Learning Objectives

Overall Objective: The overall objective refers to the entire eLearning application or the complete blended learning course. For example, it could be: "The field staff achieve a 20% increase in sales with the new tariff." (see Sect. 3.2.3). This overall objective is then divided into the so-called major learning objectives.

Major Learning Objectives: The major learning objectives are also structural elements. They refer to the subject areas or chapters within the course and thus provide a structure for the eLearning application. Major learning objectives determine what the target group needs to know and be able to do in order to achieve this sales increase. They also describe the specific actions that the learned knowledge and skills should guide.

Example

The overall objective: "The field staff achieve a 20% increase in sales with the new tariff" can be divided into several major learning objectives according to the categories of Bloom mentioned above:

Cognitive:

"The field staff are able to integrate the tariff into the overall product concept."

"The field staff can name the legal backgrounds and guidelines for the new tariff."

"The field staff know what content is in the insurance conditions."

Affective:

"The field staff understand that the new tariff is to be explained as an important retirement provision for their customers."

"The field staff see the new tariff as a contribution to securing pensions in the long term."

"The field staff grasp their personal responsibility to advise customers sensibly and sustainably."

Psychomotor:

"The field staff are able to conduct result-oriented consulting and sales talks."

"The field staff are capable of applying the associated communication rules." ◄

Major learning objectives are broken down into detailed fine learning objectives in the detailed concept. Subsequently, tasks are used to check whether the learner has also achieved these fine learning objectives (see Sect. 4.2.2).

In addition to describing learning objectives and the resulting skills and abilities, the rough concept includes formal degrees, certificates and participation certificates. Together with the overall objective, the major learning objectives provide instructions for the teaching approach to be selected now.

4.1.1.5 Teaching Approach

The rough concept includes the following descriptions of the teaching approach:

- Type of learning paths, for example: tutorial system, simulation, exercise program, microworld, or knowledge database: externally controlled (linear), self-controlled (modular), or a combination of both.
- Information-oriented or problem-oriented knowledge transfer (cognitivist or constructivist, see Sect. 5.7).
- Inductive or deductive development of learning content.
- Possible inclusion of a learning dramaturgy, such as a simulation game or a framing action; this usually evokes high acceptance among learners, but requires a linear sequence, which in turn does not allow selective access to knowledge; it also involves expensive implementation.
- Tonality: Voice modulation of different speaker types: Which characters appear in the eLearning application? How should they speak?
- Character and appearance of the leading figure, who guides through the eLearning application and provides evaluative feedback along with motivating comments.

> **Tip!**
> Include a sketch of the leading figure in the rough concept, it enhances the imagination!

Table 4.3 outlines the elements of the teaching approach that a rough concept should include, providing examples for each.

4.1.1.6 Structure

The rough concept reflects the most important elements of the structure of the eLearning application. This is best represented using a flowchart program (see Sect. 4.1.2). The structural elements listed in the rough concept are not binding for the entire production, they can be varied, supplemented or omitted later.

In the initial concept, it is crucial to determine whether the pages are interconnected or if each page stands independently. This information is vital because it informs the author's decision on whether to formulate transitions from one page to the next or to design the spoken texts in such a way that each learning page is self-contained. However, in modern eLearning, each page typically stands on its own (Fig. 4.4 and 4.5).

General page types in an eLearning application

- *Distributor pages* contain many links and serve as a so-called "Advance Organizer", providing a preview of the learning objectives and content as well as the average processing time of the respective learning pages. They can also encourage further exploration by drawing attention to exciting topics through animated menus, which is usually the case with eLearning programs with an informational character. The

Table 4.3 Explanation of the elements of the teaching approach in the rough concept

Element of Teaching Approach	Background/Basis/Agreement	Example Text for the Rough Concept
Learning Path	Affective broad learning objective: "The field staff have learned to understand the new tariff as an important retirement provision for their customers."	The learning path combines self-control with external control: Simulated sales talks are followed by exercises in which the learner can control the course of the sales talk depending on the chosen solution.
Type of Knowledge Transfer	Affective broad learning objective: "The field staff see the new tariff as a contribution to securing pensions in the long term."	The knowledge transfer is problem-oriented: Model calculations show the supply needs of potential customers. In the subsequent exercises, the learner is asked to make their own model calculations using the simulated calculation program.
Development of Learning Content	Practical orientation of the eLearning application, that is, the learner should learn based on problem situations.	Inductive approach: A problem situation is presented, then the learner finds solutions themselves. At the end, they receive a summary, which also serves as a guideline for future sales talks.
Learning Dramaturgy	Psychomotor broad learning objective: "The driving students learn to steer the vehicle safely through city traffic." Here, a learning dramaturgy is worthwhile, as the eLearning application is only intended to prepare for the driving test; it will not be needed for selective knowledge access afterwards.	A young protagonist urgently needs to bring a gift to his mother because it's her birthday. He is already late and now encounters all possible traffic situations that one can encounter during a city car ride. Each of these situations integrates a learning content on vehicle control, traffic signs, and reaction ability. Only by passing the associated task(s) can the learner continue driving.
Language Modulation	The eLearning application should be equipped with a virtual leading figure who gives motivating comments and evaluative feedback. In parallel, there is a speaker who conveys the learning content together with the screen text.	The leading figure is a cheeky companion who speaks in the jargon of the young target group. His speech texts are emotionally colored: In the feedbacks to the tasks, he shows enthusiasm, sometimes disappointment, but always ends with a motivating sentence. The speaker should differentiate themselves from the leading figure in their way of speaking, to make it clear that they are conveying the important learning content.

(continued)

Table 4.3 (continued)

Element of Teaching Approach	Background/Basis/Agreement	Example Text for the Rough Concept
Leading Figure	The eLearning application for preparing for the driving test mainly appeals to young people; therefore, a leading figure is used who should guide through the knowledge acquisition in a lively and motivating way.	The leading figure is called Radolfo and has "the license to drive". He is only interested in cars and traffic and is often irritated to come into contact with pedestrians or cyclists. Radolfo speaks in youth jargon, he also likes to imitate car and traffic noises. He has the shape of a car tire with a face in the middle. It is important to ensure that the speech texts do not annoy, that is, before the dubbing, the speech texts formulated in the script are read to selected representatives of the target group.

Fig. 4.4 Example scribble for the leading figure "Radolfo"

learner can thus mentally prepare for the upcoming lessons and benefits from a higher retention performance of what has been learned.

- *Detail pages* have few or no links and are also referred to as *content pages*. Detail pages prepare the individual learning content, explain it, and delve into it. The focus of the detail pages is on knowledge transfer.
- *Interaction pages,* also known as *exercise pages*, offer tasks with which the learner can independently check their learning progress.
- *Summary pages,* conclude a topic at regular intervals by revisiting the core content points.

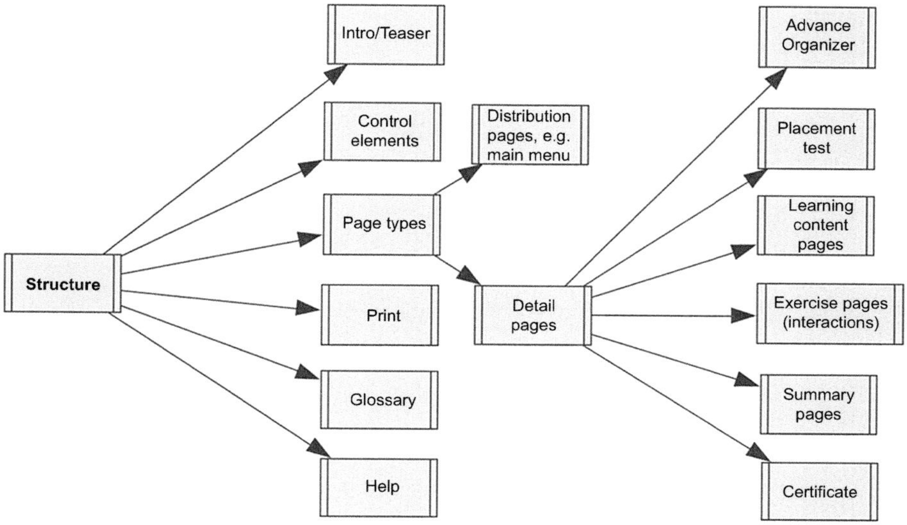

Fig. 4.5 Example of the structure of an eLearning application, created with the software Inspiration

Control elements (Buttons)

As varied as the learning objectives and target groups of eLearning applications are the operating elements used for user guidance. Some of the elements listed here are standardized; the italicized elements are recommended, but ultimately optional. The chosen control elements should be available to the learner on every page. They are essentially the learner's tool for efficient work with the eLearning application.

The most common control elements for eLearning applications are:

- Menu: The learner can access the main menu on each learning page,
- Next: Proceed to the next learning page,
- Back: Return to the previous learning page,
- End: Exit the program,
- Sound on/Sound off,
- *Repeat: Replay the current learning page,*
- *Pause: Resume learning at the same place later,*
- *Search,*
- *Help/Instruction manual,*
- Settings,
- *Notes,*
- *Print: Store learning materials as a PDF file,*
- *Bookmarks, and*
- LogIn/LogOut.

Structural Elements

Structural elements assist learners in navigating through the program independently and safely while simultaneously tracking their own learning progress. The optional structural elements are printed in italics:

- Main menu as a central, intuitive orientation system,
- *Entrance test* for recommending the learning path,
- *Table of contents* before each chapter (also known as the distribution page),
- *Modularity:* individual selection of the learning path,
- *Page tracking function:* previously visited pages (for example: "2 out of 20 pages") displayed in a small overview or already clicked links marked in color,
- *Tasks* at the end of each lesson,
- *Learning status storage,*
- *Tutor,*
- *Messages,*
- *Certificate,* and
- *Glossary.*

4.1.1.7 Navigation

Navigation refers to the user guidance through the eLearning application. There are numerous ways to implement this:

Linear Navigation

Linear navigation serves the controlled content delivery. The eLearning application guides the learner along a predetermined path through the learning unit, as shown in Fig. 4.6. Linear navigation is suitable, for example, for endless loops at trade fairs or for logically related learning sequences. However, it is rarely used in modern eLearning as it does not allow self-directed learning.

Hierarchical Navigation

Hierarchical navigation serves the modular content delivery. It has a ladder structure and clearly shows the content of the eLearning application, as vividly illustrated in Fig. 4.7. It allows the learner to navigate forward and backward within the lessons; however, they cannot jump from a learning page within a lesson to the learning page of another lesson, as the learning pages are not linked to each other. This form of navigation is well suited for users who are not very practiced in using the computer and especially with

Fig. 4.6 Linear Navigation

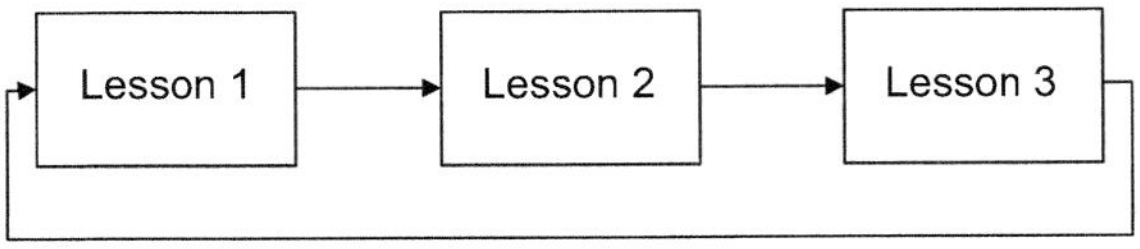

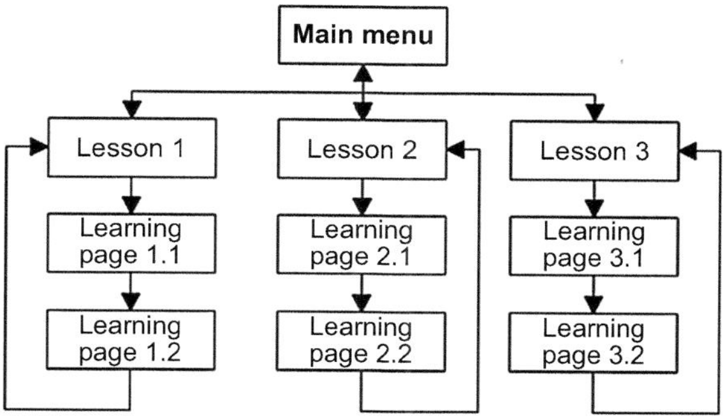

Fig. 4.7 Hierarchical Ladder Structure

networked pages, such as those found on the Internet. It is also recommended for an eLearning application whose lessons have little relation to each other, but whose learning pages within the lessons are logically related.

Hierarchical Navigation with Tree Structure

The hierarchical navigation with tree structure also serves the modular content delivery. However, it goes a step further than the ladder structure, as it allows the user to selectively access individual learning pages within the individual lessons. This form of navigation is common in current learning applications. There are also no connections between the individual lessons here. To switch from one lesson to another, the learner must access the main menu. The learning paths of the hierarchical navigation are shown in Fig. 4.8.

Networked Navigation

Similar to hierarchical navigation, networked navigation also facilitates modular content delivery (Fig. 4.9). It enables the learner to access the learning content at their discretion, without the necessity to access the main menu first. Both content-related learning modules and independent topics can be networked. This web-based user guidance is particularly suitable for knowledge systems and reference works.

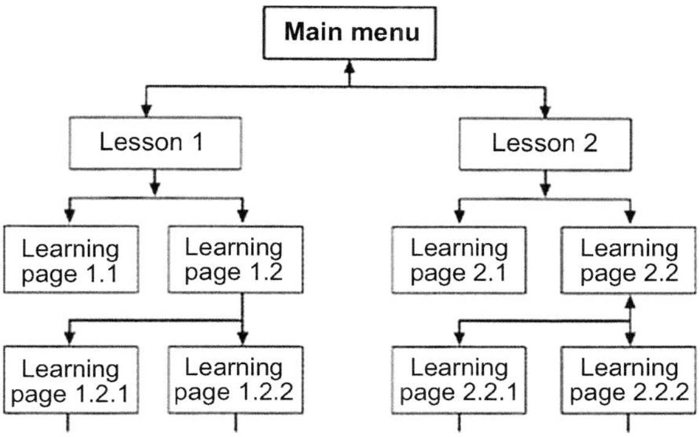

Fig. 4.8 Hierarchical tree structure

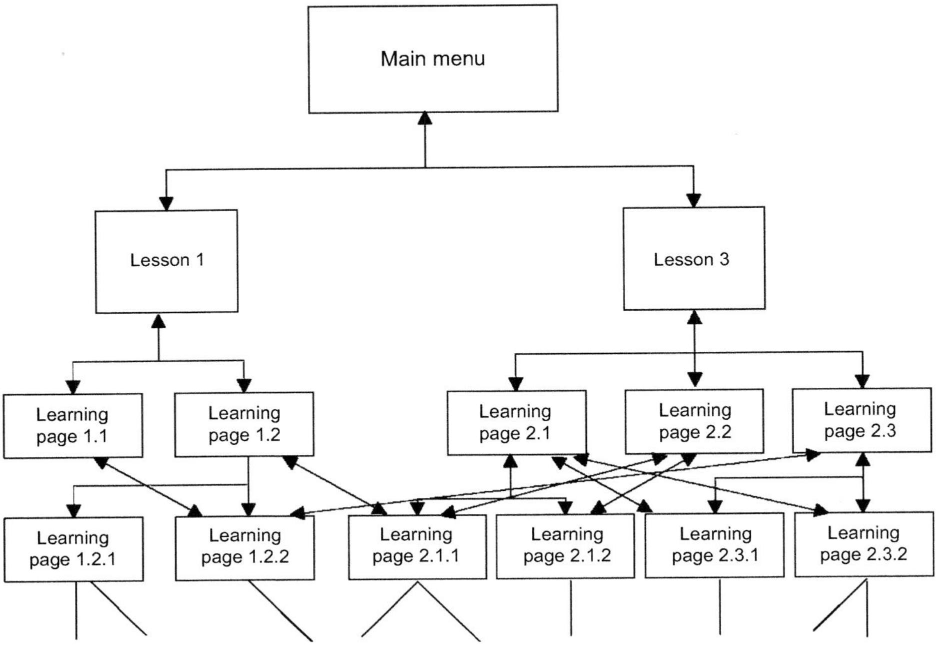

Fig. 4.9 Network Navigation

> **Tip!**
> Even within a Network structure, the learning path can be preserved by only opening a pop-up window with the targeted page when a hyperlink is clicked. This approach simplifies the learner's orientation process.

Examples of Navigation

Figures 4.10, 4.11, 4.12, 4.13, 4.14 and 4.15 illustrate how various types of navigation and control elements can be implemented as screen pages. The navigation screen for the module series VIP-S-Training from Versicherungskammer Bayern, designed for the training of savings bank employees, opens with a target wheel. This wheel allows the user to select the desired learning program. At this level, the navigation is implemented in a hierarchical ladder structure. Figure 4.10 shows the graphical implementation of the target wheel with individual theme segments. The rings refer to different learning levels: "Basics", "Basic Knowledge", and "Practical Knowledge".

On the distributor page in the main menu, the learner sees an Advance Organizer, which allows them to make an individual selection of the learning chapters, as shown

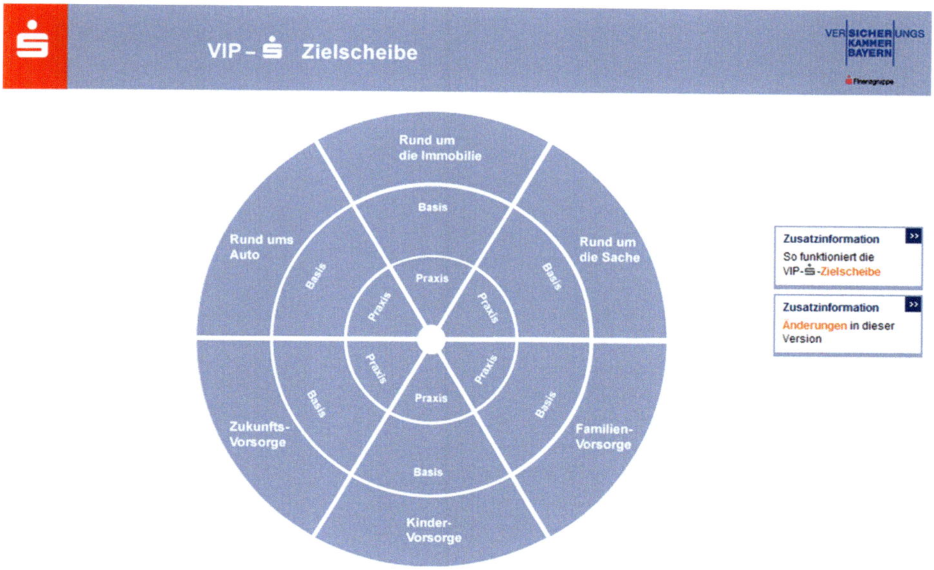

Fig. 4.10 Target wheel "VIP-S-Training", Versicherungskammer Bayern

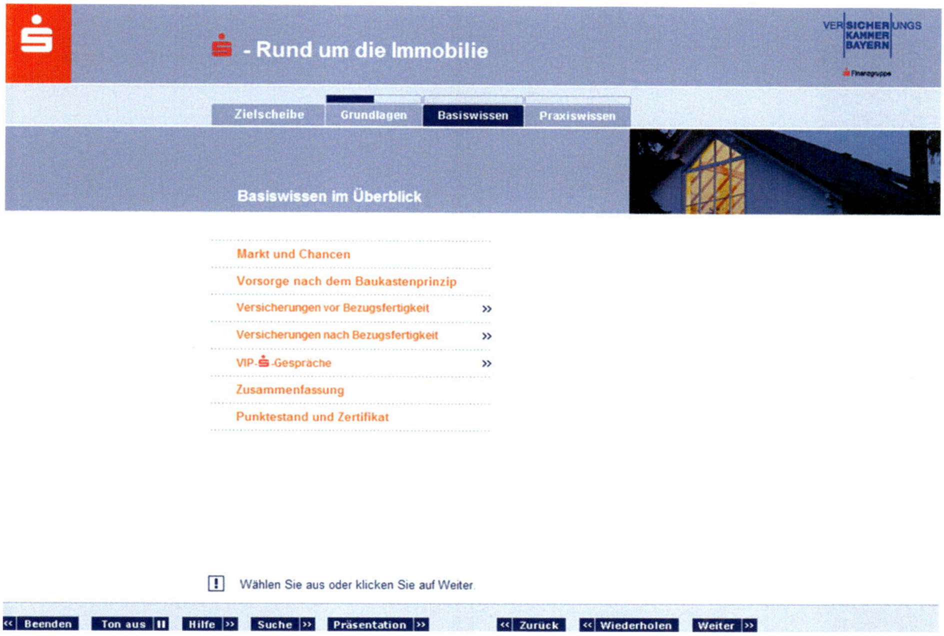

Fig. 4.11 Main menu "VIP-S-Training", Versicherungskammer Bayern

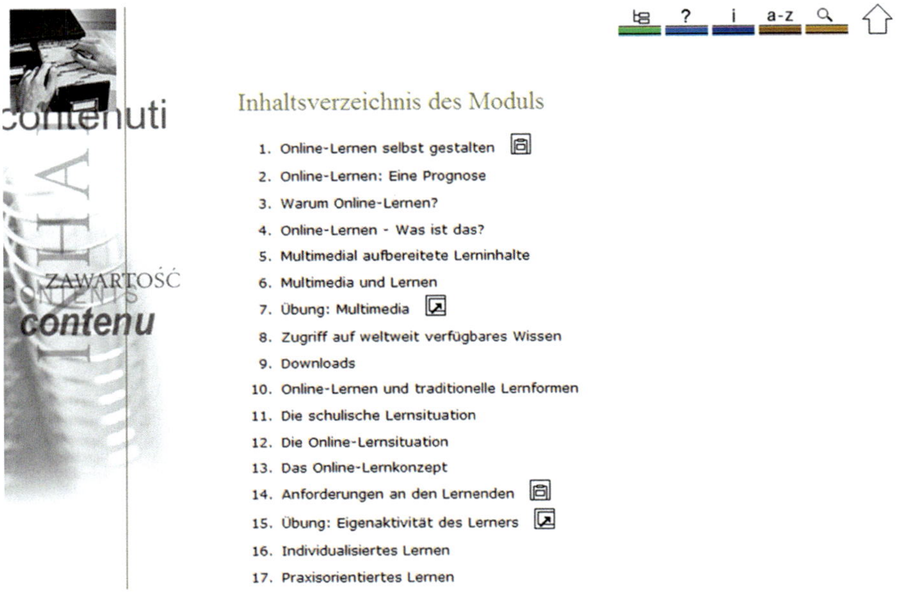

Fig. 4.12 Main menu "Designing Online Learning Yourself", bfz/bbw online, Nuremberg

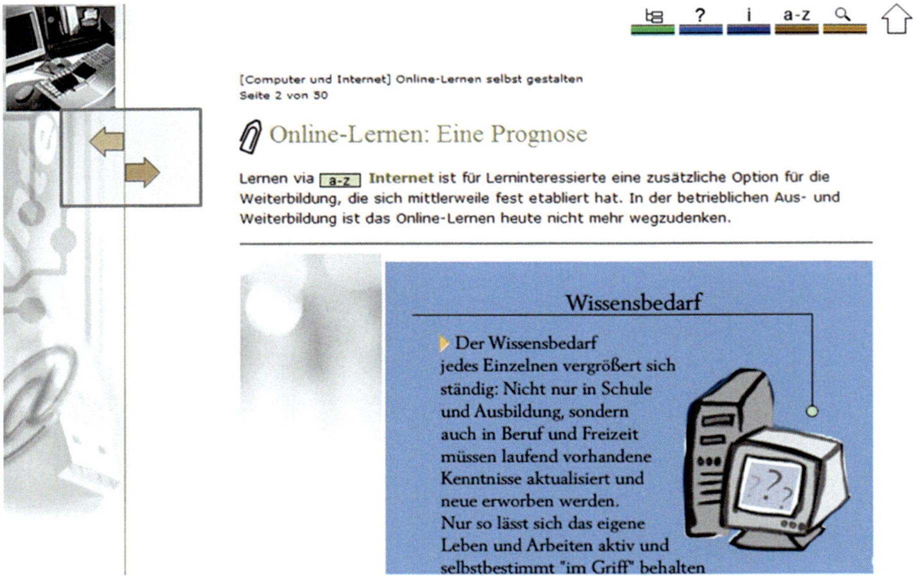

Fig. 4.13 Linear menu navigation in the course "Designing Online Learning Yourself", bfz/bbw online, Nuremberg

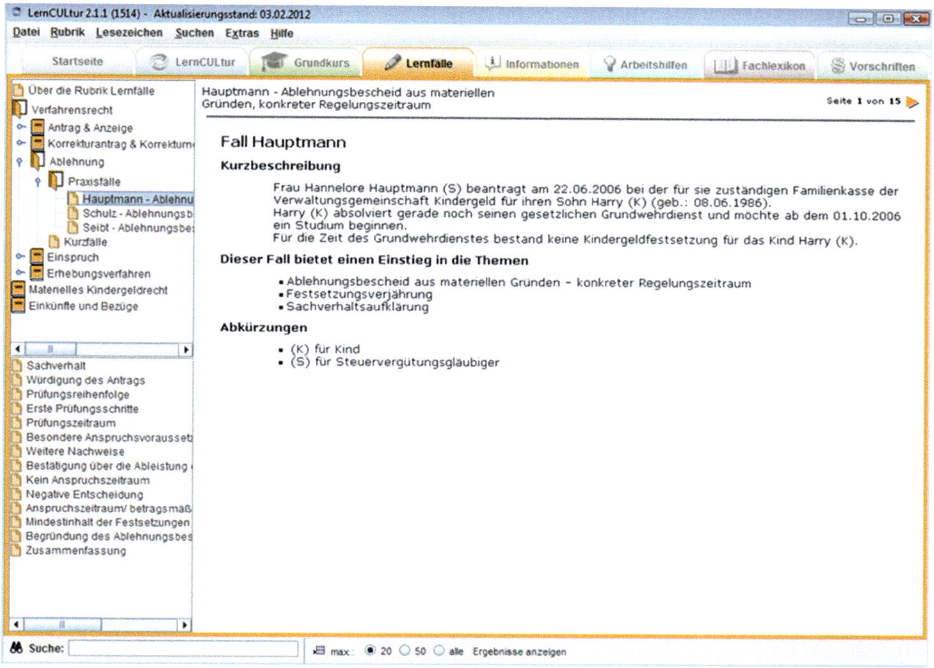

Fig. 4.14 "LernCULtur", Teleteach GmbH

Fig. 4.15 Wikipedia "Topic Portal Geosciences". (*Source*: http://de.wikipedia.org/wiki/Portal:Geowissenschaften)

in Fig. 4.11. Alternatively, they can follow the learning program linearly by clicking the "Next" and "Back" controls at the bottom of the screen. At the level of the distributor pages, the navigation follows a hierarchical tree structure.

The learning platform from Berufliche Bildungszentren der Bayerischen Wirtschaft (bfz) gGmbH uses a simple table of contents as a start menu and follows a linear tree structure from this level, as shown in Fig. 4.12.

However, the learner also has the option to access individual learning pages by using the table of contents from any screen page of the learning program. Figure 4.13 provides insight into this, as well as the strictly linear menu navigation within the learning pages.

A clear navigation with a networked structure can be found in the learning program LernCULtur from Teleteach GmbH. Figure 4.14 shows a special feature of the user guidance applied here: the so-called "3-frame architecture", in which navigation is also possible via a third linked window. Links to the lexicon open in a pop-up window.

Finally, the topic portal of Wikipedia serves as an example of a first-class networked navigation, as shown in Fig. 4.15. The user can access various content areas on the topic in the tab bar at the top of the screen in a so-called "topic portal". Optionally, links to further, topic-related articles are available in the right screen window. In addition, all the terms within the lexicon entry are linked to which there is again an article in the topic portal.

4.1.1.8 Design

In the film industry, there is a rule: A film that does not captivate the audience in the first ten minutes will not win them over in the next 100 minutes. Screen designers have even less time: Users decide within seconds whether they like the screen design or not. Thus, screen designers face several challenges. The layout or "interface design", as it is technically termed, should meet the following criteria:

- Target group orientation,
- Variety to promote motivation,
- Clarity, and
- Harmonious overall character of the illustration and navigation elements.

> "Page content and navigation should be designed so clearly that it is easy for the user to move quickly and specifically within it." Stephanie Wehner, screen designer at bfz, central eLearning department.

The rough concept outlines the general requirements for the screen design and should include the following points:

- Corporate Design (CD) or Corporate Identity (CI) of the client, including reference to specifications by a possibly existing specification sheet (see Sect. 4.3).
- Possibly a metaphor, for example: desk, residential building, sales room, consulting room, city etc. Note! The metaphor must be interpretable in the same way for all users.

- The most important control elements for navigation (buttons).
- Design peculiarities of the buttons, such as mouseover texts, which name the function of the buttons.
- Description of the basic user guidance, for example through index cards as vertical menu guidance at the top of the screen.
- The basic design of the learning pages, for example graphic on the left, text on the right, additional information in a column far right, scrollability of the pages, positioning of the navigation elements. Ideally, represent this as a rough drawing in the concept or program a template as a demonstration in the conference.

Tip!
On the checklist "Page Design" you will find practical tips for good screen design, see Sect. 10.15.

You can find more about the profession of screen designer in Sect. 2.2.5.

Reading tip!
Practical tips and hints for good design are provided by the textbook by *Christian Fries:* "Basics of Media Design". Following an introductory visual training, there are concrete information on the development of design, visualizations (including pictograms) and color areas as well as on the use of font types.

4.1.1.9 Media

Learning content is presented differently across a variety of media. This approach appeals to several sensory channels, which in turn promotes retention (see Sect. 5.7.1). All media available for the eLearning application are listed in the rough concept along with the corresponding implementation concept; an example of this is given in Table 4.4. Additionally, there are rough estimates about the number, size, and complexity of the chosen media. These details usually come from the briefing (see Chap. 3). When creating the media list, it is important to respect the copyright of the used media: rights must be obtained and sources must be cited for external media.

4.1.1.10 Technology

The following content points are included in the rough concept for the technical description:

- Deployment environment: What are the system requirements at the learners' workstations (operating system, multimedia equipment, such as headphones or similar, internet access etc.)?

Table 4.4 Rough concept: List of media

Medium:	Example implementation concept:
Screen text	Right side of the screen; text is not scrollable.
Learning documents	Stored as a PDF file, with reading and printing function.
Real images	Colour photos on the left side of the screen, also as collages of up to three photos; visual language is target group related.
Graphic	Coloured graphics (RGB mode) on the left side of the screen; like hand-drawn.
Video	Left side of the screen; 2 films of max. 2 min with conversation simulation.
Animations	Animated lead figure starts to speak, then remains static; renewed animated movement at the end of her speech text.
Sound	Noises appear together with the corresponding image, for example, the breaking of a window pane; sound can be turned off.
Audio/Spoken texts	The narrator's pronunciation is standard German. The lead figure has a colloquial youth slang; audio can be turned off, instead a small text window appears in the lower right screen area; the volume of the audios is adjustable.
Plug-ins	Windows Media Player, Acrobat Reader.

- Media formats: Which file formats are used in the eLearning application (HTML, DOC, XLS, PPT, JPG etc.)?
- Authoring tool: Which software does the media author use to create the script (see Sect. 5.6)?
- Content Management: How are the contents maintained (see Sect. 5.6)?
- Production type: Which technology is used for software development (XML (see Sect. 5.6.1), Java, Kotlin, PHP or similar)?
- Structure: Should the eLearning application be modular or linear?

Tip!
Checklist "Technical facilities and specifications" for querying system requirements, see Sect. 10.8.

4.1.2 Tools for Creating a Rough Concept

Essentially, a rough concept can be effectively represented using word processing software. If scribbles are to be incorporated into the main figure or scenarios, a scanner or smartphone and software for image editing are necessary. Digitally edited images can be directly integrated into a text document. For the representation of structure, navigation,

Table 4.5 Rough concept: tools

Image editing software:		
Adobe Photoshop http://www.adobe.de	German trial version	Highly professional image editing, training required, widely used.
Adobe Photoshop Elements http://www.adobe.de *(Products/Elements-Family)*	German trial version	Simple, creative image editing.
PaintShop Pro X4 Ultimate http://www.paintshoppro.com/de	German trial version	Fast, semi-professional image editing, affordable.
Paint.net https://www.getpaint.net	German trial version	Fast image editing at a simple level, publish and manage images, affordable.
Software for creating mind maps:		
MindManager http://www.mindjet.com/de	German trial version	Fast, diverse mind maps with interfaces to Microsoft Office software.
Software for creating flowcharts:		
Draw.io https://www.draw.io	English	Free software, fast flowcharts, intuitive to use, starts directly via Google Drive.
Edraw Max https://www.edrawsoft.com	English trial version	Professional flowcharts, precise and creative work, many functions.

and design, programs for creating flowcharts (also referred to as *flowcharts*) or software for drawing mind maps are suitable. With Microsoft's *PowerPoint* presentation software, rough concepts can be presented to the customer in a clear and engaging manner. Table 4.5 provides an overview of common tools that are helpful in creating the rough concept.

> **Tip!**
> With the "Rough Concept" checklist, both the author and the client can check the concept before submission and upon acceptance, respectively. See Sect. 10.16.

4.2 Detailed Concept

In the detailed concept, the contents from the rough concept (see Sect. 4.1.1) are organized and divided into lessons, learning units, and learning steps. The assignment is made according to the focal points as communicated in the briefing and according to content-related connections.

Tip!
Basic rule for learning on the screen: *Focus on one idea per learning page!*

When building lesson structures, the guiding objective provides orientation (see Sect. 3.2.3). All lessons and learning units should be consistently structured. That is, the Advance Organizer, learning steps and tasks should always appear in the same order. This approach relieves the learner from dealing with orientation and allows them to focus undisturbed on the acquisition of knowledge.

4.2.1 Contents of the Detailed Concept

The detailed concept lists everything that should later appear on the learning pages, supplemented by Learning objectives and structures:

- Title of the eLearning application,
- Detailed learning objectives,
- Assignment of learning content to the learning objectives,
- Selection of media and interactions for the learning objectives,
- Division into lessons, learning units and learning steps,
  Type of learning unit, for example: entrance test, content phases, simulation phase (for example of sales talks), interaction phase (tasks), final test,
- Type of learning pages, for example: Advance Organizer, content pages, summaries, tasks, glossary,
- Links to stored documents, pages on the intranet or internet as well as the
- Quantity structure with the complete number of screen pages.

Tip!
Checklist "Detailed concept", see Sect. 10.17.

The detailed concept can be implemented using different methods: With a flowchart, as shown in Fig. 4.16, a clear assignment and hierarchy of the learning content can be represented, as it has already been described in the navigation.

However, a flowchart quickly becomes confusing because a detailed concept should list among other things learning objectives, contents, media and notes. For this reason, it is advisable to use a simple table in landscape format, as shown in the example in Fig. 4.17.

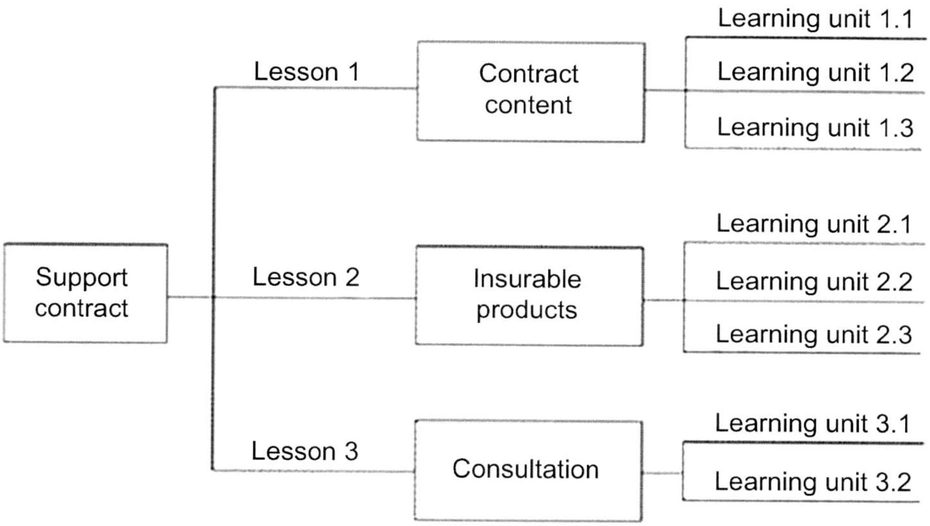

Fig. 4.16 Detailed concept as a flowchart

No.	Learning objective	Contents	Page type	Pages	Note / Media
	"The sales representatives achieve a 20% increase in sales with the new tariff" (indicative target)	Motivation: Benefits for the seller and customer	Intro	1	Photo presentation with music and motivating speaker text
1		Learning objectives Lesson 1 Menu with lem units	Advance Organizer	1	Photo collage with topic reference as a bar at the top of the screen; fade in lemma target texts successively with speaker comments
1.1	"The sales representatives understand that the new tariff should be explained as an important retirement provision for their customers." (Rough objective)	3 pillars of retirement provision		1	Graphic with three columns. Speaker text, no on-screen text, only successive fading in of the graphic labeling
1.1.1	"The advisor can explain the legal basis of the new tariff to the customer." (detailed objective)	Pension payment period	Contents	1	Timeline diagram. Speaker and screen text
1.1.2		Retirement age	Contents	1	Age pyramid. Speaker texts accompanying the successive screen structure. Screen text
1.1.3		State funding	Contents	4	Tables, speaker and screen texts
1.1.4		Summary	Add. fass.	1	Photo of active pensioners, enumeration
			Tasks	2	Exercise with sliding creel for Retirement age Multiple choice for state funding

Fig. 4.17 Detailed concept as a table, created with Microsoft Word

4.2.2 Developing and Formulating Detailed Learning Objectives

Detailed learning objectives describe individual learning contents in more detail and refer to one to three learning pages within the eLearning application. The formulation guidelines and categories for Detailed learning objectives correspond to those for guiding and rough learning objectives.

For the development of learning objectives in the cognitive and psychomotor domains, it is first necessary to distinguish between the three categories of knowledge acquisition: cognitive, affective, and psychomotor. Learning objectives in the cognitive domain follow a specific order, known as the taxonomy (Bloom et al., 1976). Table 4.6 explains the individual levels of this taxonomy and provides suitable verbs for formulating learning objectives.

Table 4.6 Taxonomy of cognitive learning objectives

Taxonomy level	Explanation	Verbs
1. Knowledge	Recall of known information, reproduction of learned knowledge, methodical and abstract knowledge	Write down, enumerate, select, confirm, represent, define, recognize, label, measure, name, reproduce, underline, list, show, recall
2. Understanding	Processing of new information; classification in a new context, transformation, translation, interpretation	Illustrate, justify, describe, interpret, discuss, explain, elucidate, formulate, point out, identify, interpret, classify, name, justify, represent, direct, paraphrase, comment, translate, clarify, compare, choose
3. Application	Use of rules and principles in defined situations = transfer of learned knowledge	Fill in, select, estimate, execute, answer, affirm, calculate, correct, use, classify, assess, develop, explain, calculate, construct, create, find, write out, estimate, negate, demonstrate, predict, choose, show, assign
4. Analysis	Dissection of a matter, of elements, relationships, orders	Derive, analyze, uncover, resolve, decide, describe correctly and completely, differentiate, extract, contrast, structure, identify, criticize, prove, justify, separate, investigate, compare, choose, dissect, disassemble, assign
5. Synthesis	Combining elements into a new whole, a system	Arrange, build, set up, report, decide, discuss, set up, debate, formulate, combine, construct, plan, connect, generalize, choose, summarize
6. Evaluation	Making judgments, whether certain criteria are met (criteria of logic and those of facts)	Attack, select, evaluate, determine, judge, assess, recognize, identify, criticize, measure, test, direct, support conclusions, avoid, defend against, choose, draw

The taxonomy is a valuable tool for formulating learning objectives, as it allows them to be reconsidered and articulated with a suitable verb. Moreover, learning objectives that are aligned with a taxonomy result in a clear task that tests the required knowledge in accordance with the learning objective. Learning objectives are operationalized in the formulation by:

- precisely describing the expected final behaviour,
- specifying the conditions under which the final behaviour is tested, and
- setting the standard for achieving the desired final behaviour.

The principles that apply to the formulation of specific learning objectives are the same as those for writing general learning objectives: use few abstract nouns and adjectives, many verbs for active formulations, and short sentences. Explain foreign words and technical terms, and avoid filler words. The verb should be meaningful and always placed at the end of the sentence. More information on the formulation of general learning objectives can be found in Sect. 4.1.1.4.

Example of a specific learning objective at taxonomy level 1

"The learner can list the differences between the warranty contracts for personal computers and those for netbooks in detail." ◀

This learning objective can be assessed with a multiple-choice task by providing several correct and incorrect answers to the contents of the warranty contract; the learner is asked to select the correct solutions. More on the different types of tasks can be found in Sect. 5.4.1.

4.3 Specifications

Specifications serve as a guide on how to successfully complete an eLearning project. However, setting up specifications is often neglected due to time constraints or perceived high costs. This is short-sighted, as specifications not only serve the current production but also lay the foundation for further developments of eLearning and similar IT projects within the company, such as the creation of an online presence. Specifications, almost like a checklist, represent a powerful tool for establishing routine in large processes. As international management consultant Fredmund Malik aptly puts it: "International air traffic would have long since collapsed if there were no checklists. They help to effectively routinize what can be routinized in a process." (Malik 2019) By investing time and costs once to develop specifications, the project team saves on follow-up costs for further concepts and especially for corrections.

Two possible initial situations can occur:

- The client already has a specification sheet in which, among other things, the corporate design or the corporate identity are defined.
- The client does not yet have a specification sheet; in this case, they are created based on the rough concept.

A newly created specification sheet thus establish the framework conditions for future productions. The criteria from the rough concept that can be applied to other projects are incorporated into this.

4.3.1 Elements of a Generally Valid Specification sheet

- Exact name and address of the company,
- Industry, product group, service offer,
- Company size and structure (number of branches, growth rates),
- Technical equipment of the PC workstations, servers and mobile devices,
- Previous use of eLearning and IT applications,
- Naming of the administrator as well as
- Design guidelines, possibly as an attached style guide.

4.3.2 Elements of a Specification Sheet as a Production Contract

A specification sheet valid for the current production integrates the rough concept. This makes it a binding production contract.

- Exact name and address of the multimedia agency,
- Naming of all project managers,
- Generally valid specifications,
- Rough concept,
- Fees, prices and budget,
- Payment modalities,
- Schedule and deadlines,
- Regulations in case of delays and cost increases,
- Description of the type of data delivery,
- Warranty conditions (for example, six months on technical defects),
- Rights of the contractor and client as well as
- Conditions of a possible contract termination.

References

Bloom, Benjamin et al. (1976) Taxonomie von Lernzielen im kognitiven Bereich. Weinheim: Beltz Verlag, 5. edn.

Fries, Christian (2016) Grundlagen der Mediengestaltung. München: Hanser Verlag, 5. edn., neu bearbeitet.

Kerres, Michael (2018) Mediendidaktik: Konzeption und Entwicklung digitaler Lernangebote. München: De Gruyter Oldenbourg Verlag, 5. edn.

Malik, Fredmund (2019) Führen, Leisten, Leben: Wirksames Management für eine neue Welt. Frankfurt: Campus Verlag.

5 What does a Good eLearning Script look like?

Abstract

Chapter 5 delves deeply into the practice of scriptwriting. All elements that a script must depict are explained in detail and presented in a practical manner with numerous examples. Additionally, the conveyance of background knowledge, such as from the fields of learning psychology and multimedia didactics, is included to develop as learning-friendly and perception-friendly screen pages as possible. The approach to scriptwriting for learning videos and the selection of the suitable authoring tool for creating an eLearning script are also comprehensively discussed.

A comprehensive eLearning script encapsulates all content elements of a multimedia application, outlining their processes and interactions. It provides detailed task descriptions for the project team members, ensuring that each participant knows exactly *what* they have to do and *how* to do it:

- The script serves as a production plan for media developers, including screen designers, graphic artists, software developers, sound technicians, video producers, and project managers of the multimedia agency.
- The client can gain a coherent understanding of the emerging learning program through a carefully prepared script.

Tip!
Changes to the script can be made at any time. However, late-stage author corrections may result in additional costs.

D. Modlinger, *eLearning and Mobile Learning – Concept and Script*, https://doi.org/10.1007/978-3-658-44695-6_5

A high-quality eLearning script…

- … adheres to the learning objectives.
- … is appropriate for the target audience.
- … maintains consistency in terms of image design and tonality.
- … is technically accurate.

For all elements of a script, the primary concern is not whether they are particularly humorous, creative, witty, or aesthetically pleasing, but whether they align with the previously defined learning objectives and are suitable for the target audience. The most crucial component in human-computer communication is the *action;* it also serves as the guideline for designing screen pages. The challenge in developing learning programs is that environments, interfaces, and objects are easier to conceptualize and depict than a fundamentally invisible communication quality. As the Association of German Screenwriters e.V. aptly describes, paraphrasing Bert Brecht: "Some are at the desk and others are in the light. But only those in the light are seen… those at the desk remain unseen." A media author who understands this resists the temptation for recognition, which could lead to compromising the principles of good scriptwriting, and instead lays a solid foundation for the upcoming production. They can take pride in their work when there are no complaints about the finished learning program, the educational objectives have been met, and the users enjoy working with it. However, media authors rarely receive feedback. Their work is considered complete once the script has been approved and production begins. It is advisable for the media author to seek feedback and incorporate it into future script developments.

> **Tip!**
> Refer to the "Script Acceptance" checklist in Sect. 10.10.

5.1 What Components does a Script have?

Previous chapters have extensively described how navigation is created within the framework of a rough concept. This navigation is part of the script and is established before the actual script pages once the rough concept has been approved. This means that the entire structure of the screen, including all available control elements, is determined before the first script page is written (see Sect. 4.1.1.6). The layout is typically designed by the screen designer, which is why it is not part of script development. However, the media author can and should influence the user-friendly design of the screen pages with their knowledge of learning psychology and especially multimedia didactics (see Sects. 5.7 and 5.8). The script should include a comprehensive description of all elements that will later appear on the screen in a multimedia format. The media author specifies the detailed content and media use per page in the script.

5.1.1 Elements and Media of a Script

- Project name.
- Module name.
- Version.
- Date.
- Author.
- History: Who worked on the script, when, which version number was created, and what was changed (see Sect. 7.4)? You can see an example of a history in Fig. 5.1.
- Table of contents: If a script is saved in several documents, a page overview is important, as shown in Fig. 5.1.
- Metadata: Provide keywords for the keyword catalog (i.e., for a search function), especially interesting for XML-based eLearning applications.
- Time indication: How long does the learner need to work through the individual learning pages and thus the lesson?

Script for the eLearning program "Sales training"

Project	"Extended warranty for ultrabooks"
Screenplay	Conditions of the Ultrabook warranty contract
Module	Basic knowledge
Version	1.2
Date	12.08.2019
Author	Daniela Modlinger

History

Version	When	From whom	What
1.0	12.08.19	DM	Screenplay first version
1.1	20.08.19	EK	Professional review
1.2	23.08.19	DM	Changes entered by EK

Table of contents of this screenplay chapter

Fig. 5.1 Example cover page for a script chapter

- Screen texts: Fully formulate and indicate to which other screen element (for example, graphic) these should appear (see Figs. 5.21 and 5.22); if there is no style guide, you should also describe how and where the text is on the screen (for example, font bold or light, position right, left, bottom or top).
- Graphic: Detailed description of the image content and indicate to which other screen element (for example, screen text) the graphic should run or appear (successively or fade in all at once); also describe where it is on the screen (right, left, bottom, center or top). If possible, create a scribble and integrate it into the text document; always indicate the source for graphics not created by yourself.
- Photo: Detailed description of the image content and indicate to which other screen element (for example, speaker text) the photo should appear (successively or fade in all at once); also indicate where it is on the screen (right, left, bottom, center or top). If possible, integrate the photo reduced into the text document; always indicate the source for photos not created by yourself.
- Speaker text: Fully formulate and indicate to which other screen element (for example, screen text) this should run and whether a special pronunciation is desired (see Sect. 5.2.2).
- Noises and sounds: Description of the type and time of appearance.
- Effects and animations: Description of the type and time of appearance and indicate how the effect or animation should run.
- Video: Exact name of the video; indicate when it should start and how long it should last; a separate video script is created for an eLearning video (see Sect. 5.5).
- Tasks, interactions: Detailed description of the task type (for example, multiple choice, see Sects. 5.2.4 and 5.4) and the process of the tasks; also indicate how many attempts are possible and which learning objective is being queried.
- Instructions for software developers: Indicate if an extraordinary screen layout takes place.
- Story: In some cases, a learning program is embedded in a narrative framework, then a short description of the story comes at the beginning of the script.

Tip!
One script page corresponds to one screen page.

In addition to the complete specification of all media, the media author describes the interaction of the individual elements in the screen and program sequence. Scripts for eLearning can be created with the most diverse tools (see Sect. 5.6). Changes are possible in the script at any time. However, later author corrections may incur additional costs (see Sects. 3.3.6and 3.4.1).

5.2 Writing for eLearning

The core rule for all types of eLearning texts is:

> One statement per screen page.

When screen text, graphic elements, and audio text on a learning page follow only *one* thought, it lays the foundation for clear content delivery.

> "Those who cannot express it simply and clearly should remain silent and continue working until they can express it clearly." Sir Carl Raimund Popper, philosopher.

The screen text significantly differs from the spoken texts (see Sect. 5.2.2). It focuses on the topic, conveys facts, and is factual. Emotions, questions, additions, and youth jargon, on the other hand, are assigned to the spoken texts. Screen texts can correspond with the spoken texts or stand independently of them. If there is an interaction, care should be taken to direct the learner's attention to a unit of information (see Sect. 5.7.1).

Modern learning programs usually follow a network or tree structure. For the media author, this means a rethink in the sense that there is no "preceding" and also no "following" page in the sense of a textbook. Phrases like "As the previous chapter showed ..." or "On the following page ..." are therefore unnecessary, both for the screen and for the spoken text. Instead, the relevant topic is referred to with a clear chapter reference.

> **Reading tip!**
> Understandability and catchy German based on 44 simple "recipes" for authors and readers is described by *Wolf Schneider* in: "German! The handbook for attractive texts", Rowohlt.

Back and Beuttler (2006, p. 215) have established nine rules of thumb for understandability based on Schneider (2006). They apply equally to screen and spoken texts, for the description of visualizations and the formulation of tasks:

- Minimize the use of adjectives.
- Maximize the use of verbs.
- Verbs can stand alone, for example, "apply" instead of "bring to application".
- Name actors, avoid passive structures; verbs like "occur" and "carry out" also promote the passive.
- Avoid abstract nouns.
- Explain or omit foreign words.

- Main topics in main clauses.
- Avoid nested sentences as much as possible.
- Arrange piles of numbers in tables.
- Repeating terms with a clear message is more understandable than varying them with "pleasing" synonyms.

Reading tip!
Back and Beuttler focus on methods of smooth collaboration between client and service provider in the "Handbook Briefing", Schäffer-Poeschel.

5.2.1 Creating Screen Texts

The author of a novel uses a different expression than the author of a textbook. The writing style of an advertising text differs from that of a company brochure. And writing for eLearning fundamentally differs from the presentation style in a textbook. The reading style is crucial for the writing style of the respective text: A novel invites you to browse, the advertising text wants to attract attention, the company brochure wants to make a good impression, and a textbook or a learning application wants to pass on knowledge. Accordingly, the respective texts are to be designed linguistically differently.

Reading tip!
Standard work for the visual design of learning material: *Steffen-Peter Ballstaedt:* "Visualizing", UTB.

In recent years, there have been many publications on writing good online texts on the web. However, the media author should not be tempted to borrow from here. Online texts differ just as much from texts in learning applications as, for example, encyclopedia entries differ from textbook chapters. It should also be considered that the learner at the computer is exposed to worse reading conditions than a learner with a textbook: Texts on the screen are read between 20 and 30% slower than on paper (Ballstaedt 1997). Factors responsible for this include the lack of resolution on the monitor, the low refresh rate, the luminance of the texts, the differences in contrast range, the constant changing adaptation of the eye from the screen to the environment, and the electrostatic charge (Hasebrook 1998). Therefore, screen texts must be written in a way that improves the reading conditions on the monitor. They should be sensibly structured, written in understandable language, and last but not least, be learning objective-oriented.

5.2.1.1 Structure of Screen Texts

Each type of screen text has its own form, which is crucial for readability:

- Content texts are composed of formulated, complete sentences.
- Summaries are presented as bullet points.
- Tasks include question sentences, solution sentences, and feedback comments.
- Box texts consist of short sentences that provide additional information or serve as glossary entries.

For improved readability, the screen text should be logically structured. For instance, according to the LATCH categories proposed by Richard Saul Wurman (1996):

- Location—strategic placement of information on the screen
- Alphabet—alphabetical organization
- Time—temporal organization
- Category—organization into categories
- Hierarchy—hierarchical organization

The structure is also reflected in the optics by:

- Choosing appropriate headings,
- Linking a maximum of three to seven text blocks with a main heading, and
- Ensuring a text block consists of three to a maximum of seven sentences.

Ballstaedt recommends starting each new screen line with a syntactic incision, i.e., not breaking apart related word groups. It should be noted that modern learning programs are usually produced for various browsers and screen resolutions, which can individually shift the running width of the screen texts. In this case, the author cannot specify a syntactically motivated line break within a running text.

5.2.1.2 Headings

Two types of headings are suitable for learning programs:

1. A heading related to the core theme of the text block to be depicted, for example, "Termination periods of the guarantee contract",
2. A question that introduces a problem-oriented situation, for example, "How do I recognize a potential customer for the conclusion of a guarantee contract?"

Emphasis can be added within the text blocks through bold or coloured printed words and italics. However, these remain accents only if they are used sparingly. For coloured printed words, use a uniform colour for highlighting within a learning program.

Tip!
Read the written text aloud: Reading aloud reveals a bumpy sentence structure!

5.2.1.3 Comprehensibility

To make it easy for the learner on the screen, the author has to make it difficult: "So, writers: Struggle!", as Schneider demands in "German!" (Schneider 2006).

Literature tip!
Learn the art of writing with practical tips and exercises in Doris Märtin's "Successful Texting!", published by Bramann.

Table 5.1 presents the most important criteria of comprehensibility with hints for their practical implementation, as Schneider also recommends in his book.

In conclusion, screen texts adhere to the four rules that Langer, Schulz von Thun and Tausch have established for the comprehensibility of texts:

1. *Simplicity*—Use clear and unambiguous words.
2. *Structure/Order*—Structure the text clearly.
3. *Brevity/Precision*—Formulate concisely and bring the statement to the point.
4. *Stimulating Additions*—Introduce invigorating elements that motivate continued reading.

Book Recommendation!
A textbook with many practical exercises: *Inghard Langer, Friedemann Schulz von Thun and Reinhard Tausch:* "Expressing oneself understandably", Reinhardt.

5.2.2 Formulating Spoken Texts

When listening, the learner exerts more cognitive effort than when reading: Unlike with eye movement, they cannot "quickly" jump back or forth with their hearing. Additionally, the spoken word is transient. Although learning performance is higher immediately after listening than through pure reading, heard contents only move into long-term memory if they are combined with corresponding screen texts or visual implementation. What does this mean for the formulation of spoken texts? Above all, it is important to ensure that screen text, visualization, and spoken text correspond with each other in content and that no so-called "text-image gap" arises.

Tip!
In some learning programs, learning pages are linked to each other. Ensure that the speaker's transitions to the next page fit.

Table 5.1 Criteria of Comprehensibility

Criteria of Comprehensibility	Background
Verbs forward	In German, the verb often only appears in the last part of the sentence, for example: "The guarantee contract with all its conditions belongs to the training." If the verb moves forward, the learner quickly grasps what it is really about: "The guarantee contract belongs with all its conditions to the training."
Resolving Sentence Brackets	In German, sentence brackets are commonly formed by separating verbs with a large number of intervening words. For example: "The warranty contract *closes* with its conditions to the subjects learned in the education for electronics sales specialist *on.*" In this sentence, 12 words separate the two parts of the verb "on" and "close". This requires the learner to remember the first part of the sentence until they reach the end. A better construction would be: "The warranty contract with its conditions *closes* to the subjects *on,* that were learned in the education for electronics sales specialist." Schneider (2006) proposed a rule of 12 syllables for this: A maximum of 12 syllables or six words should separate the halves of a split verb.
Forming Short Sentences	Reading on a screen is more strenuous than on paper, causing learners to tire quickly. Short, concise sentences can mitigate this. For example: "There are two different basic types of warranty contracts that serve different product groups by aligning their conditions with the respective product lifespan." This sentence can be divided into shorter, simpler sentences: 1. "There are two types of warranty contracts." 2. "Each type serves a specific product group." 3. "The conditions are based on the respective product lifespan." The following sentence forms improve readability on the screen: **Definitions, mnemonic sentences, enumerations** and **short declarative sentences.**
Using Prepositions Sparingly	Excessive use of prepositions can promote a nominal style, as demonstrated in the following example: "The application for a support contract is to be forwarded to the accounting department for verification of correctness via the department head." By rearranging the sentence, prepositions can be omitted: "The department head forwards the application for a warranty contract to the accounting department; the accounting department checks whether the application has been filled out correctly." By rearranging, the sentence acquires an *active* character.

(continued)

Table 5.1 (continued)

Criteria of Comprehensibility	Background
Deleting Adjectives	Adjectives can obscure clarity, making them unsuitable for a learning program. For example: "You learn to conduct **targeted** consultation talks." "Your customer is **heavily** overwhelmed with the operation of the PC." "You can **individually** adapt the warranty contract." These adjectives can be deleted without distorting the content, because: A "consultation talk" is always targeted, as it provides the customer with a recommendation. The verb "overwhelm" alone already expresses the severity of the situation; it does not need to be reinforced. A contract that can be "adapted" is therefore tailored to the individual.
Writing Actively, Avoiding Passive	Active writing identifies the actor, thus promoting the action orientation of a learning program. For example: "The customers are secured against PC failures by the support contract." This sentence can be easily written actively: "The support contract secures the customers against PC failures."
Using Numbers in Digits on the Screen	In learning programs, numbers often appear and should be presented in a learner-friendly manner: A text with many numbers is clearer as a table than in the form of running text. Numbers should be presented as digits in screen texts, as they are much faster captured by the eye. As a rule: Numbers that are usually written as digits (stamps, type designations, amounts of money) should be presented as digits in screen texts, even if they are smaller than "13" (contrary to the well-known rule: up to the number "12", numbers are written in letters).
Technical Terms	Technical terms that appear in the learning program should be explained at their first mention. If the technical language should be known to the learner, a reference to the glossary is sufficient.
Implementing References as Hyperlinks	Typically, learning programs follow a network or tree structure. Therefore, references to previous or subsequent pages and texts above or below are unnecessary. The reference is made differently, either by a specific chapter indication or by setting a hyperlink on a word in the sentence. It is crucial to choose a suitable word for the hyperlink's target. The hyperlink in this sentence is not well chosen: "You can download the conditions of the support contract as a **PDF file**." The target of the hyperlink is the "conditions", so a clear hyperlink looks like this: "You can download the **conditions of the support contract** as a PDF file."

5.2.2.1 Interaction with Screen Texts

- The core message appears as screen text parallel to the spoken text.
- Enumerations only come into the spoken text if they appear on the screen at the same time.

5.2.2.2 Rules for Formulation

- Spoken texts should be consistent, that is, important terminologies are always pronounced the same and match the terms mentioned in the screen text.
- Once chosen, terminologies should be consistently maintained during the spoken text, that is, do not alternate these with synonyms.
- Spoken texts work with repetitions, because the learner cannot easily jump back and forth.
- Concrete before abstract, for example: "For each sold support contract you receive a commission", instead of abstract: "With each support contract that you have processed with a customer, you increase your monthly payments."
- As far as possible, do not include values, numbers or current facts in the spoken text, as audio updates are time-consuming and costly.
- The criteria for the comprehensibility of screen texts (see Sect. 5.2.1.3) also apply to spoken texts: short sentences with less than 12 words, clear sentence constructions, clear sentence references and always put verb and main statement at the beginning of the sentence.
- Foreign words are to be avoided. Exception: They are learning content and are explicitly explained in the spoken text.
- Each sentence should contain at most one new piece of information.
- Audio texts have a slow speaking speed with little text and many pauses.
- Spoken texts should be written in as small sequences as possible, so that they are easier to update.

> **Tip!**
> Especially when formulating spoken texts, the correct punctuation is crucial; only then can the speaker hit the intended intonation when dubbing.

5.2.2.3 Tonality

- Consider the tone of voice in the company or target group and adjust the spoken texts accordingly.
- Dialogues should sound fluid; they ought to be read aloud before they are voiced.

Tip!
Listen to the radio! It is best to tune into a channel where a lot is spoken: listening to the radio will hone the sense of language for good spoken texts.

5.2.2.4 Directing Instructions

- Speaker Instructions for emotional colourings or tones must be precise. For instance, the media author decides on a colouring, such as: *(speaks in a tortured-cheerful manner)* "…"—this information is ambiguous and challenging for the speaker to implement; if the tone is to be varied, it is better to write: *(speaks first part of sentence in a tortured manner, ends cheerfully),* then the assignment is clear.
- Emphasize places by underlining or bolding, as brackets within the text disrupt the reading flow.
- Specific ways of speaking, emphases, types of pronunciation appear in brackets before the entire Take.
- Always write numbers in the script as digits, this makes it easier for the speakers to read.
- Indicate the pronunciation of abbreviations or technical terms, for example: *(please spell out WBT) "WBT is a modern form of learning."*
- If something is to be pronounced, it is best to write it in the script as such, for example: "Web Based Training is a modern form of learning."
- A grammatically incorrect phrase, which however represents a witty comment of the lead character, must be marked as correct, for example: *(speak text as in advertising)* "Do something against ugly!"

Tip!
When selecting speakers, avoid choosing voices that are *too* distinctive: This makes later updates difficult, for example if a certain speaker is no longer available.

5.2.2.5 Lead Character

A lead or sympathetic character appeals to the emotional level and motivates:

- The spoken texts can be humorous and cheekier than the usual language style.
- Ensure that spoken texts of lead characters do not come across as pedantic.
- Spoken texts provide tips and hints and draw attention to important facts.
- The lead character can convey emotional colourings and thus make a significant contribution to the motivation of the learner at the computer.

5.2.3 Describing Images

"A picture says more than a thousand words. In short, the media author should provide image templates: copies, Scribbles, style templates etc. No matter what it is—the main thing is, it's a picture!" Christian Ertl, Bildersprache Munich.

How do I describe images so that they are understandable to the media developer? Images that can appear in scripts for eLearning include graphics and photos. Hints for video scenes and animations can also appear in the image descriptions. The basic rule is: use as few words as possible. The clearest image descriptions are images themselves, that is, the media author should be practiced in drawing scribbles. They should also master the most important technical terms from the photo and film world in order to provide clear descriptions for photo shoots and video shoots.

5.2.3.1 How does a Scribble work?

A scribble is a sketch that roughly represents a scene or an object. In advertising, a scribble is the precursor to the layout or the final artwork. It should be so precise that the graphic designer or photographer can well imagine the depicted scene and implement it in their medium. But it should also not be too professional, because that only costs the author unnecessarily much time for detail work; it has also happened that a media author finds his carefully worked out scribbles 1:1 in the beta version, which was not necessarily his intention.

Literature tip!
Insights into the two hemispheres of the brain and instructions for visual seeing and drawing are provided by the workbook and exercise book by *Betty Edwards:* "The New Drawing on the Right Side of the Brain", Rowohlt.

Now some media authors may get scared because they can write fluently, but were no Picasso in art class. This fear is unfounded: scribbling is easy to learn with some practice. The advantage for the author is that he strengthens his visual imagination and saves his eloquence for the important topics, such as writing screen and spoken texts.

5.2.3.2 Basic Principles for Effective Scribbles

- Sketch simply and clearly, avoiding an overload of symbols.
- Representing people as stick figures is sufficient.
- Reduce to the essentials: A scribble is not finished when nothing more can be added, but when nothing more can be omitted, similar to writing.
- When scribbling video sequences, take advantage of the brain's ability to bridge supposed gaps between individual images in a sequence; only sketch the decisive moments that drive the story forward.

Tip!
As a media author, consider visiting the editorial office of a schoolbook publisher and observing the textbook editor: Creating understandable scribbles is part of their daily toolkit.

5.2.3.3 Tools for Effective Scribbles

- For paper scribbles: pencil and paper, as well as colours for graphics and images that build up successively, scanner or smartphone.
- For digital scribbles: image editing program, drawing tablet, digital camera or smartphone.

5.2.3.4 Implementing Scribbles

First, the situation needs to be analysed. For example, the following topic is to be introduced: "The salesman presents a netbook warranty contract to the customer." The essential elements are: *salesman, customer, contract* and they need to be depicted. Additionally, it is important to illustrate the relationship between these three elements. Fig. 5.2 represents this relationship in a simple scribble. The reduction to the essentials means that not even the legs of the participants are visible. With simple lines, people and actions can be represented.

Reading Tip!
Learn to scribble using techniques and examples from flipcharts in the seminar room with a book that encourages you to get started immediately: *Elke Meyer & Stefanie Widmann:* "Flipchart ART", Publicis.

Often, a single scribble is enough to record a sequence of images. The sequence is indicated on the scribble by (coloured) director's instructions, which will ultimately form the overall picture. In Fig. 5.3, the director's instructions for the order of the fades are represented as hatched numbers.

Fig. 5.2 Scribble Theme Introduction

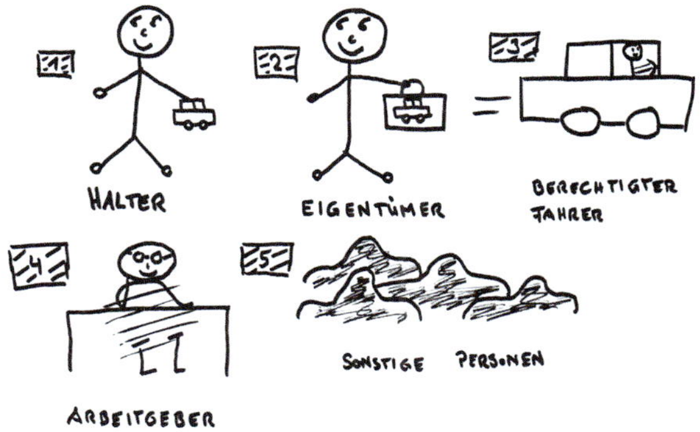

Fig. 5.3 Scribble Sequence of Images

Scribbles can also serve as templates for diagrams; the colour is not binding here, but only shows the different references. The differentiating colour scheme is indicated in Fig. 5.4 by hatching.

Some types of tasks are based on a graphic template, for example, drag-and-drop exercises. In Fig. 5.5, for example, the elements that are not insured are to be pulled out of the picture. The underlying graphic consists of individual elements with the codes S1 to S8. The hatched elements (S2, S5, S7) are the correct solutions and thus to be pulled out of the picture by the learner.

In principle, the literal image description in the script is limited to the following information:

- Position of the image element within the learning page.
- Appearance time in the course of the image page.
- For a video: the total duration.
- For photo shoots, it is helpful to add thought sentences of the protagonists to the image ideas or scribbles, which reflect the emotions.

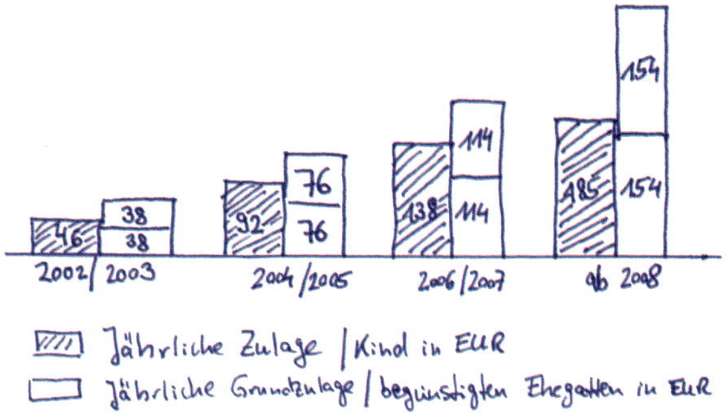

Fig. 5.4 Scribble Bar Chart

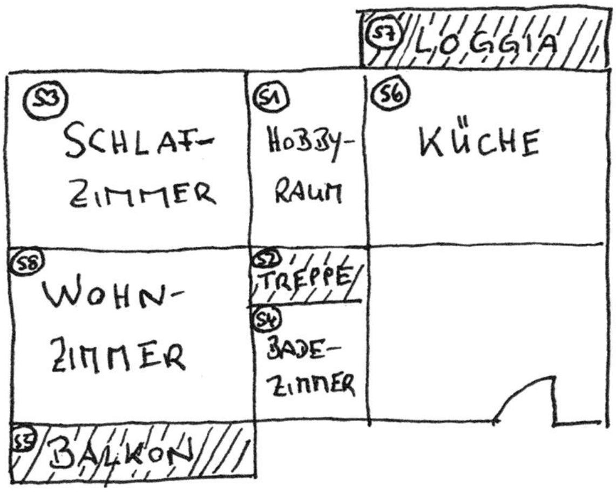

Fig. 5.5 Scribble of a Drag-and-Drop Task

5.2.3.5 Terminology in the World of Photography and Film

To describe photo and film recordings briefly and succinctly, it is beneficial to understand the most significant technical terms of photography and film. Table 5.2 provides an overview.

5.2.4 Formulation and Description of Tasks

Task texts consist of task specifications, solution sentences and numbers, and feedback after the task has been completed. Tasks test whether the previously set learning objectives have been achieved through the processing of the learning pages. The question should not be too difficult, otherwise, the learner becomes frustrated and loses motivation. However, the task should not be too easy either, as in this case, the learner does not feel taken seriously and finds further learning uninteresting. The skill of the media author, therefore, lies in formulating tasks

- to build up learning objective-oriented,
- to adjust according to the level of difficulty, and
- to formulate in a way that is appropriate for the target group.

Example

In a Multiple-Choice Task, several solution options are given. The questions could be:

- *Appropriate:* "What is the cancellation period for a warranty contract for netbooks?"

- *Too easy:* "What is the cancellation period for the 1-year warranty contract for netbooks?"—The cancellation period is already mentioned in the "1-year warranty contract".
- *Too difficult:* "What is the cancellation period for a warranty contract of product group 1A?"—The question assumes further knowledge, namely the knowledge of the "product group 1A".

Table 5.2 Technical Terms in Photography and Film

Technical Term	Explanation
Fade in	The gradual brightening of an image from complete darkness to the chosen exposure level. It is mainly used at the beginning of a sequence, as a counterpart to the fade out.
Fade out	The image gradually disappears into darkness.
Cross-fade	An image is faded out while a new image is simultaneously faded in.
Single shot	A performer is shown alone, usually in medium shots to close-ups.
Extreme close-up	The camera is directed at a Sect. of an object or person. The short distance allows for the capture of minute facial reactions on a person's face, such as frowning, winking, or similar.
Long shot	The long shot provides an overview of the entire situation. The image Sect. is somewhat closer than in the wide shot; people are usually the subject.
Medium long shot	Shows people from head to toe, corresponds to the photographic group shot.
Full shot	Shows a person from head to waist.
Medium close-up	The person is shown from the head to the upper body. This shot size best reveals a person's gestures and facial expressions; it is well suited for conversation scenes.
Close-up	The face and usually the shoulder of a person are shown; the focus is on the facial expressions.
Very long shot	The very long shot shows landscapes, sea, sunrises and sunsets, as well as buildings; people appear negligibly small.
Two-shot	Shot of two people, usually in dialogue.
Top-shot	Viewing angle from above, that is, viewed from the "bird's eye view".
Pan right/left; tilt up/down	The camera is rotated on the same level on the tripod to the right or left. With each pan, the Sect. that the camera shows changes.
Zoom	By changing the focal length of the lens (zooming), an object is displayed larger or smaller without moving the camera.

The Feedback textsinform the learner whether they have solved a task correctly or incorrectly. Usually, the speaker provides a differentiated feedback, that is, they differentiate whether the task was only partially solved correctly, point out errors and recommend repetition chapters:

- *Differentiated feedback:* "That's almost correct. Consider the target group and try again."
- *Feedback with repetition recommendation:* "Oops! The second attempt also went wrong. My tip: Repeat the chapter with the contract conditions."

Included in the task description are the details of how many attempts the learner has for the task and which of the proposed solutions is correct. If a leading figure provides the feedback, the script specifies when they appear on the screen, when they disappear and how they move. For more on task types and feedback, see Sect. 5.4.

5.3 Types of Visualisation

The media author selects the image medium that best represents the learning content. Images can serve different functions:

- Transmit information, regardless of language.
- Represent relationships.
- Illustrate processes.
- Clearly represent complicated systems, such as an engine.
- Convey large amounts of data.
- Make comparisons.
- Provide instructions for action.
- Show examples.
- Increase the memorability of learning content.
- Meet aesthetic requirements.

For all these functions, various types of visualisation are available, which the following chapters will introduce.

5.3.1 Graphics

One of the most common visualization methods is graphics. They come in various levels of detail, from the purely schematic flow chart, as shown in Fig. 5.6, to the visualization of complex processing processes, as shown in the example in Fig. 5.7.

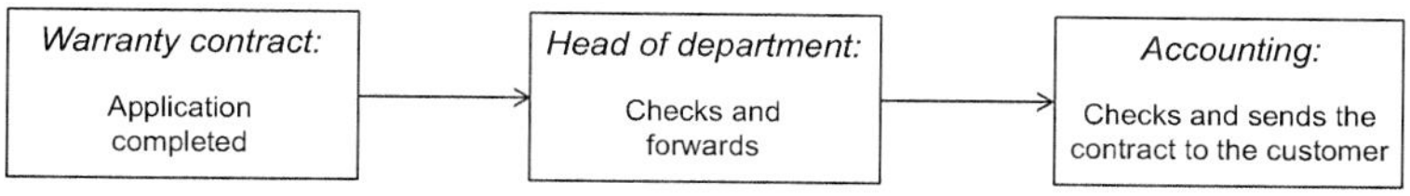

Fig. 5.6 Flow chart

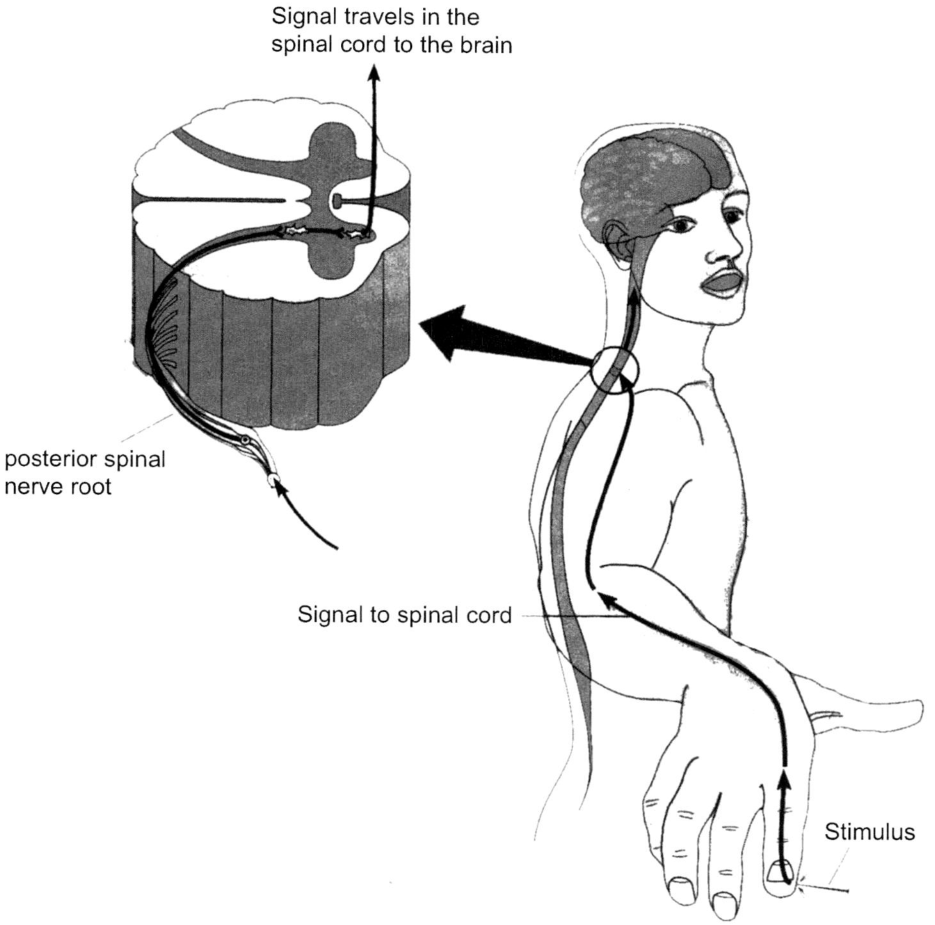

Fig. 5.7 Processing process *Source* Goldstein, Bruce (1997) Perception Psychology, Heidelberg: Spectrum Publishing, p. 434

Tip!
Always consider feasibility when developing and selecting types of visualization. If in doubt, consult with a media developer.

5.3.1.1 Other Types of Graphics

- Diagrams (flow, structure, circle, bar, column, line, scatter, point, area, ring, network diagrams, etc.),
- Tables,
- Mind maps, or
- Illustrations.

The graphic artist manually converts the author's scribbles and scans them in, or edits digital templates with a drawing tablet, either as vector or bitmap graphics.

5.3.1.2 Vector Graphics

In vector graphics, the relationship between lines and fill elements is defined, that is, lines and vertices form a surface that can be filled with colour. Advantages of this type of graphic include small amounts of data and arbitrary reduction or enlargement (= scalability) without loss of quality. A program that works in vector format is, for example, Adobe Illustrator.

5.3.1.3 Bitmap Graphics

Bitmap graphics are pixel-oriented, that is, each point (= pixel) is defined individually. The graphic artist sets the resolution for a specific image size before drawing. It reads, for example: 72 dpi (= **d**ots **p**er **i**nch), which corresponds to 72 pixels per inch (1 inch = 25.4 mm). If the image is enlarged, the amount of data increases accordingly. The program Adobe Photoshop, for example, works in bitmap format. Advantages of this software are that it allows photorealistic representations with soft focus effects and similar, and can edit photos.

To help the learner process graphic visualizations effectively, it is helpful to guide them by:

- asking the learner to find detailed information in an image,
- limiting the time for viewing the image and announcing this,
- adding pull-down menus with target specifications and explanations to the image, and
- instructing the learner to engage with the image.

A good learning page builds the graphic successively parallel to the spoken text; this allows the learner to approach the learning content step by step.

> **Tip!**
> Checklist "Image Design", see Sect. 10.18.

5.3.2 Photography

5.3.2.1 Applications of Photos

Photos are an excellent choice when the client already possesses a picture archive, perhaps from advertising campaigns. This allows for cost-effective visualisation. Photos are the preferred choice for illustrating dialogues, as learners can best understand the conversation using the example of "real" people.

5.3.2.2 Implementation Examples of Photos in an eLearning Application

- Create a photo collage, a series of images at the top or bottom of the screen from several photos.
- Display a photo collage on the left side of the screen that forms a square from four elements.
- Use photos transparently as a background for a graphic, for example, Euro bills on which a table with sales figures is superimposed.
- Display photos as circles that are connected to each other like a flow chart via arrows, for example to represent the different types of customers.
- Expressive photos form an Advance Organizer: When you click on a photo, the program links to the respective learning page.
- Photos can be used as orientation markers by, for example, first forming the Advance Organizer and then appearing as a miniature on each learning page within the chosen chapter; the learner always knows where they are.
- Photos build up successively in the left screen field, while a listing fades in on the right at the same time.
- Display photos in black and white and let them become coloured when clicked on, while speaker and/or screen text runs in parallel.
- Photos with faces that change, for example a sad face that turns into a happy face with the fading in of further screen texts and audios.
- Transparent photo that only becomes fully coloured with the fading in of screen and speaker texts.
- Assemble photos in puzzle form successively while the learning page runs.
- Timeline with small-format photos that, for example, represent the career of an apprentice up to the master.

5.3.2.3 Communication Examples for Photos

Photos can convey a variety of meanings; often a Sect. is enough to let the viewer infer the whole:

- Need for care: Medicine being administered with a spoon.
- Disability: Hand on wheelchair tyre.
- Enjoying retirement: Elderly couple walking on the beach.
- Lonely retirement: Face of an old person behind a window.
- Past: in black and white style, optionally with a yellow tint.
- Accident: broken fender.
- Court hearing: Judge's gavel.
- Decision: Tracks with switch.
- Achieving a goal: Show a photo series that shows the movement towards the goal over several learning pages, for example a mountaineer who finally places the summit cross.
- Education: School bag on a child's back.

5.3.3 Animations

5.3.3.1 Applications of Animations

- *Visualisation* of complex facts, constructions, spatial dimensions, movements, processes or actions that a real film cannot do justice to, for example the simulation of a complicated operation.
- *Entertainment* and *tutorial accompaniment* by a leading figure offer a point of identification for the learner.
- *Directing attention* on a learning page, for example by using crossfades, flashing words, fading in or out an image or a line, and growing diagrams animatedly.
- *Creating tension.*

Tip!
Leading figures do not necessarily have to be animated; often illustrated figures in different positions or photo variants serve their purpose.

Animations should generally be used sparingly and never interrupt learning units or disrupt the program flow. They should also be used sparingly because their production is expensive. Similar effects to animations can be achieved with changing sequences of images, for example by first fading in a photo and then fading it out again or by gradually building up a graphic from individual elements.

The selection criterion for an animation is always: The learning objective can only be achieved with an animation and no other visualisation. It should also be considered that a 2D or 3D animation film only runs in a small window on the screen.

5.3.4 Learning Videos

Another very popular visualisation tool is videos. Learn more about the design of learning videos and their visual application possibilities in Sect. 5.5 Learning Videos.

5.4 Tasks

Tasks serve to verify whether the learning objectives defined in the detailed concept have been achieved by the learner. Typically, tasks are set at the end of a learning unit and as a large block of tasks at the end of the entire learning programme. In some instances, tasks also serve to classify the learner before they can even start the learning programme; in this case, we refer to it as an entry test. There are numerous variants available for the type of task. The choice of task type depends on the learning content to be tested and on the techniques used for knowledge acquisition. If a learning programme works with simulations, it is advisable to also use these as a task type. Regardless of the task set, feedback is essential! This is what a learning programme owes its "student".

> **Tip!**
> Indicate in the menu the processing time for the tasks or task blocks; this helps the learner to stay "on track".

5.4.1 Types of Tasks

There are numerous kinds of task types. However, all tasks can be traced back to a few basic types, which are listed below with examples of variations. This collection does not claim to be exhaustive; rather, it is intended to provide inspiration and impulses for further creative task variants.

5.4.1.1 Multiple Choice Tasks

Multiple choice tasks present several solution options, from which the learner should select the correct one(s). Choices can be presented as sentences, numbers, photos or other elements. They all follow these three patterns:

- *Single-Choice:* Simple selection from several alternatives; this also includes "Yes/No tasks" or "True/False tasks". The learner is asked a question and the only solution options are "Yes" or "No" or "True" or "False". Yes/No tasks are not often used as they can be guessed correctly 50% of the time. Fig. 5.8 provides an example of a single-choice task.
- *Multiple-Choice:* Multiple selection from several alternatives.

Fig. 5.8 Example of a single-choice task, VIP-S-Training, Versicherungskammer Bayern

Table 5.3 Example description of a cross-choice task in the eLearning script

	Netbook warranty contract	Smartphone warranty contract
Cancellation period 6 months		X
Cancellation period 3 months	X	

- *Cross-Choice:* Multiple selection from several parallel alternatives; in the example, the learner clicks on the correct assignments—for example by clicking on the box for "Netbook warranty contract" and "Cancellation period 3 months". Table 5.3 provides an example of the description of a cross-choice task in the eLearning script.

5.4.1.2 Drag-and-Drop Tasks

The term "Drag-and-Drop" originates from English and translates to "drag and drop". Often, you will also encounter the term "Pick-and-Place" or, in short, "PNP". Drag-and-drop tasks contribute more to the transfer of learned material than selection tasks, as the learner must think through the connections in detail. There are numerous variants of this:

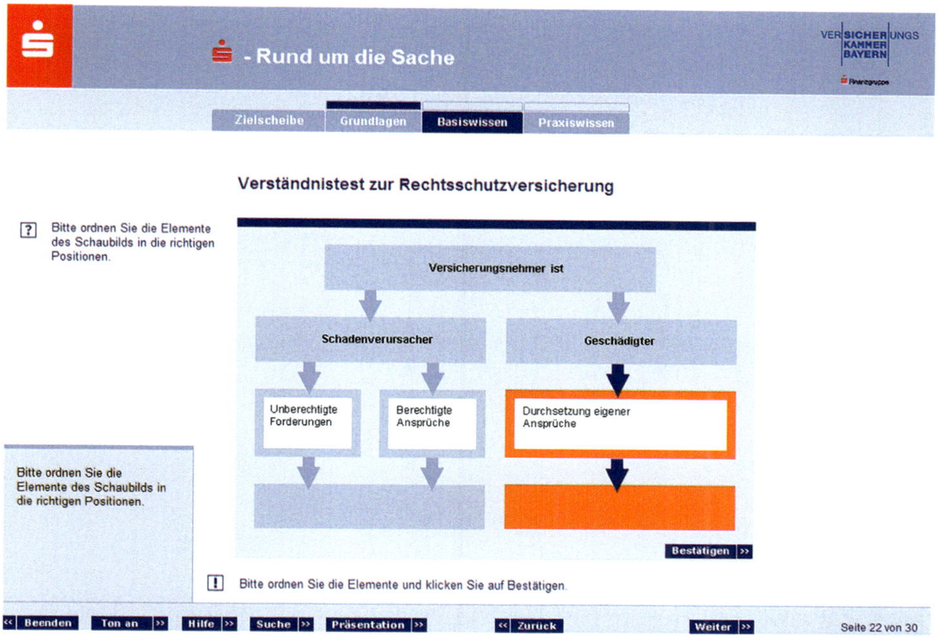

Fig. 5.9 Example Drag-and-Drop task "correct positioning", VIP-S-Training, Versicherungskammer Bayern

- *Forming a sequence:* Several terms, photos, boxes or similar are arranged in a disorderly manner and should be brought into the correct order by clicking on an element and dragging it to the right place. Fig. 5.9 provides an example of what a task to form a sequence might look like.
- *Filling in a gap text:* A list of terms appears next to the gap text and the learner must drag the correct terms to the appropriate place in the gap text.
- *Assignment tasks:* The learner assigns certain images, elements or text passages to the corresponding images, elements or texts, as shown in the example in Fig. 5.10.
- *Place by ear:* The learner hears a word and drags the correct one from a row of given words into a predetermined placeholder in the gap text. This variant is particularly suitable for foreign language acquisition.
- *Sliders:* The learner clicks on a slider and drags it to the correct place, for example on a scale or a number line.

5.4.1.3 Marking Tasks

Marking tasks provide the learner with certain elements within an exercise. The learner should identify the correct elements by clicking, for example by:

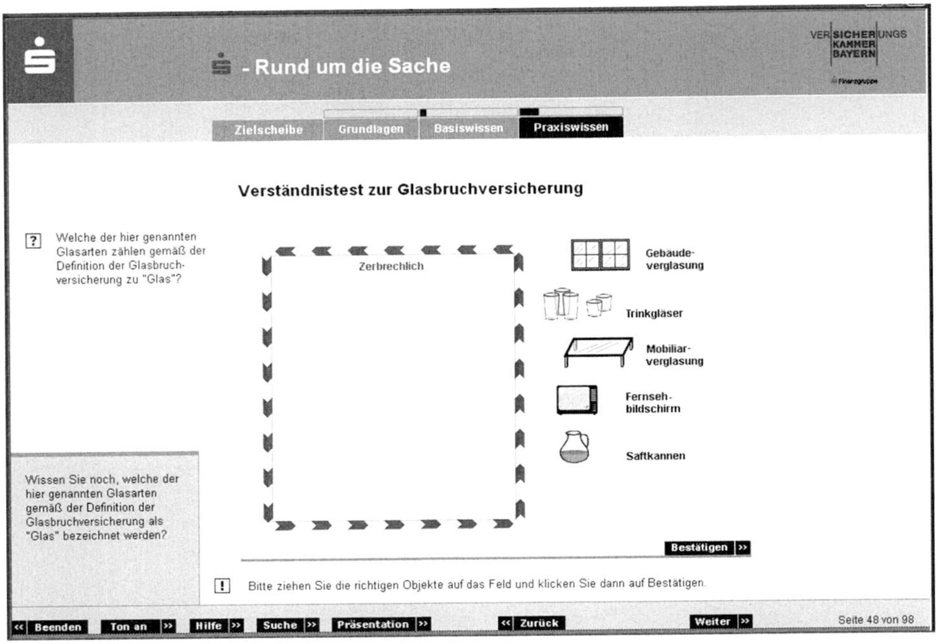

Fig. 5.10 Example Drag-and-Drop task "correct assignment", VIP-S-Training, Versicherungskammer Bayern

- turning arrows on or off,
- turning points on a timeline or scale on or off, or
- turning images, text boxes or other elements on or off.

For example, the learner could click on all parts of a computer that would be replaced for free under a warranty contract.

5.4.1.4 Tasks with Free Input

In Tasks with free input, an empty field is provided in which the learner independently types their solution without any specifications. This task can be well implemented when the solution space is relatively small, that is, when as few correct spellings as possible are possible for the solution word sought. Because the system must analyze every entered term to see if it could fit the solution. Therefore, free text entries with long sentences or even paragraphs should only be offered in tutorial learning systems. There they end up as a submission task directly with the tutor, who corrects them and sends them back to the learner. Fig. 5.11 shows a task with free input.

Fig. 5.11 Example "free entry of numbers", VIP-S-Training, Versicherungskammer Bayern

Examples of Free Inputs

- Numbers and digits,
- Letters,
- Solution words matching the question in a gap text, and
- Heard words in a gap text. ◀

5.4.1.5 Game Tasks

Tasks based on classic board games are very popular. It is advisable to enhance a learning program with various game tasks to maintain the learners' motivation. Here is a small selection of game tasks:

- Memory,
- Crossword puzzle,
- "Hangman" game, and
- Picture puzzle.

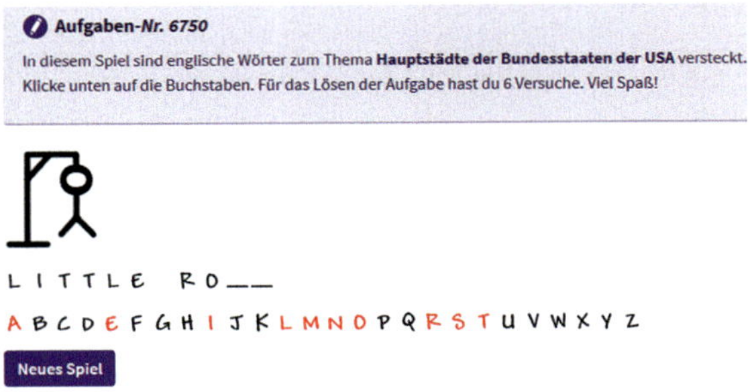

Fig. 5.12 Hangman game
Source https://www.englisch-hilfen.de/spiele/galgenraten19.html

A very engaging hangman game on the topic of "US capitals" can be found on the website "Learn English for free". Fig. 5.12 demonstrates how it works: The player clicks on a letter. If the letter is correct, it appears in the solution word. If it is incorrect, a line is added to the "hanging man" (https://www.englisch-hilfen.de/spiele/galgenraten19.html).

5.4.1.6 Listening and Speaking Tasks

Especially for foreign language acquisition, listening and speaking tasks are highly suitable. The learner listens to a spoken text and then repeats it into their microphone. The learning program evaluates whether the pronunciation is correct. All presented task types can be combined in such a way that instead of the question appearing on the screen, a speaker delivers the question in the foreign language to be learned, and the learner solves the task on the screen as usual.

5.4.1.7 Simulations

Simulations replicate real-world scenarios, devices, processes, or similar. For example, the learner may be asked to reproduce a procedure observed in the learning program in a simulation exercise. This makes simulations very conducive to exploratory learning and also allows the conveyance of extremely complex knowledge content. An example is the virtual hip replacement by Edheads (https://edheads.org/page/hip_resurfacing). The learner is asked to prepare the patient themselves and guide the surgical instruments until the painful hip is completely renewed, as can be seen in Fig. 5.13. And all this with a click of the mouse.

5.4.1.8 Tasks in Virtual Realities

Virtual Realities (VR) are created by computer, through image, sound, movement (shaking, acceleration simulation etc.) and—in room installations—also smell. There are various ways to enter VR: with glasses that have small screens for each eye, via (rear) projections and in rooms with 3- to 6-sided stereo projection; input devices include: 3D or 6D mouse, joystick, trackball, data glove or other haptic devices. VR is mainly used for learning complex actions or for product development, such as:

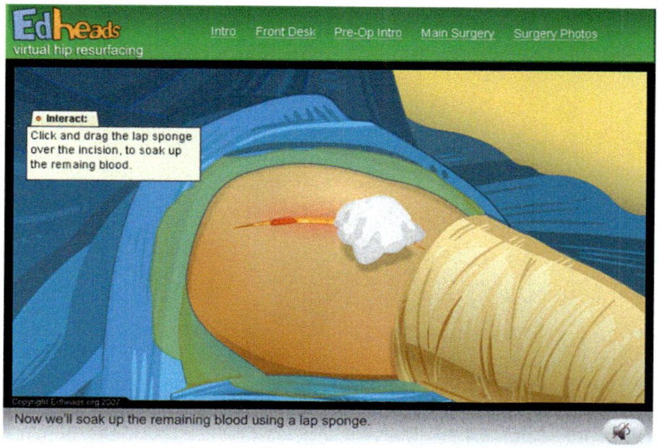

Fig. 5.13 Example "Simulation of a virtual hip operation" (© Edheads.org)

- Operation of large machines (flight simulator, harvesting machines),
- Crash simulations (product development in the automotive industry), or
- Operations on the living body (medicine).

The unique aspect of VR is that the learner can directly intervene in this world and change it via the input devices; this way, they learn almost as if on the "living" object.

5.4.2 Feedback

Tasks provide learners with feedback on their progress and allow them to control their learning path individually. These tasks are supported by appropriate feedback. Praise and point gains reinforce the correct completion of tasks. Mistakes lead to constructive feedback, which also offers opportunities for correction. Well-chosen and implemented feedback is one of the most important motivational factors in the learning program.

> **Tip!**
> Audio feedback, such as noises or spoken texts, should generally be switchable to accommodate various application conditions.

5.4.2.1 Forms of Feedback

- Speakers, for example, the leading figure,
- Sounds, for example, a crash noise for errors and a bright bell for correctly solved tasks, and
- Screen texts.

5.4.2.2 Areas of Application for Feedback

- Task completely solved correctly,
- Task partially solved correctly,
- Task completely solved incorrectly,
- Task incompletely solved,
- Task not solved at all,
- After each input, or
- After a series of inputs.

Tip!
Feedback can be cheeky and funny. However, it should never sound negative or derogatory.

5.4.2.3 Goals of Feedback

Examples of feedback that meet certain goals can be found in Table 5.4.

Tip!
Checklist "Feedback", see Sect. 10.19.

Table 5.4 Goals of feedback with examples

Goals of Feedback	Examples
Motivation of the learner.	"Well done! You really understood the contract duration!"
Recommend repetition of learning pages.	"That was quite good already. For reinforcement, you should revisit the chapter on notice periods. It's also very quick."
Recommend repetition of the task and link with the corresponding learning pages.	"You can do it, I'm sure of that. Just repeat the task and show me!"
Point out mistakes.	"You have correctly assigned the contracts, but the notice periods are not quite right yet. Try again."
Give a hint to the solution/Show the model solution of the task.	"It's getting there. Think about the different product groups in your next attempt. Then you'll have the ball in the goal!"
Address the number of attempts.	"Top class! On the second attempt, you remembered which of the components are eligible for warranty!"

5.5 Learning Videos

Both businesses and universities, as well as other institutions, are increasingly relying on the use of learning videos in training and further education. This is primarily due to the fact that a learning video can highlight particularly important action elements, for example, through zoom, slow motion, still images, or focusing. With all these techniques, the attention of the learners can be specifically directed.

> "For the topic of pension insurance, we used sequences from our successful TV commercial. This created a good identification opportunity for our learning employees and highly motivated them at the same time." Timo Rettig, Project Management eLearning, Versicherungskammer Bayern.

For the successful development of a learning video, it is recommended to proceed in a structured manner. The following project steps can help:

1. Check the technical requirements of the learners: A video should only be used where sufficient screen resolution and smooth video playback can be assumed. If only inferior playback quality is possible on the part of the learners, a learning video should generally be avoided.
2. Check if usable video material is already available on site. If yes, can this possibly be edited with good editing software and enriched with new elements (see Sect. 5.5.7)? As shown in the following chapter, the production of a learning video is usually complex. Therefore, for economic reasons, existing image and learning materials should always be the first choice or serve as basic material for further processing.
3. Formulate a learning objective for the video.
4. Describe the learning concept in which the learning video should be integrated. This could be, for example, a blended learning concept, consisting of an eLearning application and face-to-face training. It is important that learning videos, like animations, neither disrupt the program flow nor interrupt the learning units.
5. Create a concept, script, and shooting schedule. Possibly write a camera script.
6. Develop instructions for viewing the learning video and specific work assignments that precede or follow the learning video.
7. Assemble the team, consisting of production management, actors, camera team, and experts for post-production.
8. Shoot the video, with direction, film recordings, sound, and lighting.
9. Edit the film material on the computer and prepare it for playback on the internet on a website, within a learning program on a learning platform, within a learning app, or on CD-/DVD-ROM.

A concept for a learning video consists of topic finding, exposé, and script. For topic finding, it is important to focus on moments, scenes, and events that are conducive to the learning objective of the video—preferably those from the everyday learning and working environment of the learners. Whenever possible, you should film with a smartphone. But remember to always ask the involved persons for permission to film.

5.5.1 Areas of application for learning videos

Learning videos cover a wide range of applications depending on the learning objective, learning environment, and teaching approach. The most important of these are summarized here:

- A learning video can be a model by visualizing *complex theoretical facts* and processes in a comprehensible and detailed manner. It transports authentic situations in a comprehensible and detailed manner, thus giving the viewer the opportunity to expand their knowledge through observation. For example, the future customer advisor of a bank first observes how they can identify subtle buying signals from a customer before they have to prove themselves in reality. In this respect, learning videos are well suited for any type of *behavioral training.*
- On the other hand, learning videos can be *problem-oriented.* This allows learners to be specifically sensitized to certain challenges in practical everyday action and trained in their *value awareness.*
- Learning videos are very suitable for creating *tension.*
- Learning videos can also be used as a *task* by having the learners shoot a video themselves. The learner thus acquires *self-constructed knowledge* about a learning object and at the same time increases their media competence. In addition, the learner's video can be used as a basis for discussion in the further learning context.
- Learning videos are an ideal *communication tool,* allowing learners to watch lectures, lectures, or similar as a (live) video in the context of their learning.
- By having the tutor communicate with the learners via a video played on the learning platform or by explaining learning content in a personal way via video, a learning video also supports *blended learning concepts.*
- Through the scenic, pictorial representation, learning videos optimally promote *situated learning* and *change of perspective.*

5.5.2 Project Planning and Image Rights

Every video project begins with planning. Similar to an eLearning project, this process is closely tied to budget planning. The following items should be considered for effective budget planning:

- Technical equipment (for example, camera, microphones, lighting and computer technology, see Sect. 5.5.5),

- Personnel costs (for example, project management, authors, actors, speakers, lighting technicians, sound engineers and editors), and
- Rent for the locations where filming will occur.

Depending on the size of the learning video production, it must be determined whether the video should be produced in-house by specialists or if it would be more efficient to outsource the production to an external service provider.

Image Rights
A film, like a photo or a graphic, is an image. Therefore, it is crucial to clarify or obtain the corresponding image rights of involved persons and locations before using the filmed material (see also Sect. 8.2).

5.5.3 Concept and Script for Learning Videos

If an eLearning application is to be supplemented with a learning video, a separate video script must be written, preceded by an exposé. The exposé defines all important parameters for your video shoot. Always create an exposé as it saves a lot of extra work and discussions during the shooting itself. A common word processing software, such as *Microsoft Word,* can be used as a working tool.

Similar to the rough concept for an eLearning program, basic formal parameters must be defined for learning videos:

- Videos always have a time indication. For example, a bar with a slider at the bottom of the video window shows the video's duration and how much of it has been played so far.
- Videos should offer the learner the following options: pause, repeat smaller sequences, and fast forward by moving the slider forward.
- Ideally, when hovering over the slider, a pop-up window should indicate which video scene the learner would enter when clicking on the slider.
- Videos should be modular in structure so that the learner can individually enter scenes.
- Complex images, especially those with novelty value, require sufficient viewing time; for each setting, at least five seconds are assumed.
- Important content should be repeated, shown as a still image or in slow motion.
- Close-ups and close shots require short setting times.
- Long shots or wide-angle shots have longer setting times (rarely in learning videos).
- If a video is used as a film-like intro or outro, it must be possible to optionally turn it off or skip it.
- Be careful when dubbing videos: The more background noise there is when filming in real situations, the worse the sound quality of the actual learning content to be transported.

5.5.3.1 Outline for a Learning Video

In the outline, you establish the foundational data for the video production. Important aspects of the project, such as film duration, brief summary, budget, addresses, etc., are included. These can be compiled in a simple table. The most important elements of an outline are:

- Foundational data,
- Production data,
- Working title of the video,
- Description of the *setting,* i.e., the *location,* where the video is being shot (for example, a bank branch and its exact address) (See Figs. 5.14, 5.15 and 5.16),
- Description of the *locations*, i.e., the individual *scene locations* (for example, the counter in the bank branch, the cash register, and the consulting room),
- Brief summary of the video in two to three sentences (see Fig. 5.17),
- Names of the individuals appearing in the learning video (see Fig. 5.17),
- Brief characterization of the individuals appearing in the learning video (see Fig. 5.17),
- Physical description of the individuals appearing in the learning video (see Fig. 5.17),
- Precise time indication of the duration of the learning video, and
- Technical data (see Fig. 5.16 and Sect. 5.5.5).

Generally, you should consider at the outline stage that videos should not be too long. Since the learner views the action "passively" and no interactions are possible, attention can only remain stable with a relatively short film duration, thus ensuring content retention. This is particularly true the higher the degree of animation. A learning video should have a **maximum length of two to three minutes**. With this short format, you cater to the network habits of learners: They prefer to be active users, often click further, share what they find on the net with other users, and are always looking for new, interesting things.

Exposé Film *IGEL-Conference 2019*

Framework data	
Client	***Ludwig-Maximilians-Universität Munich:*** Contact person and address ***IGEL - International Society for Empirical Literary Studies:*** Contact person and address
Production/Director/Screenplay	***Drehbuchtext. de:*** Daniela Modlinger, M.A. / Lange Straße 13 / D-96047 Bamberg
Camera / Sound	Patrick Ranz / Klenzestr. 11 / D-80469 Munich
Date / Version	September 2, 2019/V01
Author Expose	Daniela Modlinger

Fig. 5.14 Fig. 5.14 depicts the beginning of an exposé listing the framework data. In screenplay work, the section containing the framework data is also referred to as the 'header'.

Production data	
Working title	***IGEL* on the water** – International Literary Society meets on Lake Chiemsee
Filming period	September 30, 2019 - October 04, 2019
Film editing period	October 07, 2019-October 11, 2019
Budget	EUR 5,500 plus 19% statutory VAT and travel expenses
Setting	Fraueninsel, D-83254 Breitbrunn am Chiemsee
Locations	▪ Seminar room E01 ▪ Buffet in the dining room ▪ Ferry boat

Fig. 5.15 Fig. 5.15 exemplifies possible production data for the filming of a video: the working title, timeframe, budget, as well as setting and locations.

Technical data	
Medium	Digital video film
Editions	Web film for integration on the ***IGEL*** website: http://www.arts.ualberta.ca/igel and on DVD
Technical requirements	DSL/W-LAN/DVD player
DVD movie length	approx. 15 minutes
Web movie length	approx. 4 minutes
Music	Music I: classical music with a solemn style Music II: Light music with a lively character

Fig. 5.16 Fig. 5.16 is an example of listing technical data in the exposé.

Movie content	
Brief summary	The conference and its various events are viewed from the perspective of two protagonists. The video film is enlivened by regular comments from the protagonists.
Names of the protagonists	Helena Cruz, Frédéric Duplan
Character of the protagonists	Helena Cruz: young woman, seminar participant; doctoral student of Brazilian origin who is in Europe for the first time. Mother tongue: Portuguese, speaks English well, but with a clear accent. Frédéric Duplan: a young man from the French part of Canada who is currently working on his habilitation in literature. Mother tongue: French, also speaks good English with a clear accent.
Appearance of the protagonists	H. Cruz: South American type, long dark hair, very smart clothes. F. Duplan: Northern European type, short blond hair, rather alternative clothing.

Fig. 5.17 Fig. 5.17 is a sketch of the film's content with a summary and description of the protagonists in the exposé.

5.5.3.2 Developing a Story

The pivot and fulcrum of the video script is the story. It has a **beginning,** a lively **middle part** and an **end.** Mostly, individuals are part of the story, the so-called "protagonists". A good story is characterized by being **extraordinary**, **unexpected** or **current** or all together. Therefore, take the time to develop a logical story. Sometimes you may want to present too many topics and ideas in a learning video and run the risk of embedding too many plot lines into the video. The film loses its thread and the learner loses orientation. This can be easily avoided by trying to formulate the action in a single sentence. This reveals any subplots that distract from the actual topic.

The following aspects contribute to the development of a compelling story:

- Does the topic include an **extraordinary**, long-awaited, or even an entirely unwanted **outcome**, for instance, from negotiations or similar?
- Is there an unexpected **turn of events**, a problem, or perhaps even drama?
- Has an **extraordinary**, atypical **statement** been made on the topic during a discussion (for example, at a company's annual meeting) or speech?
- Does the topic follow a **current development** that directly affects learners in their professional or academic life or learning context (for example, compliance with the new General Data Protection Regulation in all operational processes)?

But how do you proceed if you have to create a learning video on the careful and secure recording of sensitive customer data in a specific software application for the umpteenth time?

You may have considered a *chronological structure*. That means, you describe the input procedure according to the temporal sequence. However, this can quickly become monotonous for the learners.

It becomes more engaging if you provide the learner with a *specific beginning* and a *specific end*. The **beginning** orients the learner, draws them into the process being presented. It introduces potential participants and outlines the video's objectives. The beginning should be entertaining and provide the learner with as much information as possible to immediately engage them.

Tip!
The attention span of learners during a "passive" film viewing is extremely short. Therefore, learning videos, even more than screen pages of a learning program, need to be concise. The message must also be clear and understandable.

Depending on the concept for the learning video, a protagonist guides the learner through the video-based learning sequence. This allows learners to better identify with the video content. Protagonists are usually people, but they can also be objects, such as a wind turbine on the topic of "alternative energies" or personified technical devices or objects from everyday professional life.

The main part then revolves around **movement**. Instead of a monotonous sequence of actions, it is better to incorporate problems, surprises, exciting innovations, and the like.

With the **end**, the learning video reaches its goal. This can, for example, be accompanied by a reference to a final test in the learning program, an invitation to delve deeper into the topic in face-to-face training, or a look at future applications and developments. Consider the Five-Shot Rule No. 5: the "Wow-Shot" (see Table 5.5).

Tip!
Take a cue from the professionals on TV! During post-production when editing the film, they regularly ask: "Why should I keep watching in the next minute?"

The story is crucial in every video. It does not matter whether it is a

- learning video,
- screencast,
- documentation,
- information film or similar.

A screencast refers to the process of recording screen activity on a computer using specialised software. The objective is to create a video guide that helps users understand the functions and processes of a particular software.

5.5.3.3 Script for a Learning Video

Once the exposé is established and a compelling story has been developed, the core of the learning video conception, the script, comes into play. The script outlines *how* the story of the learning video should unfold, and *when* and *where* it should take place. It provides a factual and sober description of the film. The "Five-Shot Rule" (see Table 5.5

Table 5.5 The Five-Shot Rule

1.	WHAT is happening? What is going on? (Close-up of a detail and an action.)
2.	**WHO** is doing it? Who is it about? This can also be an object. (Close-up of the person who is acting.)
3.	**WHERE** does the action take place? (Explanatory subtitle or spoken text to accompany it.)
4.	**HOW** do the action and the acting person relate? (Maintain the narrative thread.)
5.	**WOW-SHOT:** an impressive image at the end. The Wow-Shot is a camera setting that spontaneously inspires, touches, convinces or similar. It can also be a still image or an O-Ton. The O-Ton is the *original* sound, for example in an interview in front of a running camera.

and example), which outlines the five most crucial camera settings (Schneider and Raue 2012, p. 44), can assist with this.

Example

Consider filming an employee while they enter customer data into the new database:

1. **What?**
   A close-up of the input window for the customer's name and address, with the mouse pointer positioned in the input field and the first letter of the name being entered.
2. **Who?**
   A close-up of the employee's face as they look relaxedly at the monitor.
3. **Where?**
   A wide shot of the situation: The employee is sitting at the computer, the input mask on the monitor is visible; everything appears clear and tidy.
4. **How?**
   The camera looks over the employee's shoulder.
5. **Wow-Shot?**
   The camera shows the input mask again in close-up: It appears as it did at the beginning, only now all input fields are filled and a clearly visible green feedback check mark signals that the customer's data has been correctly recorded. ◀

The script begins, just like the eLearning script, always with the *head*. The *head* is identical to that of the exposé. You only need to adjust the date and insert the current version number. The main part of the script, or the *body*, consists of a logical sequence of video scenes. Each new scene begins with the frame data. This could be the name of the first appearing speaker or the description of the new setting or location. These details appear in capital letters. Fig. 5.18 shows what the first page of a video script could look like in a simple table form. Always indicate whether it is a day or night shot and whether it is an indoor or outdoor shot. This information is later required for the shooting schedule. The time specifications in a video script are made in steps of tenths of a second.

To make a learning video engaging and stimulating, various types of camera settings are available. These describe the image Sect. that the camera captures each time (see Sect. 5.2.3.5 *Terms of the Photo and Film World* and Table 5.2 *Technical Terms Photo and Film*). Each camera setting conveys a certain perspective of the people or the action. Therefore, ensure to use the settings in a way that they emphasise the statement of a scene or set certain accents in it. This gives the video more dynamics, and the learner is more involved in the action.

On average, a script comprises about as many pages as the video lasts in minutes.

Timeline/Location/ Remark	Intro
Minute 1:00 - 1:30	FADE IN/MORNING MOOD AT LAKE CHIEMSEE
PRIEN/FERRY TO THE ISLAND OF WOMEN	Record MUSIC II TOTALE: You can see the landing stage in Prien with ferry, people boarding the ferry.
OUTSIDE / MORNING	HALBNAH: Departure board in Prien with picture of Lake Chiemsee and journey times TOTALE: Passengers on the ferry, talking animatedly / ferry / departure of the ship / departure jetty CUT HALF TOTAL: wake CUT HALBNAH: The presenter stands at the railing and tells the story:
MODERATOR	"Welcome to the 10th IGEL International Congress in Munich. It will take place on the enchanting Fraueninsel in Lake Chiemsee."

Fig. 5.18 Example page of a video script in table form

Tip!
Rule of thumb: 1 page of video script = 1 min. of playtime

The easiest way to create the video script, just like an eLearning script or an exposé, is to use a common word processing software. If you also organise the content into a simple table, it can be structured more easily.

Tip!
A professional film script software is, for example, *SESAM-Dreh;* it is chargeable, but available in German: http://www.sesamsoft.de. Only available in English, but free is *FinalDraft:* http://www.finaldraft.com.

5.5.3.4 Speech Texts and Dialogues for Learning Videos

A learning video can be provided with or without sound. However, it is common nowadays to include voice-over in a learning video. If the budget and time do not allow for a separate speech text, music is usually added at the very least. Therefore, you should pay special attention to the rules for speech texts in the script. The learner needs heightened concentration to follow the spoken word because what is heard is characterized primarily by its transience. Listening attentively to radio contributions can help train one's own sense for writing successful speech texts.

> **Tip!**
> Pay attention to the **text-image gap!** It arises when the spoken text *does not* match the video image shown at the same moment. This discrepancy could confuse the learner.

For developing successful speech texts in learning videos, please refer to Sect. 5.2.2, *Formulating speech texts*, and Table 5.1, *Criteria of comprehensibility*.

Writing Dialogues
It is quite conceivable and sensible to create a learning video in which conversations between two participants occur. The dialogues formulated for this purpose are an essential part of the script for a learning video, as they…

- Convey facts and information,
- Make the characters lively, natural, and spontaneous, and
- Establish relationships between the characters.

> **Tip!**
> More on formulating speech texts can be found in Sect. 5.2.2.

Writing dialogues also follows certain rules, because even if a dialogue in a cinema or television film sounds authentic, it is actually always artificial. Dialogues should therefore neither sound stilted nor clumsy. This demand certainly challenges the media author. The goal is to develop a conversation that combines harmony and authenticity. And you can practice this:

- Recall recent conversations with a colleague. Try to write down the dialogue word for word in its "orality".
- If the colleague agrees, you can also digitally record the conversation and then transcribe it to get a feel for spoken language. In technical jargon, this recording and transcribing is called "transcribing".
- Always formulate dialogues completely.
- Keep your dialogues short to maintain the viewer's attention.
- At the beginning of dialogue writing, it is enough to write for a maximum of two people. Bringing a third person into the conversation is only suitable for experienced, routine dialogue writers.

- Dialogue writing also includes giving special instructions to the actors, such as "whispers", "gets annoyed", "gets loud" or "is pleased".

Tip!
The best countercheck for whether a dialogue is successful is to read the dialogue out loud with another person, for example, a colleague.

As a rule of thumb for the time required: one hour of writing time per half page of dialogue. By the way, half a page of dialogue corresponds to about half a minute of film. These values are quite useful for planning the workload when creating a learning video. An example dialogue from a video script is shown in Fig. 5.19.

5.5.3.5 Function of a Leading Figure

Perhaps the learning video should have an explanatory or instructive character. In this case, it is advisable to use a leading figure. This figure accompanies the learner through the events in the video. The leading figure should emotionally involve the learner, indeed, get them on board and motivate them. The leading figure should stand out from the rest of the speech text; how this works is shown in Sect. 5.2.2.5 *Leading figure.*

5.5.4 Filming Schedule

Consider the following scenario: You have packed the camera equipment, the script is in your folder, the actors arrive at the agreed meeting point, and filming can begin. You set up the scene and focus on the first script scene, which reads: "Two people are sitting on a bench in front of the house, discussing the application training seminar." The next scene reads: "The two actors are in the seminar room, rehearsing a job interview." For this, you move your equipment into the building, adjust the lighting, and continue filming. The following scene reads: "During the break, the two main actors meet again on the bench in front of the house, with the woman crying because she doubts herself so much." Then you move the equipment back to the yard in front of the building, adjust the light,

	TOTALE: 2 passengers on ferry
PASSENGER 1	HALFNAH: Passenger 1: "Excuse me, may I ask you something?"
PASSENGER 2	HALFNAH: Passenger 2: "Of course, I'd love to."
PASSENGER 1	NAH: Passenger 1: [IGEL: pronounces "Eitschel"] "Are you by any chance going to the IGEL Congress?"
PASSENGER 2	NAH: Passenger 2: "But yes. [Short pause, then astonished] You too?"

Fig. 5.19 Example of a dialogue page in the video script

Film production IGEL conference / Fraueninsel: 30.09 to 04.10.2019

DATE	TIME	PLACE	ACTION
01.10.19	19.00 h – 20.00 h	Women's Island	TAKE 10: Concert
02.10.19	11.00 h – 12.00 h	Women's Island	11th TAKE: Keynote Speaker *James Pennebaker*
02.10.19	13.30 h – 15.00 h	Women's Island	12. TAKE: Round table with *Founding Fathers/Mothers*
02.10.19	15.30 h – 15.40 h	Women's Island	13th TAKE: Protagonists of the conference during a fictitious farewell crossing
02.10.19	16.00 h – 16.15 h	Men's Island	Ferry to Prien
02.10.19	16.15 h – 16.30 h	Prien	Footpath: Ferry → Parking lot

Fig. 5.20 Example of a filming schedule as a table

and so on. If you also want to film all scenes in the yard, but some of them take place in the evening and some in the morning, you again face the problem of setting up and dismantling the equipment. To avoid this unnecessary effort, you need a proper filming schedule. The filming schedule serves an important function: It organizes the scenes by locations and times of day. This means that if you have set up your scene in the yard in the morning, for example, you film all scenes that are to be played in the morning light in the yard. Only then do you move the equipment into the building to film all the indoor scenes there. In this way, you progress much faster and more effectively. With a filming schedule, you know what conditions to expect at the filming location and how you can respond to them. This is referred to as the so-called "filming economy". Fig. 5.20 shows a simple filming schedule. The settings are organized by filming locations. This can be seen at a glance from the different color coding. In addition, the respective date and exact filming times are given.

> **Tip!**
> A filming schedule organizes the scenes to be filmed by location and time of day. The scenes for a video are not filmed chronologically according to the script, but according to the filming schedule.

Since the scenes are not filmed chronologically, it is important to ensure consistent transitions between consecutive scenes. This is referred to as "continuity". This ensures that all details of the respective settings match each other. If the continuity is not consistent, it is referred to as a "continity error". Classic continuity errors include changes in the actors' body posture, deviations in clothing or equipment, and jumps in the displayed time. For example, if the protagonist leaves the house in a blue shirt, he should not be wearing a yellow shirt in the subsequent scene on the bench in front of the house.

Tip!
To identify continuity errors, review the already filmed video material and take notes.

5.5.5 Technical Aspects of Learning Video Production

If you plan to shoot a video for digital presentation as part of an eLearning application or as standalone learning material, you will need specific technical equipment. From a technical standpoint, successful video production requires three key elements:

1. Imagery,
2. Sound, and
3. Lighting.

To begin, you will need a digital camera or a smartphone. Ideally, you should acquire this equipment from a specialist dealer, as the camera or smartphone must be compatible with the computer equipment for later post-production (see Sect. 5.5.7). The camera or smartphone may have an integrated microphone, or you could use an external, standalone microphone for the video shoot. The sound quality significantly improves with an external microphone. Generally, there are two types of microphones: A **dynamic microphone** is robust and suitable for use in harsh environments, but it is not very sensitive to sound. A **condenser microphone,** conversely, is highly sensitive to sound but delicate in use. An additional pair of headphones allows the cameraperson to monitor the recorded sound. A tripod ensures steady images.

Lighting is also crucial for the video shoot. It can produce various effects, such as softening the skin or creating hard edges. Therefore, understanding the key properties of light and the techniques for optimal light management is essential when filming. Certain times of day are more conducive to filming than others. The **white balance** of a camera or smartphone should be adjusted. External light sources should be carefully chosen, depending on the desired image quality. Also, any noise produced by the light source should be considered, as it could affect the sound of the recording.

The filmed material can be stored on various storage media, such as an integrated hard drive in the camera or smartphone, an inserted SD card, or an integrated flash memory. The transfer of the film material from the camera or smartphone to the computer for later post-production (see Sect. 5.5.7) should always be conducted via cable to ensure fast data transfer.

The required performance of the computer depends on the chosen camera system. For a PAL-DV system or a smartphone, a standard computer setup is sufficient. However, if you are filming HDV material, the computer must be high-performance.

5.5.6 Organisation of the Video Shoot

After the conceptual and technical preparations, the practical preparation of the shooting location begins. Table 5.6 summarizes the most important activities for this.

> **Tip!**
> Professional actors can be found on the following web portals, among others: http://www.kuenstlercasting.de and http://www.model-kartei.de.

Table 5.6 Preparing the shooting location

Inspect the shooting location/ Adjust shooting concept	Ideally, you should visit the shooting location *before the actual shoot* once without camera equipment, helpers or actors. The shooting concept may need to be rewritten afterwards.
Legal situation/ Obtain shooting permission	Especially for video shoots on private property, you must obtain shooting permission in advance. That's why the preliminary inspection of the shooting location is so important: Sometimes a seemingly public place turns out to be private property.
Public places	A place is public if it is freely accessible and in common use. This also includes private property without fences or access controls **Example:** A station forecourt is public. Therefore, you can film a station from there, i.e. from the outside, *without shooting permission.*
Private places	A place is private if it has access controls or fences. In this case, you may not film *without shooting permission.* **Example:** A station is not public property. It is owned by Deutsche Bahn. Consequently, you can only film a station *inside with shooting permission.*
Filming people	You can film everything in public places, including passers-by and people. However, the *right to one's own image* applies. This means that the person filmed must agree if you want to publish their image—for example in a learning video or on a website.
Find actors	For simple learning videos, you can ask around among your colleagues or the target group of learners: Most people enjoy participating in a video and have a lot of fun with it. If you want to include higher quality scenes with people, you should use professional actors.

5.5.7 Postproduction

The raw film material that you have collected during a video shoot is usually not very meaningful and can be boring on its own. Every now and then a beautiful picture, a successful setting, an important detail shows up. But in between, there are also many irrelevant or even blurry or shaky shots. Therefore, to create an appealing learning video, it is necessary to sort out, arrange and supplement. In film technology, this is referred to as **postproduction.** Thus, in professional circles, postproduction is considered the actual creative work that makes the film a film. Nowadays, postproduction takes place on the computer. The first step is to transfer the filmed video material from the digital camera or smartphone to the computer and save it there. On the computer, you shape the raw material from the shoot into a finished video film using various techniques. For example, you can cut a video or make a montage. This means that you rearrange the individual video sequences. Furthermore, you can set image effects, such as zoom, slow motion, still images, overlays or repetitions. Postproduction also includes dubbing, for example with sounds or a spoken commentary.

For postproduction, you use a film editing software. There are numerous free and paid software offers for PC and Mac on the market. With the free *Shotcut*, for example, you can import and view video files on the PC, cut videos with the timeline, assign a title, add music and much more. *Lightworks* is also a free program, but as a real professional tool, it requires a lot of familiarization time. A video editing software with many functions, but still easy to use, is available from 130 EUR, for example *Magix Video deluxe* or the professional tool *Adobe Premiere Pro* on subscription for around 25 EUR per month. For postproduction on Mac, there is also the free *iMovie*. A real professional tool for Mac with many functions is *Final Cut Pro* at a price of about 330 EUR.

At the end of postproduction, the videos can be output in various file formats, such as in the MPEG-4 format.

5.5.8 Rapid eLearning via Learning Video

Modern technology now allows the creation of learning videos using simple digital cameras. The production method discussed here is technically referred to as "Rapid eLearning". For instance, a scene from everyday office life can be filmed and uploaded to a computer with minimal effort, providing a quick and straightforward approach to eLearning. The films can be edited using basic editing software and uploaded to a learning platform. It is crucial to ensure that the output format of the editing software is compatible with the learning platform's requirements.

Another method for creating quick training videos involves filming screenshots or presentations. This can be done in a simplified style directly in *Microsoft PowerPoint*. Software programs such as *Camtasia* or *Adobe Captivate* are also suitable for this purpose. All Rapid eLearning tools are intuitively learnable and allow the user to create a learning video from screen pages in a few steps. The completed video can then be uploaded to a smartphone, an online video portal, or the company's own learning platform.

5.5.8.1 The Camera Script

For Rapid eLearning videos and videos in authentic situations, the processes cannot be precisely defined in advance. A simple digital camera or a smartphone with an integrated microphone is used for recording. This approach results in a kind of "minimal production", without a script and without post-production. In this case, it is sufficient to create a so-called "camera script". The camera script ...

- defines the approximate course of the shooting and
- illustrates the most important camera positions in a number of possible situations.

Example

An authentic situation could be, for example, a shoot at the counter of Deutsche Bahn in a train station. A customer is supposed to ask about the conditions for a saver fare ticket, and you want to capture an unfiltered answer on your digital camera. The camera script specifies that the camera should always keep **the customer** in front of the Deutsche Bahn counter **in focus**. If you are working with two cameras, you define the division of settings for each camera. ◀

5.6 What Tools are used to Create a Script?

The media author requires a tool for script creation that eliminates the need for software development and simultaneously serves as an interface for technical implementation into multimedia content. For this purpose, so-called authoring tools have been developed in recent years, the operation of which varies in complexity. The market for authoring tools has become so vast that choosing the right tool is a real challenge. Recently, eLearning all-rounders, or "jack-of-all-trades", have been advertising for users. However, one should remain sceptical of providers who promise that their authoring tool is "team-capable" and "ensures didactic quality". Team capability is still a human characteristic, and didactics, as the art of teaching, is closely related to the learning content, which is created anew for each eLearning application. Particularly, company- or profession-specific knowledge acquisition loses quality in a standardized didactic format.

Tip!
When choosing an authoring tool, a media author should consider how large the field is in the input mask in which they are supposed to write their texts. If the input fields are too small, clarity is quickly lost.

A tool is not a human and therefore cannot "actively involve in the production process"; rather, it is the case that the human uses the tool for production. It is also worth considering the latest trend to make scripts superfluous with mature authoring tools. The question is what result you want to have in the end. For a captivating cinema film, a script is still the best prerequisite, despite the highly developed technology in the film industry and despite the flood of multifunctional digital cameras on the market, with which every home user can shoot their own film. The secret is: The story in a film has to work. Transferred to eLearning, this means: The didactics must work so that the learning objective is achieved. For the media author, this means: They must remain vigilant. The trend cannot be stopped and certainly not reversed. In the future, the media author will have two possible customer groups:

- Companies with a limited budget that resort to authoring tools with adaptable but still pre-configured eLearning courses; here the media author develops the concept and advises the client's subject authors with their media didactic and learning psychological know-how.
- Companies with a budget that allows a learning objective and target group appropriate eLearning production; here the media author develops the concept and script as before, while a multimedia agency usually takes over the technical implementation.

To fully map the amount of authoring tools available on the market would exceed the scope available here. Therefore, at this point, examples are classified into categories, supplemented by a description of how the respective tool is to be assessed from the author's point of view.

Tip!
Common authoring tools with a short description are listed in the eLearning weblog by *Tim Schlotfeldt:* http://www.tschlotfeldt.de/elearning-wiki/Autorentool.

5.6.1 Exploring XML

Common authoring tools are increasingly adopting the XML format. XML, standing for "Extensible Markup Language", is a universal data format that facilitates data exchange between different types of systems over the Internet. In essence, XML allows for the separation of page content, layout, and navigation by:

- Marking up texts, also known as Generic Markup. This is similar to changing the typeface through formatting templates. For instance, in Microsoft Word, headings have a specific point size and are printed in bold.

- Defining document types. This function is also comparable to Microsoft Word, where document types such as "business letter" or "specialist book" are defined, providing a template for different contents.
- Assigning a data exchange format to arbitrary data. This allows, for example, the data of a transfer to be exchanged between different banks by verifying whether all required XML elements, such as account number, bank code, and amount, are present.

The advantage of XML-based content pages is their modularity. As a result, they only need to be created once and can still be output in different formats, such as a PDF file, a Word document, or a slide presentation. Additionally, it is possible to display the contents defined according to XML at different points in the learning program. This significantly reduces the effort involved in updates and changes and accelerates their implementation.

5.6.2 Text Processing

Interestingly, despite the availability of mature authoring systems on the market, classic text processing remains the most used authoring tool. The advantage for the media author is clear: they can easily and clearly design their script pages and integrate illustrations or scribbles directly into the document. From the perspective of multimedia agencies, it has the advantage that the author takes over part of the software development, as they often receive specially configured Word formatting templates from the agency, which can be read directly as an XML file (see Sect. 5.6.1). A table form with indices for screen or spoken texts and other screen elements is common. Fig. 5.21 illustrates this table form.

A simpler script template as a table in a document page of Microsoft Word is shown in Fig. 5.22. When writing scripts in Word, the media author usually does not specify the position of individual elements on the screen, as their arrangement in the layout has already been determined by the screen designer in advance and documented in the rough concept or style guide.

5.6.3 Authoring Tools

Long-standing, widely used authoring tools such as Adobe Director, Adobe Authorware, MatchWare Mediator, and additional tools like Adobe Flash and Shockwave are no longer available on the market. Even Adobe Dreamweaver, which for a long time was very well suited for developing learning applications with the additional module

Index: 4121	**Provision according to the Modular principle**	**Info**
Search words:		
Building blocks, product overview, product range, brief overview		

Headings:
T4121Page=Modules "Child provision"

Screen texts:	Graphics and photos:
T4121b=Think about bundle sales! All the components together form the "child provision". *T4121g=Please click Next.*	Draw a kit box with four building blocks, see scribble (file: Scribble_G4121.jpg); fade in the building blocks parallel to the speaker texts. At the end, the box is completely filled with all four labeled building blocks. The backgrounds of the individual building blocks should be highlighted with a transparent symbol, as shown in the square brackets of the scribble. G4121a=Placeholder for kit box and building blocks G4121b=Building block 1 appears, labeled with "logo "S"/logo"-Premium savings G4121c=added G4121b: Building block 4 also appears, labeled "Training insurance G4121d=supplemented G4121b: Building block 2 appears additionally, labeled "Supplementary health insurance" G4121e=added G4121b: Building block 3 appears additionally, labeled with accident insurance

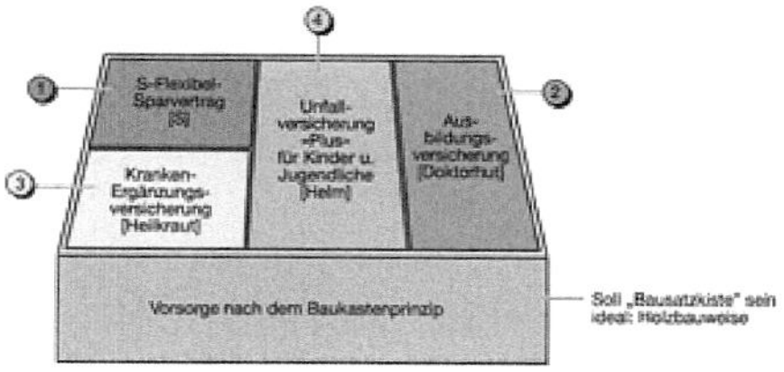

Directed by:	Speaker texts:
+G4121a +A4121a #	*A4121a=The "child provision" consists of four components.*
....	....
+A4121g +SVIP0015a +T4121g #	*A4121g=Ha, your customers will be amazed when you introduce them to these powerful products. But before we get to the training insurance, let's first balance out the parties involved in the insurance contract.*

Expiration of the page:
All headings are visible when you enter the page. The page builds up parallel to the audios. Figure is displayed after A4121f, together with A4121g and T4121g.

Navigation Next	Navigation Back

Fig. 5.21 Example script page in Microsoft Word with indexing via macros, according to the template of M.I.T e-Solutions GmbH

<Screen no.> Screen name

Headline	[Enter headline here]	
Pictures	[Enter file name of the pictures here]	
Links/Buttons	[Enter hyperlinks and buttons here]	
Text	[Enter screen text here]	
Audio	[Enter speaker text and sounds here]	
Animatio-other	[Enter comments, stage directions, animations here]	

Fig. 5.22 Template for a script page as a table in Microsoft Word

"CourseBuilder", now only covers its main area, namely the creation of websites. However, Adobe bundles most software tools to present various media and content on the computer in a creative, interactive, and didactic way. The most important authoring tools, which require little familiarization time for creating quick eLearning applications, are shown in Table 5.7. For complex, didactically and media-psychologically well-founded digital learning courses, however, basic knowledge in software development is required. In this context, a professional software developer takes over the technical production of the learning course, while the author focuses on conception and script writing.

Tip!
Visit Learntec, which takes place annually in Karlsruhe in January or February. This trade fair for didactics and technology around eLearning presents the latest developments in authoring tools, learning management systems, and digital learning applications.

Table 5.7 Overview of Authoring Tools

Authoring Tool	Properties
Adobe Captivate (https://www.adobe.com/de/products/captivate.html)	eLearning applications created with Captivate are generally based on PowerPoint slides. This approach simplifies the creation of eLearning content, but it also limits the didactic preparation. However, Captivate offers numerous functional elements, enabling the creation of a solid eLearning course. These elements include voice recordings, knowledge queries, and mechanisms to ensure that a lesson has been completed by the learners. The 2019 release allows for quick adaptability of the learning courses on mobile devices and the insertion of Virtual Reality. Captivate is SCORM and AICC compatible, which allows the finished learning course to be uploaded to a learning platform. With "Captivate Prime", Adobe also offers a learning platform (an LMS).
Adobe Creative Cloud (http://www.adobe.com/de/creativecloud.html)	The Creative Cloud by Adobe combines all applications that enable the user to carry out diverse creative processes on the PC. Thus, the Creative Cloud bundles tools for video and photo production, website creation, app development, and the creation of video stories for social media.
Toolbook by SumTotal Systems (http://tb.sumtotalsystems.com)	Toolbook is based on the programming language "OpenScript" and provides many standard types and templates, but does not allow the development of learning games and simulations. Media such as graphics or animations can be created directly in Toolbook. The learning curve is low if you rely on the templates or standard types; it is high if you design learning pages individually, as this requires knowledge of software development. The learning content created with Toolbook is SCORM compatible; the user language is English.
TurboDemo by balesio (http://www.balesio.com/turbodemo/deu/index.php)	TurboDemo aims to create simple, fast eLearning courses. The tool is used to take screenshots of software applications and to virtually film the associated mouse movements. With numerous functions, the screenshots can then be bundled as a learning application. SCORM compatibility allows uploading to a learning platform.
WBTplus by M.I.T e-Solutions GmbH (http://www.mit.de/autoren-tools)	M.I.T delivers WBTs with the additional tool WBTplus, which allows the customer to update and change their eLearning application independently, even without programming knowledge. New numbers, statistics or colour elements can be easily integrated. The format templates for WBTplus are based on the basic layout defined for eLearning production. Efficient work is facilitated by the change history, which shows who has worked on the module, and by the tasks that can be assigned to colleagues and appear in the editing window. The structure of the learning program can be clearly changed by moving, inserting and deleting pages in the table of contents. All changes are automatically applied to the entire program. Figure 5.23 shows an example screen for revising text in the learning program.

Fig. 5.23 Example "Text Editor of WBTplus" by M.I.T e-Solutions GmbH

5.7 Learning Psychology

Media authors should be familiar with educational psychology contexts if they aim to develop learning programs that promote sustainable knowledge acquisition. Table 5.8 lists the three basic learning theoretical models for multimedia learning programs along with their core elements.

It is noteworthy that around the same time *constructivism* replaced *instructional learning*, multimedia learning began to establish itself as a new medium alongside the classic forms of knowledge acquisition. Like a cogwheel, constructivist learning theories and modern learning programs interlock, their *hypertext structure* encouraging learners to construct their own learning paths. In practice, a synthesis of cognitive and constructivist learning approaches is often seen, assuming the learner's self-control and simultaneously providing suitable media for knowledge acquisition. For example, the learner can contact a tutor if they encounter difficulties in constructivist knowledge acquisition.

Table 5.8 Overview of learning theoretical models

Learning Theoretical Model	Core Elements
Instructional Learning (guiding, teaching)	Passive, receptive learning, can also be stimulus-response learning; especially in the early stages of computer learning programs, so-called "drill-and-practice" methods ("programmed instruction") were used, but this quickly led to fatigue; in the end, the learner has learned, but not necessarily understood (cf. cramming vocabulary as opposed to understanding the word formation of a foreign language).
Cognitive Learning (perceiving, thinking, recognizing)	Information-oriented learning, where learning content is processed independently and not conditioned by "right/wrong" messages. The selection of the learning environment or teaching media is based on the individual perception, understanding, and processing patterns of the target group.
Constructivist Learning (building, erecting)	Active, self-directed learning in a problem-oriented, situational context, often as a social process; knowledge is not transported as in the cognitive psychological approach, but the learner constructs his knowledge acquisition himself; in addition, there is the claim to acquire and apply new knowledge in multiple contexts and from various perspectives.

Tip!

You can find more information about the most important learning theories on the website of *Daniel Rey*, which deals with topics around eLearning: http://www.elearning-psychologie.de.

5.7.1 Perception and Attention on the Screen

A detailed discussion of the human brain's perception and attention processes is beyond the scope of this book. However, the following chapter briefly describes the most crucial findings of perception psychology that a media author needs to understand in order to design a learning program that aligns with the learner's viewing, reading, and thinking habits.

5.7.1.1 Visual Perception

The brain is primarily responsible for human perception. Simplistically, it consists of two halves: The left half is responsible for language acquisition, logical and analytical thinking, and for storing words and numbers. Conversely, the right half of the brain is responsible for pictorial thinking, understanding contexts, and experiencing colours, feelings, shapes, and rhythms.

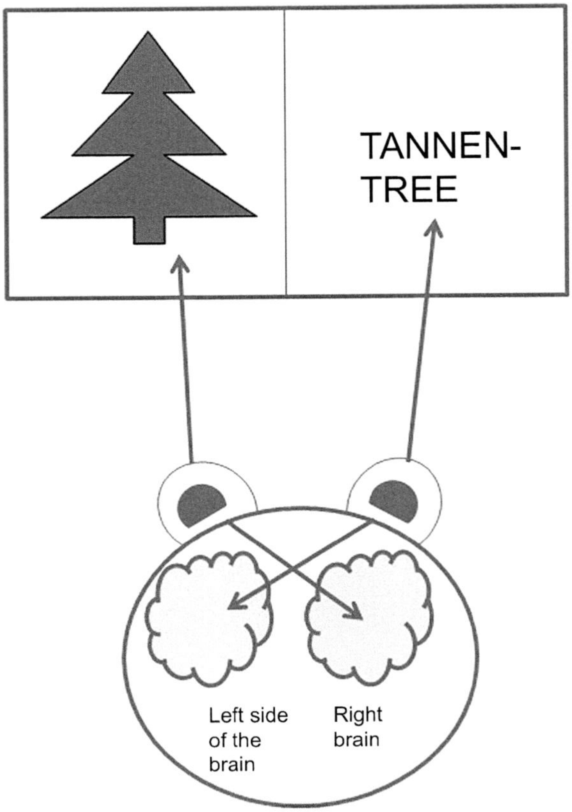

Fig. 5.24 Perceptions of the right and left brain hemispheres

Interestingly, what the eye sees on the left is processed by the right half of the brain, as illustrated in Fig. 5.24. For practical implementation in a learning program, this means: If an image is on the left side of the screen, it is perceived directly by the appropriate half of the brain.

Tip!
Place visualizations on the left side of the screen and texts on the right side of the screen to align with human perception most effectively.

5.7.1.2 Guidelines for the Presentation of Elements on the Screen

Perception times vary; for instance, the time it takes to recognize a geometric figure is shorter when it is spatially represented. Accordingly, less time is needed to recognize a text with a linear rather than spatial representation. For the media author, this means that geometric learning content should be as three-dimensional as possible; however, spatial gimmicks with text modules should be avoided.

5.7.1.3 Auditory Perception

Hearing requires constant concentration, partly because the learner cannot control the pace of information intake. In general, all sensory organs show signs of habituation and fatigue after prolonged use, which reduces attention. These fatigue symptoms can be mitigated by alternating between presenting learning content audibly and visually. Learners process auditory information more easily when written text appears on the screen simultaneously; they can then relax more, as the transience of the spoken word is no longer predominant. Studies on this topic show that students achieved better scores with simultaneous speaker and screen texts than students who only heard the same texts. Further studies show that heard information is better stored in long-term memory. Therefore, it is crucial to pay attention to the psychologically correct preparation of audio texts: Speaker texts that convey important learning content for the course should always be supplemented with screen texts in the script. Additionally, the learner should be able to repeat audios as often as they wish.

> **Tip!**
> Present images with audio texts! As soon as a sensory channel is addressed twice with the same information, it can lead to disturbances, for example when an image is accompanied by screen text—both address visual perception.

5.7.1.4 Tactile Perception

Learning through the sense of touch has not yet been fully implemented in eLearning. In this process, the spinal cord transports sensations picked up through the skin as information to the brain, where they trigger a perception. A simple example of painful learning through touch: A child who has once burned their fingers on a hot stove will in the future ensure that the stove has cooled down before touching it (see Fig. 5.7). Virtual learning worlds are already working with the simulated grasping of objects, which should approximate real touching. However, there is still a significant amount of research and development needed for this type of learning.

5.7.2 How to Motivate for eLearning?

A learner using an eLearning application is in a unique situation: they are required to self-motivate, as the external prompts common in traditional teaching are absent. So, how can a learner's motivation be fostered, enhanced, and sustained? The answer lies in intrinsic motivation. This implies that the learner is driven to acquire knowledge through the computer from within, rather than being externally guided. Various methods can support the development of intrinsic motivation for using an eLearning application:

- A clear goal definition at the start of the learning program, for instance, by asking the learner to write their personal goal for this learning session in their "note field".
- Continuous feedback, that is, feedback on the learning progress in relation to the learning objectives defined by the program. Additionally, the feedback should encourage the learner to compare their current performance with the initially defined personal goal.
- Incorporating the acquisition of knowledge into a learning story or a learning novel that closely relates to the knowledge acquisition. For example, the learning story for consultant training in the electronics retail trade involves a family. In each new problem situation, a different family member visits the specialty store, representing a specific customer group.
- Dramatic actions with the potential for discovery, surprise, or experiencing the unexpected. Numerous implementation scenarios are available, such as simulations, role-playing games, elements of suspense, cartoons, or simply humorous depictions. For instance, in a dramatic action, a scruffy-looking teenager enters a high-end furniture store to look at designer sofas. In the end, it is revealed that he has ample money and purchases an entire setup. The learning task is not to judge customers by their appearance and not to base the quality of advice on it.
- Offering incentive systems to the learner. This could be, for example, a certificate at the end of the course that they can print out; the certificate might even serve as authorization to participate in a further seminar or a sought-after company excursion.
- Organizing competitions, for instance, by ranking all learners in a top-5 list based on points.
- Incorporating new technology into the eLearning application. This typically generates excitement, for example, to learn in a virtual reality that can only be accessed with glasses and a data glove. However, it should be noted that new technologies lose their appeal as soon as they become commonplace.

Reading Tip!
For more on motivating online learning, see: *Hartmut Häfele and Kornelia Maier-Häfele:* "101 e-Learning Seminar Methods, and Strategies for Online and Blended Learning Seminar Practice", managerSeminars.

5.7.3 Learning Techniques at the Computer Workplace

The appropriate learning techniques facilitate sustainable knowledge acquisition via eLearning. Therefore, it is advisable to include an information page on this topic in the learning program. The recommended techniques are:

- Establish a learning goal.
- Recognize your existing knowledge on the topic.
- Identify which questions about the learning content persist.
- Consider how the acquired knowledge should be applied in practice.
- When embarking on Internet explorations (termed as Websafari), note down the exact goal of this Websafari with a red pen on a piece of paper to avoid getting lost.

The learner should record the results, either by hand or—if available—in a personal note field in the learning program. Over time, this allows the learner to monitor their learning progress and adjust the learning objectives accordingly.

5.7.3.1 Additional Tips and Tricks for Learning at the Computer

- Ask learners who have already completed the eLearning for their experiences and seek recommendations for focus areas.
- Form learning groups with colleagues who are working on the same learning program; possibly agree on common break times, as this is when casual conversations about what has just been learned can help consolidate the knowledge.
- Check whether the time estimates in the learning program for the duration of individual learning units align with your own time expenditure for learning; consider any deviations in further learning time planning.
- Allocate fixed learning times.
- Limit computer-based learning to a maximum of two hours a day.
- If possible, learn on a computer where only the learning program is loaded; this minimizes potential distractions from email queries, quick internet searches, calendar scheduling, etc.
- Inform colleagues that you are learning and do not wish to be disturbed, not even by the phone. This may take some getting used to, but fixed learning times will soon become routine.
- Take regular breaks: After a maximum of one hour, reserve 10 minutes for walking around, getting fresh air, or having a coffee. This allows the newly acquired knowledge to settle better.
- Eliminate internal distractions by eating and drinking enough before the learning session or by having drinks available at the workplace. This way, you do not need to interrupt your learning.
- Clear the desk, as clutter can be distracting ("This is particularly important today, I still have to do this" etc.).

5.8 How to Prepare Multimedia Elements in a Didactically Meaningful Way?

All didactic considerations must first align with the customer's corporate identity as defined in the specifications (see Sect. 4.3). These considerations are followed by the requirement that the screen is the communication surface through which the learner interacts with the program. The screen should therefore be intuitively understandable and attract positive attention. In essence, screen elements must be *self-explanatory* and *meet the expectations of the learners.* The first glance at a screen can be compared to the first entry into a seminar room:

- Does it have a conducive learning atmosphere?
- Are all the necessary tools for the lesson available?
- Is it a pleasure to enter this "classroom"?

Lastly, when preparing multimedia elements, consider that the greatest retention of what has been learned is achieved when all senses are engaged simultaneously during the course of the learning program and the learner also has ample opportunities for interactive actions (for example, solving tasks or acting in simulation rooms).

5.8.1 Design and Arrangement of Screen Elements

The design and arrangement of screen elements primarily aim to meet perceptual and learning psychological criteria. The basic rule is the definition from Sect. 5.7.1: Images to the left, texts to the right on the screen. The once decided room division and arrangement of the individual screen elements, i.e., the screen design, should be consistent throughout the entire learning program. This prevents cognitive overload of the learner, as they do not have to reorient themselves each time and can devote their attention undisturbed to the learning content (see Sect. 4.1.1.8).

5.8.1.1 Design of Screen Text

Due to the significantly higher resolution of printed letters compared to those on a screen, screen texts are read up to 30% slower than texts on paper. Therefore, it is crucial to pay special attention to the reader-friendly design of screen texts (refer to Sect. 5.2):

- Structure the content into related paragraphs.
- A paragraph should consist of a minimum of three and a maximum of seven sentences.
- A line should not contain more than ten words.
- The recommended font size is at least 12 points, although this is not commonly practiced.

- The line spacing should be 1½ to 2 lines for a 12-point font.
- On the screen, a sans-serif font, such as Arial, is the most readable.
- The fonts should not have shadows or contours.
- A uniform font type should be consistently used throughout the learning program.
- Hyperlinks should change color once they have been clicked; this includes terms in the table of contents that are linked to a specific chapter, for example.
- When hovering over hyperlinks, a small pop-up window should appear indicating where the link leads.

5.8.1.2 Design of Images

Sect. 5.3 delves into the design of images, whether they are graphics, photos, animations, or videos. Essentially, the learning effectiveness of an image is dependent on the viewer. An advanced learner may find an illustration refreshing, while for a beginner, it significantly contributes to understanding. Comprehension of an image can be enhanced through targeted image design, such as asking the viewer to find specific details within the image. Not only does the image itself influence the learning process, but also the level of engagement with it. According to Weidenmann (1994), images can serve various teaching functions. The media author's task is to adapt their visualization suggestions to these functions. An overview of teaching functions and the associated design possibilities is provided in Table 5.9.

Table 5.9 Overview of teaching functions of images

Function	Goal	
Image	Visualize the learning content that the screen moderator's speech text describes.	Dialogue text in audio, conversation scene as image.
Organization	Provide an overview of the learning content.	Flowchart, Advance Organizer.
Interpretation	Enhance the understandability of the learning material.	Explanation that the warranty contract is designed differently depending on the product group; image to go with it: An apprentice stands opposite a customer who is just buying a netbook. He has two warranty contracts in his hand and looks desperately at the two papers. This represents the problem situation: Which warranty contract does he have to fill out for the netbook?
Transformation	Provide original new creations of images that serve as mnemonic devices for remembering terms or statements.	An insurance company offers a product bundle to insure a family all around. A large tree appears to the audio text and for each product a branch; this image is a mnemonic device for the "family tree".

When designing visualizations, it is also crucial to consider the target group. In their book Flipchart ART, Meyer & Widmann (2014) assign specific visualization elements to the following recipient groups:

- Educators and craftsmen: Concrete, manageable, playful, and colourful.
- Business economists, technicians, and engineers: Numbers and developments with models and graphics, flowcharts, and tables.
- Executives: Quick overview as a visual that should follow the latest technology.
- Men in general: factual images.
- Women in general: Colours, shapes, unusual.

5.8.1.3 Colouring of Images

The colouring for the screen pages of an eLearning application should consider the corporate identity (see Sect. 4.3) of the client and generally be restrained so that the colour does not distract from the content. This also has the advantage that intensive colouring can be used specifically to direct the learner's attention to a certain stimulus. Colour can also be used effectively as an orientation element, for example by marking the same processes with the same colours. Overall, the colour distribution should be limited to five to seven different colours with clear meaning.

5.8.1.4 Design of Pictograms

As a specific type of images in multimedia applications, pictograms are to be highlighted. These are usually found on the buttons (also referred to as "icons") for navigation through the learning program. Pictograms can convey content at a glance or trigger an action, similar to the well-known traffic signs, without having to resort to language. To capture a pictogram, no eye movement should be necessary.

5.8.1.5 Properties of Pictograms

- Self-explanatory
- Clear and simple
- High recognition value
- Unambiguous
- Distinct contrast from the background
- Similarity in style and execution within an application

In this form, pictograms essentially provide a "quick shot into the brain" (Ballstaedt 1997). Pictograms are very interesting for eLearning applications because they are universally understandable, regardless of the mother tongue, due to their symbolic nature. A good example of the global comprehensibility of pictograms is provided by the control commands in Windows applications: The little house for the "Home" function in Microsoft's Internet Explorer is now known to every child.

> **Tip!**
> For a checklist on "Image Design", see Sect. 10.18.

5.8.1.6 Design of Audios

Audios include spoken texts, sounds, music, and noises. The basic rule is: All audios must be optionally switchable off. Not every learner has their own room for working on the learning program and could therefore disturb their colleagues by playing audios loudly.

5.8.1.7 Spoken Texts

Spoken texts in an interactive teaching medium should be designed in such a way that they fulfill a supportive function for processing. This includes running at a medium speed and being spoken with pronounced intonation. The learner should be able to take notes at any time, for example by accessing their own note file via a corresponding button. They should also be able to control the course of the audio text themselves, by stopping, repeating, and fast-forwarding or rewinding as desired. The self-control of the listening process is also necessary because not everything received can be processed and thus absorbed at the first listening.

5.8.1.8 Sounds

Sounds or tones can be used for feedback when speaker feedbacks are omitted for cost reasons. The sounds should be carefully selected: They should be pleasant for the learner and differ depending on whether they give positive or negative feedback.

5.8.1.9 Noises

To promote learning in reality, the use of noises is suitable. For example, in the simulation of the operator guidance of a large machine, the noises that are actually heard during operation can be played.

5.8.1.10 Music

Music can have a meaningful recognition effect in an eLearning application, for example by playing a short sequence as soon as the summary appears or when the learner has been sitting at the computer for an hour and should take a break. Music is also an effective instrument to create an identification surface for the learner, for example when the melody of their own company known from advertising is found in the eLearning application.

References

Back, Louis & Stefan Beuttler (2006) Handbuch Briefing. Stuttgart: Schäffer-Poeschel, 2. Auflage.

Ballstaedt, Steffen-Peter (1997) Wissensvermittlung. Weinheim: Beltz Verlag.

Baumgartner, Peter et al. (2002) Auswahl von Lernplattformen. Innsbruck: StudienVerlag.

Bloom, Benjamin et al. (1976) Taxonomie von Lernzielen im kognitiven Bereich. Weinheim: Beltz Verlag, 5. Auflage.

Edwards, Betty (2017) Das neue Garantiert zeichnen lernen. Reinbek: Rowohlt Taschenbuch Verlag, 17. Auflage.

Goldstein, Bruce (1997) Wahrnehmungspsychologie. Heidelberg: Spektrum Verlag.

Häfele, Hartmut & Kornelia Maier-Häfele (2016) 101 e-Learning Seminarmethoden: Methoden und Strategien für die Online- und Blended-Learning Seminarpraxis. Bonn: managerSeminare, 6. Auflage.

Hasebrook, Joachim (1998) Multimedia-Psychologie. Heidelberg: Spektrum Akademischer Verlag.

Langer, Inghard, Friedemann Schulz von Thun & Reinhard Tausch (2019) Sich verständlich ausdrücken. München: Reinhardt Verlag, 10. Auflage.

Märtin, Doris (2019) Erfolgreich texten! Frankfurt a. M.: Bramann Verlag.

Meyer, Elke & Stefanie Widmann (2014) Flipchart ART, Erlangen: Publicis, 4. Auflage.

Rey, Günter Daniel (2009) E-Learning. Wien: Hans Huber Verlag.

Schneider, Wolf (2006) Deutsch! Das Handbuch für attraktive Texte! Reinbek: Rowohlt Taschenbuch Verlag.

Schneider, Wolf & Paul-Josef Raue (2012) Das neue Handbuch des Journalismus und des Online-Journalismus. Rororo, Reinbek.

Weidenmann, Bernd (1994) Wissenserwerb mit Bildern. Bern: Huber Verlag.

Wurman, Richard Saul (1996) Information Architects. Berkeley, CA/USA: Gingko Press.

Mobile Learning 6

Abstract

Chapter 6 deals with Mobile Learning as a significant manifestation of learning with electronic media. To approach the topic of Mobile Learning, the term itself is first delimited and defined more precisely. This is followed by didactic and technical considerations that lead to the overall concept for a Mobile Learning application. In addition, the chapter highlights the advantages and disadvantages of Mobile Learning and takes a look at the possibilities of practical implementation in this field.

6.1 Significance and Distribution

Why does a book about concepts and scripts for eLearning require its own chapter on the topic of "Mobile Learning", which is essentially also based on electronic learning? In fact, eLearning on a computer or laptop fundamentally differs from learning on a mobile device, as this chapter will vividly illustrate. In principle, it is comparable to the time before the invention of the printing press. Books existed, but not in such large numbers. When people wanted or needed to learn something, they attended a "pre-lecture" by a scholar. With the advent of the printing press and the books that were thus available to everyone at any time, listeners became self-readers, which had dramatically revolutionary societal effects, in whose democratic understanding we are still located today. Currently, the triumph of smartphones across all social strata has completely transformed the design of our everyday life and simply *revolutionized* personal communication, i.e., fundamentally changed it in a short time. This has a corresponding impact on learning, since learning and communication are inseparably linked. As educators and learning psychologists, we are called upon to develop and provide concepts for this, in order to continue to

D. Modlinger, *eLearning and Mobile Learning – Concept and Script*,
https://doi.org/10.1007/978-3-658-44695-6_6

support, motivate and guide our learners through the learning process in a beneficial and safe manner.

Regardless of any scientific-pedagogical evaluation, whether Mobile Learning will be meaningful and sustainable or not, the goal is to meet people with Mobile Learning where they prefer to be—on the smartphone! Indeed, everyone is now on the smartphone, even if it is usually most noticeable among students. In Germany, many schools have imposed a ban on mobile phones, for example, Bavarian schools are considered a mobile-free zone (see https://www.netzwerk-digitale-bildung.de/information/schule/smartphones-im-unterricht). Even though the ban naturally aims to achieve something positive, namely maintaining concentration in class and protecting students and teachers from unauthorized photo and film recordings and their uncontrolled distribution on social networks, there is also the danger of a pedagogy that disconnects itself from societal reality.

In the corporate environment of adult education, a different picture is already emerging. The "eLearning Benchmarking Study" of the eLearning Journal from 2018 shows a clear growth in the use of Mobile Learning. Almost 30% of the companies surveyed already use Mobile Learning in their own training and further education, and another 30% are planning to introduce Mobile Learning in this area (see https://www.elearning-journal.com/2019/06/20/mobile-learning). Also in the so-called developing countries, there is a chance to overcome the Digital Divide with Mobile Learning. There, citizens are more likely to have a mobile device, i.e., a smartphone or mobile phone, than a computer, a tablet, a television, or a radio. Data from the US research institute for global developments "Pew Research Center" show a widespread distribution of mobile phones: 83% of the inhabitants in developing countries are equipped with them; the share of smartphones is 45% (see https://www.pewresearch.org/global/2019/02/05/smartphone-ownership-is-growing-rapidly-around-the-world-but-not-always-equally). Particularly widespread are the so-called "Feature Phones". They usually do not have a touchscreen and do not work with the Android or iOS operating systems. Since they do not have an open operating system, no apps can be installed. Nevertheless, Mobile Learning applications are conceivable. Because a Feature Phone can offer both Phone Messaging Services like Whatsapp and Social Media portals like Facebook, thus enabling mobile collaborative learning and direct contact with the teacher.

All aspects of Mobile Learning presented in the following are incorporated into the overall concept, as described in Sect. 6.7.2. The scriptwriting for Mobile Learning corresponds to the explanations in Chaps. 5to 8for eLearning.

6.2 Concept and Delimitation

6.2.1 The Learners

Learners with mobile devices are referred to as "M-Learners" or "Mobile Learners". In principle, this is anyone who uses learning applications on the go, whether online or offline. In contrast, "eLearners" learn with the help of electronic media, which are usually *not* mobile, such as a computer. For example, you find eLearners at permanently installed learning terminals with elaborate simulations. This type of learning application has too high a computational demand for mobile applications, such as on a smartphone. For more on the distinction of terms regarding learning hardware, see Sect. 6.2.3.

6.2.2 The Learning Method

Just like eLearning, Mobile Learning is often associated with the method of self-learning in the common view. However, this is true neither for one nor for the other form of learning; rather, both the integration into a presence training concept or into the classroom are common, as well as comprehensive instructions and supervision within the framework of a self-learning concept. In this respect, eLearning and Mobile Learning simply act as another learning method, alongside textbooks, study booklets, and the like.

6.2.3 The Hardware

The term "mobile" in a figurative sense simply means "movable". Even a book is "mobile" in this sense, just like a large laptop. In general language understanding, it has become common to equate mobile learning with "cell phone learning". However, the term "Mobile Learning" requires a much more nuanced view of the hardware used for this purpose. Nowadays, cell phones are usually smartphones with numerous functions that make them akin to mini-computers. Nevertheless, their functionality is not comparable to that of a tablet. In short, classifying hardware in the field of mobile learning is quite challenging, not least because the types of devices overlap and their development is progressing rapidly. Current trends include internet-enabled refrigerator apps in the "smarthome" and "wearable devices". The latter are, for example, smartwatches for the wrist, Google Glass glasses with a screen on the inside, clothing with built-in communication that, for example, sends tweets, or small, waterproof action cameras from GoPro that are attached to the body (Tremp et al. 2017). Wearable devices and apps in the household and home are part of the so-called "Internet of Things".

Reading tip!
For more on "Wearables" and the broad spectrum of "Mobile Learning" topics, refer to the vivid compilation by *Claudia de Witt* and *Christina Gloerfeld* in the "Handbook of Mobile Learning".

Table 6.1 Hardware categories for mobile learning

Category	Hardware Properties
Stationary	Long-term stationed, wired, heavy, powerful computers, usually with external hardware components such as mouse, keyboard, storage media and the like.
Portable	Usually laptops, netbooks and ultrabooks, which are designed for transport to be used independently of a specific location. The hardware components external to stationary computers are integrated here in the device. Complex commissioning by placing the device on a surface, opening the screen and booting the operating system.
Mobile	Devices that can be moved like portable devices, but can be used without a surface, for example while standing or moving. Special features are short-term activities, such as taking a photo, googling information or communicating via Whatsapp, and the personal, close connection with the device, which is expressed not least by carrying it around the clock close to the body. Easy handling of the device through second-fast, direct, open access to applications, while the respective operating system is permanently available.

Since the boundaries between mobile devices such as smartphones, tablets, netbooks, smartwatches etc. are generally fluid (Tremp et al. 2017), a clear structure is needed to determine which hardware is actually to be assigned to eLearning. In Table 6.1, three helpful categories are listed, which support the classification of the respective terms (cf. Aichele 2016, p. 52 f.):

As Table 6.1 shows, laptops—although they were designed for mobile use—are more similar to a permanently installed computer than to a smartphone or tablet (Riesenbeck 2017).

Another important differentiation of the hardware for mobile learning is shown in the different types of interaction: While computers and laptops work with a mouse or keyboard with touchpad, mobile devices are characterized by direct human interactions such as swiping, moving, tapping or voice input.

6.2.4 The Learning Application

Mobile Learning is closely linked to the term "app", which simply means "application". In the past, these apps were small calculators, simple painting and drawing programs or even the household book. In Mobile Learning, learning programs are therefore "learning apps". They can be used in two system forms:

1. Learning app as a self-contained system (see Sect. 6.6.3: VHS learning program with user identification).
2. Learning app as an open system (see Sect. 6.6.3: Anton learning app without user identification).

6.2.5 Additional Terms

The following terms frequently appear in the context of mobile learning:

- MALL = **M**obile-**A**ssisted **L**anguage **L**earning: This refers to language acquisition through mobile devices.
- Game-Based Learning = This refers to the acquisition of knowledge through play. It involves the integration of game elements into the learning context, which is typically devoid of such elements. This process is often referred to as "gamification".
- BYOD = **B**ring **Y**our **O**wn **D**evice (refer to Sect. 6.4.2 for more details).
- VR = **V**irtual **R**eality.
- Robot = This refers to a type of learning computer designed to exhibit affection in communication with humans. The goal is to facilitate personalized, adaptive learning.
- Instant Learning = This concept involves learning in any situation and at any location, facilitated by QR codes and location detection in smartphones. As Roth aptly describes in his book "Mobile Computing", "The equipping of a user with portable devices can extend to the point where physical reality is 'enriched' with additional data, a phenomenon known as Augmented Reality. For instance, data for repairing a machine can be accessed via the screen of a data helmet. This allows a service technician to repair machines that they were previously unfamiliar with." (Roth 2005, p. 5) This concept could revolutionize learning, as it primarily focuses on immediate knowledge provision rather than long-term retention. However, it is important to note that the term "Instant Learning" is a registered trademark and refers to a specific learning method.

6.3 Didactic Aspects of Mobile Learning

6.3.1 Transformation of Traditional Teaching

Before delving into the unique didactic aspects of learning with mobile systems, it is important to consider the fundamental changes in knowledge acquisition that occurred around the turn of the millennium. The still prevalent teaching practice originates from a time when only the person at the front of the room had a book from which they read or taught. For quite some time, all students and participants in educational programs have had their own books and media, rendering this type of frontal teaching ineffective (see Sect. 6.1). This is true not only for lecturers and teachers but also for parents and politicians. The new challenge is boundary setting. The traditional classroom, where knowledge acquisition was controllable, is dissolving. With the advent of the smartphone, it is no longer possible to control what, where, by whom, and with whom learning takes place. Ilona Buchem refers to this as a "digitally shaped self-learning culture". Learners acquire their knowledge from Wikipedia pages, YouTube tutorials, and journalistic texts in blogs (Buchem 2015), or they search for users who are interested in the same topics, for example, via keyword-based hashtags on X (Dittler 2017, 2017a). The role of the teacher has evolved into a coach who can clarify the incomprehensible and deepen the new, self-discovered learning content through exercises with the participants. The learner is primarily active. Through their participation, they contribute to swarm intelligence, an important didactic aspect of mobile learning. Furthermore, mobile learning adds didactic value to the teaching process in two ways: learners bring their everyday smartphone skills, and the mini-computers adhere to the human principle of movement (Bachmair 2009). Finally, mobile learning provides a significant opportunity to facilitate constructive knowledge acquisition: on-site, where the learner is, in an explorative manner.

Reading Tip!
Numerous authors discuss the topic of mobile learning with smartphones, tablets, and the like in "Smart and Mobile" by *Katja Friedrich et al.*, primarily in the context of school education. The book highlights problems in didactic, organizational, and technical terms and suggests ways to overcome them.

6.3.2 Specific Characteristics of Smartphones in the Didactic Context

Smartphones have unique features that significantly deviate from the previously established norms of work, learning, and communication, as shown in Table 6.2. These characteristics must be carefully considered when developing a didactic concept for mobile learning.

6.4 Technical Aspects of Mobile Learning

6.4.1 Specific Characteristics of Smartphones in a Technical Context

Mobile devices are the suitable hardware for mobile learning applications. They possess specific properties that influence the development of a learning program.

Summary of the Specific Characteristics and Requirements of Mobile Devices (based on Linnhoff-Popien and Verclas 2012a, b, p. 10 f. and Aichele 2016, p. 56)

Table 6.2 Specific characteristics of smartphones in the didactic concept for mobile learning

Specific Characteristics	Didactic Implications
Frequently used apps	The most frequently used apps on smartphones are communication tools like Whatsapp, Facebook, or Instagram. A didactic concept for mobile learning should consider this usage pattern. For example, by consistently linking learning with communication opportunities and offering collaborative learning, i.e., learning in a group, as a standard.
Short attention span	Given the generally short attention span on smartphones, it is advisable to modularize learning content so that learners can engage with it in small time units. Particularly, spontaneous, short-term learning interactions are suitable for mobile learning.
Typical input methods	Input methods on smartphones include swiping, tapping, handwriting (on a small display), keyboard, and voice. Smartphones are therefore ideally suited to actively involve learners with targeted interactions, whether to acquire knowledge, retrieve it, or intuitively follow navigation.
Small screen	The guiding questions here are: • What can be omitted? • How should the small units of information be organized? • Which headings should be chosen? • How can learners be oriented?
Functionality	The multifunctionality of smartphones can significantly increase learning motivation. For example, learners can take a photo of something, upload the photo they just took online, and share it with others, all using a single device.

- Small size and resolution of the display,
- Short battery life,
- Low processor performance,
- Limited storage capacity,
- Special method of data input,
- Limited number of interfaces for external devices,
- Standard: sound, headphones,
- Standard: WLAN,
- Heterogeneity, e.g., different operating systems like Apple iOS or Google Android,
- Scalability of the mobile application: This question arises as more diverse devices are to be used for mobile use of a learning app.
- Security of the mobile application: the separation of private and professional data and the security levels for these data,
- Integration of the mobile learning application into the existing IT environment of the company or educational institution: adapting processes that are generally not designed for mobile use.

6.4.2 Mobile Device Management

Almost every company and institution has an IT department responsible for the operational and institutional computers and the devices connected to them. It ensures the flawless technical condition of the devices so that they can be used without any problems at any time. This field of activity expands with the increasing number of mobile devices to "Mobile Device Management". This is responsible, among other things, for all technical tasks related to mobile phones, laptops, and smartphones. If conceptually intended, Mobile Device Management also includes the personal mobile devices of the learners, which need to be integrated into existing structures of companies and institutions (Tremp et al. 2017). Using your own computer or smartphone for knowledge acquisition is referred to as "BYOD—**B**ring **Y**our **O**wn **D**evice".

Opportunities and Risks of BYOD

If data protection and the internal rules of educational institutions and companies allow it, the possibility of BYOD could significantly contribute to saving costs. Already half of the companies surveyed in the 2018 eLearning benchmarking study rely on BYOD (see https://www.elearning-journal.com/2019/06/20/mobile-learning). From the learners' perspective, this is a welcome solution: everyone prefers to use their own device for all possible tasks, because that's where they know their way around best. Since learners are familiar with their smartphone and like to use it, costly and time-consuming training on how to handle certain technical devices is also eliminated. However, in return, users also expect to be able to access company data as a matter of course within their learning process, even if this data is "sensitive" and confidential. However, this is opposed by the high security requirements of today (Tremp et al. 2017). For example, a travel provider develops a learning program for an insurance product that will not come onto the market until the following year. In advance, the travel provider wants to train its employees and selected travel agents in the travel agencies on the insurance product. However, confidentiality should apply to the training so that the competition does not get wind of it. In cases of this kind, the use of BYOD reaches its limits. The central questions are: *Who* owns the device? *Who* is responsible for it? Who bears the *costs* for the technical maintenance of the device, and above all, *who*should maintain it? In this context, a possible remuneration of the learners for the time of use within the framework of vocational training or further education must be discussed (Tremp et al. 2017).

6.4.3 Mobile App Management

The hardware for mobile learning requires Mobile Device Management to ensure smooth operation. Similarly, the learning applications used, the learning apps, also require "Mobile App Management". Among other things, Mobile App Management ensures that learning apps are secured on the respective smartphone, authenticates the learners and, if necessary, switches the learning app on or off, both for provided smartphones and for BYOD. In addition, the question of liability for criminal actions and the use of prohibited content by the learners arises. Mobile App Management also includes the careful compliance with the GDPR (Tremp et al. 2017).

6.4.4 Costs

In the technical concept, it is necessary to weigh up whether it is more efficient to use BYOD or to purchase smartphones for all learners in terms of costs. The cost estimate includes the effort for the respective Mobile Device Management and Mobile App Management as well as the comparison with the costs that would arise if print learning materials were issued.

6.4.5 Internet Access

The Internet provides a significant added value to smartphones compared to traditional mobile phones. The ongoing auctions of the 5G mobile network, which will further expand Internet access, are beneficial. This is because almost all smartphone applications rely on Internet access. Without the Internet, the added value of using a smartphone is virtually non-existent. However, there are still regions on Earth where comprehensive Internet access is not yet standard. Even in Germany, complete network coverage has not been achieved. For instance, in areas of Franconian Switzerland, often there is no access to mobile data.

Tip!
Major mobile network providers offer network maps online that can be used to check the availability of mobile data (see: https://www.vodafone.de/hilfe/netzabdeckung.html and https://www.o2online.de/service/netz-verfuegbarkeit/netzabdeckung).

In addition to potential gaps in network coverage, there are users who own a smartphone but rely on free Wi-Fi hotspots in cities and municipalities. These users include, for example, refugees or teenagers. These aspects of Internet availability must be considered in the technical concept by offering an offline version of the learning application for times when Internet access is unavailable. Since smartphones rarely have interfaces for external storage devices, users must be provided with a location to upload the offline version of a learning app when they have temporary Internet access. This could be, for example, their own company, an educational institution, a city centre, or similar.

Reading Tip!
For more in-depth information on the technical structures and architectures of mobile apps, the overall technical basis, and especially security in mobile application systems, refer to the technical book by *Hansruedi Tremp et al.*: "Mobile and Distributed Computing".

6.5 Pros and Cons

Table 6.3 compiles the advantages and disadvantages of using mobile learning in the overall concept of a mobile learning project:

6.6 Mobile Learning in Practice

6.6.1 Specific Learning Content of Mobile Learning

Due to the unique technical and communicative aspects of mobile learning, the nature of the knowledge conveyed fundamentally changes. According to Dittler (2017, 2017a), companies and educational institutions will primarily impart action and orientation knowledge about managing the ubiquitous and constant flood of information in the future. This shift aligns with the changing role of the teacher, who will transition from traditional teaching to supporting learners as a coach in constructivist knowledge acquisition.

The essential component of school education, the classic **"Literacy"** as a core competence for knowledge acquisition, will not be achievable with mobile learning in the strictest sense. Literacy refers to general reading and writing skills, such as text comprehension, understanding of meaning, linguistic abstraction ability, and written expressive power. However, mobile learning does not provide the technical prerequisites for writing longer handwritten or typed texts on a specific topic. While discussions with other learners and lecturers on a topic or text are possible, any participant can exit the discourse at any time without providing reasons. The closed classroom, where a discourse is carried out within a certain group until the end, contributing to the learners' understanding, is not available in mobile learning.

Different standards apply to mobile learning. According to Kerres and Claudia (2006), **"Computer Literacy"** is required in return. It describes the ability to operate computers, installed software applications, and associated devices. Computer literacy also includes understanding the concepts behind computer technology and software applications, but programming is not a requirement, just as "Literacy" does not require the ability to write novels.

Table 6.3 Advantages vs. Disadvantages of Mobile Learning

Advantages	Disadvantages
Input and output paths and components (keyboard, screen, etc.) are compactly integrated.	Mobile devices are technically not expandable if a learning app requires this. Retrofitting would be so complex that it is not worth it. Consequently, when developing learning apps, one is even more bound to the technical prerequisites than with computers and laptops (Aichele 2016).
A large amount of learning material can be carried without physical strain. Additionally, learning can occur without extensive prior planning. This allows for effective use of waiting times in everyday life (Mitschian 2010).	Mobile learning always requires an active internet connection; often personal tariffs are tied to a certain data volume, which is heavily used in mobile learning.
Direct, immediate communication between tutors and learners is possible, as a smartphone is always carried around as a very personal device and is physically close to the body (Aichele 2016).	Due to the connection to the internet, learners are always online and can easily divert their attention from the learning app to other apps. There is a risk of being "lost in hyperspace" and "lost in social media".
Smartphones are used, therefore acquisition costs are comparatively low compared to laptops and computers.	Technical limitations regarding display size, resolution, storage capacity, and processor speed.
Individualized applications (learning apps).	**Limits of learning apps:** Active language production is not possible everywhere (public space/open-plan office). Handwriting of longer texts.
Exam preparation and entrance exam for a study place abroad are possible on site, for example with appropriately certified apps, universities, and examiners. Supporting technology: Live tutor via video transmission and projector. Cost savings for students who would otherwise have to pay a lot of money for a semester stay in the target country of the study to take a corresponding entrance exam.	Incidental learning as in traditional face-to-face training is omitted, for example cultural mediation in foreign language teaching or the personal experience, expertise, and body language of a teacher as a role model, for example in sales training. Also missing is the opportunity to try out in "real situations" in front of others, be it in dialogue or conversation or also in the group.

6.6.2 Forms of Mobile Learning

Smartphones are compact technical powerhouses that combine many functions. With a smartphone, learners can take photos, film, play audios, access the internet, and interact with their location via GPS. In short, they can communicate, inform, publish, and publicize (Gatterer 2013). This versatility results in numerous forms of mobile learning:

- Flashcard programs,
- Picture stories,
- Narrative videos/explanatory videos,
- Knowledge on demand with QR codes,
- Games, including competitive ones,
- Wikis,
- Geotagging with GPS (photos with the geographical coordinates of the shooting location), and
- Collaborative learning, where learners teach each other using social media, for example, via WhatsApp chats or simple video transmission of lectures and fellow learners via FaceTime or WhatsApp video call.

6.6.3 Examples

6.6.3.1 VHS Learning Portal

The VHS learning portal provides various learning applications for learning German, preparing for school graduation, and learning to write, read, and calculate. While the primary target group is refugees, the portal is open to anyone interested, as it is free of charge (see https://www.vhs-lernportal.de) (Table 6.4).

6.6.3.2 ANTON—A Learning Platform for Schools

ANTON is a free, ad-free learning platform for various school subjects. Its development is co-financed by the European Fund for Regional Development (see https://anton.app/de) (see Table 6.5).

6.6.3.3 The "Nature View" App from the Museum of Natural History, Berlin

The "Nature View" app from the Museum of Natural History, Berlin, is not a typical learning app. Instead, it encourages users to explore their environment using their smartphones, specifically the nature within the urban space of Berlin. Users can record and identify bird calls or create their own information cards with photos, audio, and GPS data. The goal is to promote digital environmental education (see http://naturblick.naturkundemuseum.berlin) (Table 6.6).

The "Nature View" app can serve as inspiration for developing similar learning apps for vocational training. For instance, trainees could use a car learning app with a QR code on their smartphones to acquire exploratory knowledge on a real engine block. However, according to Beranek (2015), the following framework should be observed when creating learning apps for exploratory knowledge acquisition on site:

Table 6.4 VHS Learning Portal: Various Learning Applications

Feature	Practical Implementation
Access/Download	Search engine: "VHS learning app" → Click on "A1-German course—VHS learning portal": App opens. No download required.
Registration	Email or mobile number; then click on the confirmation link on the mobile phone or in the email account; = closed system, as authentication takes place.
Offline Offer	Offline app via Google Play Store or Apple App Store; login like online app (no new registration); one-time download of individual or all lessons. Small messages appear, prompting the user to allow permissions for access to photos, voice recordings, etc., i.e., GDPR is taken into account.
Navigation	Clear, reduced menu page; Navigation with fingertip inputs and fingertip scrolling (pulling up or down on the display). Within a lesson, linear navigation without jump options.
Use of the Added Value of Mobile Learning	Input is adapted to the immediate, direct methods of mobile devices, but without swipe technology. Direct feedback on every required input and solved task.
Consideration of the Special Features of Mobile Learning	Operability with only one finger possible, while the rest of the hand holds the device. Minimal learning sequences. Through the "continue learning" button, you can interrupt at any time and rejoin. Ideal for the often only short-term use of apps on smartphones. Assignment tasks can be solved by fingertip. For input tasks, a keyboard window directly appears at the bottom of the screen.

- Provide a structured **file storage**for the photos, texts, etc., with indexing, indicating where and when these were found.
- Enable the GPS function on the smartphone.
- Assign app permissions, e.g., "allow access to photos".
- Utilize the multifunctionality of smartphones, including: camera, microphone, thermometer, barometer, hygrometer, GPS, magnetometer, motion detector, near field communication.
- Install a QR code generator, for example at: http://www.qrcode-generator.
- Ensure secure passwords are used.
- Respect rights to personal images (e.g., by obtaining the consent of passers-by for photo or video recordings on the go).
- Respect copyrights of images, lettering, texts, or music recordings captured on the go.

Table 6.5 ANTON—Learning Apps for School Subjects

Feature	Practical Implementation
Access/Download	The app can be installed from the Google Play Store or Apple App Store by searching for "math learning app" and clicking on "ANTON". Alternatively, enter "ANTON App" directly into a search engine, click on the result link, and start learning immediately. No download is required.
Registration	Choose a username. Neither an email nor a phone number is required, resulting in an open system without authentication.
Offline Offer	With "ANTON Plus", you can choose an annual contribution between 8 EUR and 250 EUR.
Navigation	The menu page is clear and reduced, with navigation via fingertip inputs and scrolling. Within a learning unit, navigation is linear without jump options. Despite the reduced design, it is clear and appealing to learners.
Use of the Added Value of Mobile Learning	Input is adapted to the immediate, direct methods of mobile devices, but without the swipe technique. Each learning page has a work instruction as audio and screen text. Knowledge acquisition is constructive with minimal knowledge texts and subsequent successive display of several tasks for a small learning unit. After each small task unit, there is quick and motivating feedback that corresponds to the target group. A bonus system awards coins for correct solutions, which can be used for "reward games". Incorrectly solved tasks within a learning unit result in an immediate error message with the option to "try again" (as often as desired); clicking on "Solve" displays the solution immediately. The task-based learning, combined with target group-oriented feedback and the coin bonus system, follows the playful approach to learning with smartphones.
Consideration of the Special Features of Mobile Learning	Operation is possible with only one finger, while the rest of the hand holds the device. Learning units are small. Interruption at any time is possible; the learning status is saved and displayed in the topic menu with "Last viewed". This is ideal for the often short-term use of apps on smartphones. For input tasks, a keyboard window directly appears at the bottom of the screen. A special feature is that the keyboard only has the keys necessary for solving the respective task.
Avatar	Target group appropriate, there are pre-configured avatars that can be individually adapted.

6.6.3.4 Outdoor Rally "Actionbound"

Similar to the app "Naturblick", "Actionbound" incorporates an additional competitive element, positioning it within the game-based learning area (see https://de.actionbound.com). The application is free for private users, while companies are charged a small fee. To set up an outdoor rally, one simply needs to visit the Actionbound website, sign up, and create a so-called "Bound" in the browser with various tasks, such as solving puzzles and competing with others. For trainers, tutors, teachers, and education providers, Actionbound is particularly interesting as it automatically documents the learning

Table 6.6 "Nature View" App Features

Feature	Practical Implementation
Access/Download	Available on Google Play Store or Apple App Store. Search "Nature View" → Click on "Nature View": App can be installed. Alternatively, enter "Nature View App" into a search engine → click on result link and use immediately. No download required.
Registration	No registration required.
Offline Offer	No offline version available.
Navigation	Clear, simplified menu page. Navigation with fingertip inputs and scrolling (pull up or down on the display). Special feature: navigate by swiping right and left.
Use of the Added Value of Mobile Learning	Input is adapted to the immediate, direct methods of mobile devices, including swiping technique. Uses multifunctionality for exploring urban nature: recording audios, taking photos, generating information via GPS.
Consideration of the Special Features of Mobile Learning	Operability with only one finger possible, while the rest of the hand holds the device. Minimal information units can be displayed by tapping on question mark or photo buttons. The "field book" is available for personal observations. The app is ideal for working with the smartphone, which can be taken anywhere on nature explorations and put into operation immediately.

process, even with multiple participants (Beranek 2015). An application like Actionbound is well suited for introducing newly recruited employees of medium to large companies to the operation and its departments, as well as the processes in collaboration. They get to know their future workplace in a playful way. Actionbound is certainly more motivating than passively following a PowerPoint presentation and having to remember many new, theoretical contents. It is also an interesting learning medium in the cultural and language mediation for refugees or foreign students. By participating in an outdoor rally, they get to know the city and engage in conversation with the local people.

6.6.3.5 Quizlet

The learning app "Quizlet" provides flashcard sets for a wide variety of school subjects. In addition to its use in schools, it is also conceivable for use in company training and further education (see https://quizlet.com) (Table 6.7).

6.6.3.6 Deutsche Bahn

A prime example of the implementation of numerous multimedia didactic aspects in mobile learning is the learning application "PRiME" by Deutsche Bahn. Table 6.8 illustrates how PRiME implements the individual requirements for target group-appropriate and system-adequate mobile learning in practice (cf. Schumacher and Wode 2017):

Table 6.7 Quizlet

Feature	Practical Implementation
Access/Download	Search engine: "quizlet" → Click on result link: App opens. No download required.
Registration	Email → then click on confirmation link in email account; directly via Google or Facebook → immediately work or learn with the app; = closed system, as authentication takes place.
Offline Offer	Offline app via Google Play Store or Apple App Store; chargeable: around 35 EUR per year.
Navigation	Simple, reduced menu page; navigation with fingertip inputs and fingertip scrolling (pull up or down on the display). Special feature: Various interactions can be performed by swiping.
Use of the Added Value of Mobile Learning	Input is adapted to the immediate, direct methods of mobile devices, including swiping technique. Uses the common "Social Media" component of smartphones to contact fellow learners, lecturers or teachers, or to compete with them in small knowledge games.
Consideration of the Special Features of Mobile Learning	Operability with only 1 finger possible, while the rest of the hand holds the device. Mostly short learning sequences, individually created, as each user of the app can also act as a producer of new learning cards. For input tasks, the corresponding keyboard window appears directly at the bottom of the screen.

Tip!
You can view examples of apps from a wide range of educational topics at "LearningApps.org" and also use them for your own educational offer free of charge. You can also easily create your own apps there. However, please note the data protection and copyright guidelines of the provider: https://learningapps.org.

6.7 Overall Concept for a Mobile Learning Application

At its core, the process of producing mobile learning corresponds to the processes in an eLearning project, as described in this book: project progress, conception phases and script. Mobile learning is characterized above all by its small to minimal, often almost atomic learning units. Therefore, the conception is limited to an overall script with comprehensive framework data for production and a script that, just like in eLearning, comprehensively describes the individual pages (see Chap. 5). The following preliminary

Table 6.8 Mobile learning at Deutsche Bahn with PRiME

Conceptual aspect	Practical application
Communicative approach that aligns with user behaviour on smartphones.	Fast, immediate support, expert exchange and virtual colleague meetings in the community. For this, PRiME has integrated its own messaging and chat app.
Physical relief: Deutsche Bahn employees require ongoing information tailored to their work area in their daily tasks. These are part of a complex, unwieldy and heavy set of rules. However, the entire set of rules is never needed.	Information and documents can be broken down into the smallest possible, atomic units and saved as Word or PowerPoint files. They are also reusable. For this, an editor is available for lecturers and authors with a simple, Windows Explorer-oriented two-window navigation plus horizontal menu bar.
Individual and short learning units that accommodate the acquisition of knowledge on smartphones or tablets.	The employees can assemble elements that are relevant to their work area themselves in their learning environment. At the same time, the comprehensive source document is still available as a reference. For example, a wagon technician only includes the information in his personal learning environment that concerns the maintenance of those vehicle types for which he is responsible.
Constructive acquisition of knowledge by encouraging learners to generate and share their own knowledge.	Integrated text, photo and video functions with which employees can share work processes with colleagues via the community integrated in the app.
Change in the role of teachers, trainers, authors.	The employees share information and knowledge in the community. This results in a swarm intelligence that authors, teachers and trainers pick up to continuously optimize learning content and learning environment in a target group-appropriate manner.
Data security in the mobile learning context.	The network offers employees two options for data release: for individual users or for a group they define themselves. PRiME has its own project server, so no data is sent to external service providers.

considerations examine whether mobile learning is actually the best choice for the learning objective pursued with the learning application. All results of the preliminary considerations flow as content into the overall concept (see Sect. 6.7.2).

6.7.1 Preliminary Considerations for the Overall Concept

Initial Situation

The initiation of a projected mobile learning production depends on the answers to the following two questions:

1. Why do we want to use mobile learning?
2. What is the added value for the company or the learners?

Costs
Before creating the overall concept of a mobile learning application, two fundamental decisions regarding costs should be made:

1. Should we equip the learners with smartphones? Or should we rely on the BYOD concept (see Sect. 6.4.2)?
2. Should we develop the learning application ourselves? Or should we purchase a learning app?

Equipping learners with smartphones can be a significant cost factor. However, this could reduce the printing costs for the regular updating and distribution of printed teaching and learning materials. A careful cost calculation is helpful in making this decision.

When considering whether to develop the learning application yourself or to purchase it, an overview of the offerings from online stores that sell mobile applications may be helpful. Well-known online stores include Apple's "App Store" (https://www.apple.com/de/ios/app-store) and "Google Play" (https://play.google.com/store). When you access the website, enter "learning" in the search window to get an overview of numerous learning apps. Once an app is selected, a short description, user ratings, and comments are displayed. This allows you to quickly and inexpensively find out the range of functions, the provider, and the cost of the application. However, registration for the respective app is required to learn about the functional *content*. For this purpose, research on online portals is more time-saving, for example, using the search term "education" on the English-language portal: https://www.appbrain.com. In addition to user ratings, you will find rankings and especially screens that provide insight into the content of the selected app (Aichele 2016).

Benchmarking
Whenever possible, mobile learning applications from other providers should be examined and analyzed to determine whether they contain aspects beneficial for your own learning project or structures that you definitely do not want to adopt. This process is referred to as "benchmarking" in technical jargon.

Framework Data
The following framework data should be clarified before creating the overall concept (cf. Friedrich et al. 2015, p. 95):

- Is the existing network infrastructure sufficient for the mobile applications?
- Should mobile devices be purchased, and if so, which ones?
- Should we use smartphones as *teaching* and/or *learning*tools?

- Is there a "Mobile Device Management" system (see Sect. 6.4.2)?
- Is there a "Mobile App Management" system (see Sect. 6.4.3)?
- Should learning apps be installed as group licenses, and if so, which ones?

6.7.2 Content in the Overall Concept

Target Group

Orientation towards the target group is crucial because, ultimately, the effective and efficient use of the mobile learning application is the primary goal of an educational project in this area (see Sect. 4.1.1.3).

Educational Concept

- A mobile learning strategy forms part of the overall educational concept. It must be determined whether mobile learning operates independently within specific learning apps or whether it should enhance face-to-face training or a more comprehensive eLearning program. In the latter case, the exact scope, that is, the proportion of teaching units, needs to be defined, as well as the learning content to be covered by mobile learning.
- The implementation of mobile learning in education and further training necessitates a precise description, for instance:
  - Developing the lesson based on the learning app,
  - Preparing learners for the activities: informing learners about the learning content they can anticipate in the app and how they can integrate it into their education and further training,
  - Structuring collaborative learning: outlining the nature and method of communication among learners within the group as well as with the lecturer or tutor.
- An educational concept delineates which didactic elements should be covered by mobile learning. Given the specific technical capabilities of smartphones, the following are particularly suitable:
  - introducing topics,
  - deepening topics,
  - securing knowledge, and
  - promoting motivation.

Supporting these are various learning methods, including small exercises, vocabulary training, and tasks such as taking photos or videos on the go and incorporating them into the lesson.

- The examination organization must be generally regulated. The mobile context requires special consideration, for instance, when conducting tests with smartphones. Due to internet access, all solutions are theoretically available online. With BYOD

(Bring Your Own Device), they could also be stored on the device. One option for a regulated examination is to conduct it offline in a learning center, but this would contradict the principle of "learning on the go". The alternative is to modify the task so that a knowledge *transfer* occurs that cannot be found through a simple online search.

Languages
Mobile learning implies that the learning app can be used anywhere and by anyone. Therefore, it is advisable to provide multiple language versions if possible.

Navigation
The navigation of a learning app on a smartphone should generally be simple due to the small display. For instance, the German Adult Education Association utilises targeted user guidance with straightforward, linear navigation in its learning apps (see Sect. 6.6.3). The optimal navigation for a learning application depends on various factors, including device-specific input methods. These methods differ significantly between computers and smartphones, as demonstrated in Table 6.9:

Given the specific input methods on smartphones, the following aspects should be considered for the navigation of learning apps:

- Intuitive operability according to common input methods, such as tapping instead of mouse click, swiping, and controlling by voice input. Despite the simplified navigation, the learner must always know where the next tap or swipe will lead, if necessary with the help of small, context-related hints.

Table 6.9 Comparison of input methods between computer and smartphone

Computer/Laptop	Smartphone
External or built-in physical keyboard for number and letter input and navigation with arrow symbols.	No physical keyboard, but touch function for number and letter input on a display keyboard. Sometimes implemented as a reduced keyboard, as seen in the learning app ANTON (see Sect. 6.6.3).
Mouse to activate functions on the display by clicking.	No mouse and therefore no click option, but activation of functions by finger touch.
Mouse for scrolling, opening, and closing.	Swipe with fingers or hand across the display to scroll, open, and close.
Display formats of opened files can be changed with mouse-selected menu commands.	Display formats of opened files can be changed by flexible movement to "portrait" and "landscape" of the smartphone.
Audio input with external or integrated microphone for voice control of input commands. Activation by mouse click on the voice input function.	Audio input is simpler compared to a computer or laptop, as a smartphone can be held to the mouth to speak directly into the integrated microphone. Immediate activation of the voice input function by finger touch.

- Classic eLearning applications usually orient themselves on the Microsoft Office or Wikipedia navigation. With mobile learning, the navigation adapts to the small screen and is arranged at the edges of the screen. From there, the menus can be opened and closed horizontally and vertically by tapping and swiping.
- Scrolling far down on a page was previously rather undesirable in learning programs on a computer or laptop, as this can easily make the view confusing and an additional reach for the mouse is necessary. However, since the "scroll" on smartphones works by finger touch, it is quick and intuitively usable. This has established it as a desired navigation element.
- The device navigation should clearly distinguish itself from the app-related navigation.
- The learning application must be scalable to smartphone size.
- Applications on smartphones impress with their immediacy and speed of operation. However, this also runs the risk of inadvertently closing an application without previously saving the learning status. Therefore, it is always recommended for learning apps to display the message "Really close?" before the app is actually closed. This gives the learner the chance to save their learning status after all.

System Consistency

The same methodology used in the context of knowledge acquisition should also be applied in tests and exams. If the educational concept includes the use of mobile learning, this should also be considered in knowledge assurance, thus maintaining system consistency.

Updating Learning Content

The overall concept should ideally address a content management system (CMS) for lecturers or teachers.

Data Protection

Careful data protection is a must in all professional fields of action and should be documented accordingly in the overall concept. For example, a GDPR preface page could be added to the learning app. You can find more on this in Sect. 8.2.4.

References

Aichele, Christian & Marius Schönberger (2016) App-Entwicklung – effizient und erfolgreich. Wiesbaden: Springer Vieweg.

Bachmair, Ben (2009) Medienwissen für Pädagogen. Medienbildung in riskanten Erlebniswelten. Wiesbaden: Verlag für Sozialwissenschaften.

Beranek, Angelika & Simon Zwick (2015) Actionbound – laufend lernen. In: Friedrich, Katja et al (Eds.) smart und mobil, München: kopaed, pp. 217–228.

Buchem, Ilona (2015) Mobiles Lernen und die Ent-/Didaktisierung der Lernräume. In: Friedrich, Katja et al. (Eds.) smart und mobil, München: kopaed, pp. 43–61.

De Witt, Claudia & Christina Gloerfeld (Eds.) Handbuch Mobile Learning, 2018. Heidelberg, Dordrecht, London, New York: Springer.

Dittler, Ullrich (Eds.) E-Learning 4.0, 2017. Berlin, Boston: Walter de Gruyter Oldenbourg.

Dittler, Ullrich (2017a) Die 4. Welle des E-Learning: Mobile, smarte und soziale Medien erobern den Alltag und verändern die Lernwelt. In: Dittler, Ullrich (Eds.) E-Learning 4.0. Berlin, Boston: Walter de Gruyter Oldenbourg, pp. 43–67.

Friedrich, Katja et al. (Hrsg.) smart und mobil. Digitale Kommunikation als Herausforderung für Bildung, Pädagogik und Politik, 2015. München: kopaed.

Gatterer, Christian (2013) Mobile learning – Smartphones im Unterricht. Saarbrücken: Akademie Verlag (jetzt: Berlin: Walter de Gruyter).

Kerres, Michael & Claudia de Witt (2006) Perspektiven der „Medienbildung". In: Fatke, Reinhard & Hans Merkens (Hrsg.) Bildung über die Lebenszeit. Wiesbaden: Verlag für Sozialwissenschaften, S. 209–220.

Linnhoff-Popien, Claudia & Stephan Verclas (2012a) Mit Business-Apps ins Zeitalter mobiler Geschäftsprozesse. In: Linnhoff-Popien, Claudia & Stephan Verclas (Eds.) Smart Mobile Apps. Heidelberg, Dordrecht, London, New York: Springer, pp. 3–16.

Linnhoff-Popien, Claudia & Stephan Verclas (Eds.) Smart Mobile Apps, 2012b. Heidelberg, Dordrecht, London, New York: Springer.

Mitschian, Haymo (2010) m-Learning – die neue Welle? Mobiles Lernen für Deutsch als Fremdsprache. Kassel: university press.

Riesenbeck, Wilke (2017) Betriebliche Aus- und Weiterbildung 4.0. In: Dittler, Ullrich (Eds.) E-Learning 4.0. Berlin, Boston: Walter de Gruyter Oldenbourg, pp. 172–189.

Roth, Jörg (2005) Mobile Computing. Grundlagen, Technik, Konzepte. Heidelberg: dpunkt.verlag, 2. aktualisierte Auflage.

Tremp, Hansruedi, Tobias Bruderer und Daniel Hess (2017) Mobile und Distributed Computing. Norderstedt: BoD.

Schumacher, Gerd & Bianca Wode (2017) Praxisbeispiel: Deutsche Bahn. In: Dittler, Ullrich (Eds.) E-Learning 4.0. Berlin, Boston: Walter de Gruyter Oldenbourg, pp. 190–208.

7 How do I Organize the Work on the Script?

Abstract

Chapter 7 deals with the organization of a media author's working day. Topics such as time management, archiving, version maintenance of corrections, and source citations concern both the media author and the leader of an eLearning project. The information on sensible contract design and economic fee calculation is specifically aimed at the independent media author.

Creating scripts for eLearning involves dedicating oneself to a multifaceted project for an extended period. Outside of conference times with the project team, the media author works independently. These conferences only constitute a minimal part of the total time required. For the remaining majority of the project time, the media author needs strict self-management to deliver a high-quality script in the end.

Most media authors work freelance, which presents the challenge of managing self-employment in addition to project-related organization. In most cases, a freelance media author is not well-prepared in terms of business management. However, they cannot avoid dealing with this topic. Specifically for these cases, the Federal Ministry for Economic Affairs and Energy (BMWi) has developed an information and learning program with several modules. This program guides beginners from the decision for self-employment through financial and business planning to legal business formation. In addition to the learning content, numerous information and addresses are available, as well as printable checklists. Fig. 7.1 shows the start page of the learning program with an overview of the content of each module.

D. Modlinger, *eLearning and Mobile Learning – Concept and Script*,
https://doi.org/10.1007/978-3-658-44695-6_7

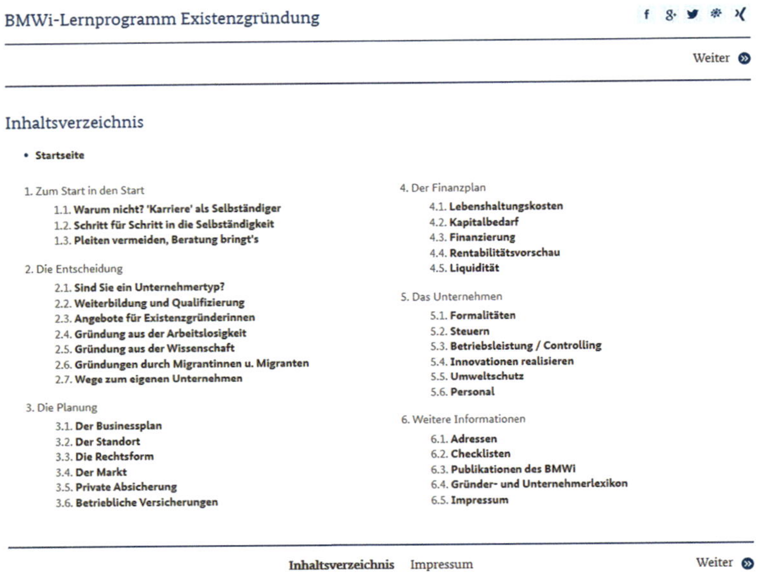

Fig. 7.1 Start page of the BMWi's business start-up learning program

> **Tip!**
> At: http://www.existenzgruender.de/static/etraining/existenzgruendung/inhalt.html the BMWi's "Existenzgründungsberater" learning program is available for free.

7.1 Design of Offer and Contract

The path to the offer begins with the call of the project manager of a multimedia agency, who offers participation in an eLearning project. This conversation is the first step to the offer: The media author should have a checklist ready to ask for the following information:

- What number of learning hours is planned?
- Is there already a quantity structure?
- If there is a quantity structure, how many screen pages are estimated per learning hour?
- Should the screen pages be pure information pages, i.e., relatively static?

- Should the screen pages be interactive, so that they encourage the learners to actively acquire knowledge?
- How many tasks are planned per learning hour?
- Should the tasks include differentiated feedback?
- What should the visualization look like (graphics, photos, animation, illustration, learning video)?
- Are learning objectives and contents already given?
- How many days are estimated for the briefing?
- How many days are estimated for the script acceptance?
- Who will cover the travel expenses?
- How is the effort to be assessed? (What does the client want to pay? Should the learning application be produced more cost-saving or elaborate?)
- Are there already conceptual guidelines or approaches?
- How has learning been done so far? Is there already a textbook, a teaching booklet, a teaching film, or an eLearning application on the topic?
- What basic text is available? Is everything provided or does research need to be done (content, images)?
- Will the learning program be dubbed?
- Is special knowledge required on the part of the media author? (If yes, then a higher fee should be charged for this.)
- Time frame—can one assume a usual working day (see Sect. 7.1.1) or should one expect a hectic ten-hour day and weekend assignments? (For the latter, a higher fee should be charged.)

The outcome of the initial conversation is integrated into the proposal. Typically, the media author also receives project-related documents, enabling a more accurate effort estimation. The proposal should be detailed, providing fee information for:

- Daily rates: briefing, script approval (including a breakdown of individual fees),
- Interactive screen pages (including a breakdown of individual costs),
- Static screen pages (including a breakdown of individual costs),
- Tasks with yes/no feedback (including a breakdown of individual costs),
- Tasks with differentiated feedback (including a breakdown of individual costs),
- Travel expenses, and
- Author corrections (refer to Sect. 3.4.1).

Tip!
Refer to the "Information conversation" checklist, see Sect. 10.20.

7.1.1 Fee Calculation

To calculate an appropriate fee, the following helpful brochures and information are available:

- *iBusiness Fee Guide:* This guide, regularly published by Hightext Verlag, contains fees as well as production and licensing costs for the development of interactive applications (including app developments) in German-speaking countries. The values are determined from current surveys. It is 194 pages long and includes tables and charts. It costs 49.80 EUR and its ISBN is 978-3-939004-33-2.
- *Calculating and Selling Intellectual Work* by Dorle Weyers: This brochure introduces strategies for successful economic work to humanities and social scientists. Although it primarily targets women, the practical recommendations for fee calculation, customer care, value enhancement of one's own work, marketing measures, as well as cultural and political action are also beneficial for men. It is 70 pages long, costs 5 EUR, and its ISBN is 3-936536-02-3. It is available at: https://shop.digitalcourage.de/broschuere-kopfarbeit-kalkulieren-verkaufen.html.
- *Self-Employed Guide* by ver.di: This online portal evolved from the "Guide for Freelancers" by Goetz Buchholz from 1998. It provides basic information for all those who work freelance in art and media. The guide comprehensively covers what a media author needs to know: fees and contracts, legal issues, financing options, collaborations, insurances, etc. The contents are detailed and easy to understand, enriched with many addresses as well as practical tips and hints. As it is available on the web, the contents are always up to date: https://selbststaendigen.info/.

For the calculation, it is not sufficient to base it solely on the pure working time. For instance, if one aims to achieve a certain daily rate to avoid making a loss, they should avoid the following naive calculation for, say, 60 screen pages: Suppose the daily rate is 500 EUR. The media author calculates 7.5 hours of work for this day, during which they plan to create 10 screen pages (1 screen page = an average of 45 minutes of work). Their offer states: *3000 EUR for 60 screen pages* (they need 6 days at 500 EUR, on each of which they create 10 screen pages). But what does reality look like in everyday work? The phone rings, the computer crashes, urgent emails need to be answered, and internet research on the new topic consumes time. In the evening, the author has only finished 5 screen pages, even though they were fully occupied for 9 hours. In the end, they need 12 days for the 60 screen pages, for which they receive 3000 EUR; this reduces their daily rate to 250 EUR. And they also fall behind in terms of time. Therefore, buffer times for the following activities must be included in the calculation:

- Administration,
- Coordination,
- Discussion,
- Phone calls,
- Printouts,
- Proofreading,
- Archiving,
- Acquisition,
- Gathering information on current developments,
- Solving computer problems and similar.

The calculation of a daily rate should therefore be based on a maximum of 5 hours of pure work time (= writing time and conception time) and allow for a 3-hour buffer. A media author can manage an average of 5 hours of pure writing time per day; after that, concentration, mental freshness and creativity decrease. A useful guide for fee calculation and other questions about the profitability of freelancers in the multimedia industry is available with the online portal "Consultation Network for Solo Self-Employed by ver.di" (see https://selbststaendigen.info/).

7.1.2 Contract Design

When designing the contract, the media author should clearly agree on the following points:

- How many correction rounds are included in the fee?
- What is meant by correction rounds? (For example, specify that additional costs will be incurred for author corrections, see Sect. 3.4.1)
- How should travel expenses be accounted for?
- In what form should the work be delivered to the agency (print, digital, or both)?

The parameters mentioned in Sect. 7.1.1 for fee calculation should be included in the contract. This provides clarity about the contract contents and makes clear which individual tasks are covered by a flat hourly fee or daily fee.

Example of a contract addition for a media author

"The fee includes: familiarization with the project, research, creation of the complete script with screen and audio texts as well as graphic suggestions, quality assurance, 2 correction rounds on the part of the client, electronic and printed script delivery, careful archiving as well as travel and postage costs." ◀

7.1.3 Sending a Sample Chapter

Tip!
Checklist "Script Acceptance", see Sect. 10.10.

For every new project, the media author should send a sample chapter of the script to the multimedia agency and ideally also to the client. The other project members can judge from these first script pages whether the direction is correct in terms of learning objectives and tonality, as defined in the rough concept (see Sect. 4.1). The scope of a sample chapter is about ten percent of the total number of pages. Before the media author releases the sample chapter, they should carefully check whether they have correctly implemented all the learning content agreed upon in the briefing and in the rough concept.

7.2 Effective Time Management in the Project

Every project participant is co-responsible for ensuring that an eLearning production remains within the planned financial and time frame; this also applies to the media author. In addition to the project manager, they have the largest share of time management to handle, as they must plan well how long they need for writing, for example, 100 script pages and for the associated conception. For planning, they can use the information provided in Sect. 3.3.5 on the duration of concept and script development. They now have the choice between forward and backward scheduling (see Sect. 3.3.5). Backward scheduling is recommended, where the available time is distributed over weeks and days starting from the end date. The buffers to be included for fee calculation are also valid here (see Sect. 7.1.1). The advantage of backward scheduling: The author immediately sees if there is not enough time and can agree on a new end date with the client and multimedia agency; if this is not possible, a co-author can alternatively be brought in. Under no circumstances should the author say "I will somehow manage" when the time budget is too tight. It is better to ensure a predictable, stable working time frame in advance.

Classic (paper) planners are available as tools for time planning, as well as electronic calendars, such as Microsoft's Outlook. The electronic calendar has the advantage that you can be reminded of appointments and thus have a follow-up system. In addition, appointments can be assigned to different categories and marked accordingly in color. This gives a clear overview in the monthly view of when which projects start and when they end.

In addition to the overall project schedule, detailed plans should be made for each week and each day. This allows the media author to consistently assess whether they can meet the time frame. If changes occur, they should adjust their schedule and inform the

To-do list Date: ______________

To-do	Prio	Profit
1.		
2.		
3.		
4.		
5.		
6.		
7.		
8.		
9.		
10.		

Fig. 7.2 Form template for the daily to-do list, sorted by importance and profit

project manager. Proper daily planning is the most crucial tool in time management. For instance, the priority list presented in Fig. 7.2 suggests that a maximum of 10 activities or tasks per day should be listed. Subsequently, levels of importance from "1" to "10" are assigned, with "1" being the most important. In the next round, each activity or task is assigned the expected monetary gain, again from "1" for the most gain to "10" for the least gain. The tasks are then tackled according to the expected gain. This approach is an effective method to learn to properly assess times and priorities and to follow a business-oriented thought process. It is worth a try!

As previously described in the fee calculation, a media author should plan for a maximum of five full hours of pure writing time per day. Additionally, they need buffers for administrative tasks, research, breaks, and conversations, or even for reading trade journals or daily newspapers to stay informed about political and economic developments. Continuous intellectual gain should not be underestimated, as general knowledge is very important for writing eLearning programs.

A few words about the "writer's block," which affects every author sooner or later. This can occur due to overload: there are so many projects piled up on the desk that the author can no longer think clearly due to time pressure and can no longer work creatively. They distract themselves and start cleaning their garage while the clock relentlessly ticks towards the deadline. But it could also be that their energy has simply depleted and they can no longer come up with anything creative. However, one can extricate oneself from this entanglement with the right techniques:

1. *Set priorities* with the just introduced to-do list, sorted by importance and profit.
2. *Work focused:* Once the priority list is set, it is important to shut off external disturbances (inform family members, colleagues) and note down internal disturbances ("I really need to ...") on a separate sheet and work them off later; working according to the priority list does not always work immediately, but can be learned over time with consistent application.
3. *Find optimal personal working hours* and adjust activities accordingly:
4. When do I make decisions faster – in the morning or in the evening?
5. When do I concentrate best – in the morning or in the afternoon?
6. When do the most distractions usually come at me from outside?
7. *Find rhythm and regularity* in daily routines, for example, check the mail in the morning when starting work, write the priority list, get a coffee and start; always show up at the coffee corner at the same time – then family members or colleagues know when to exchange news and discuss problems. Advantage: Disturbances during focused work are eliminated.
8. *Kill your darlings:* Authors' favorite formatting work on documents should be recognized as time eaters and with self-discipline be postponed to times when one can no longer concentrate so well.
9. *Reward and motivate* for regular, priority-oriented work, for example, the author has a weekend really free due to optimized processes and plans their personal leisure highlight for this weekend.

Essentially, every person approaches their daily tasks differently. In the book "Arbeitsblockaden erfolgreich überwinden: Schluss mit Aufschieben, Verzetteln, Verplanen!" by Claudia Guderian (2008, mvg-Verlag), you can determine your personal work structure and learn corresponding strategies to counteract delays.

7.3 Sources and Archiving

The provision of sources and the archiving of files and correspondence are crucial tasks when a media author aims to organise their work in a time-saving and quality-assuring manner.

7.3.1 Citing Sources

"Where did you get that number from?", the client asks during the script approval. "I got it from the briefing, just a moment, here ...", the media author replies, searching and flipping through pages, only to add: "I cannot find it right now, but I am sure it is in the documents at the office. I will check it this evening and email it to you." The client is satisfied and the media author can cancel their table reservation at the Italian restaurant for that evening. Such situations can only be avoided by consistently citing sources. During the writing process, this seems unnecessary, as all books are at hand, the basal text is filed, and a folder with the links to the project has been created in the browser. But during the script writing process, it is easy to forget exactly where in all the texts, links, etc., a certain piece of information was found. The subsequent search is time-consuming and annoying.

Therefore, all sources should be cited in the script document. In the word processing program Microsoft Word, for example, you can enter as a comment where a passage comes from. The media author should create two versions of the document: a working script with comments for their own use and a ready-for-approval script for the client and the agency, from which all comments have been deleted. The media author demonstrates their professionalism when they can immediately give a clear answer to the question asked at the beginning.

7.3.2 Archiving Correspondence

Similar to the sources, the same applies to the correspondence. In large projects, a lot of communication takes place and when something does not go according to plan, a scapegoat is quickly sought. It is fortunate for those who carefully archive their correspondence and do not let the transience of email communication tempt them to delete quickly. All correspondence for a project should be saved in the project folder on the hard drive by creating well-structured folders and subfolders, as shown in Fig. 7.3. Emails should be saved as PDF files; then they are no longer changeable and thus have documentary character.

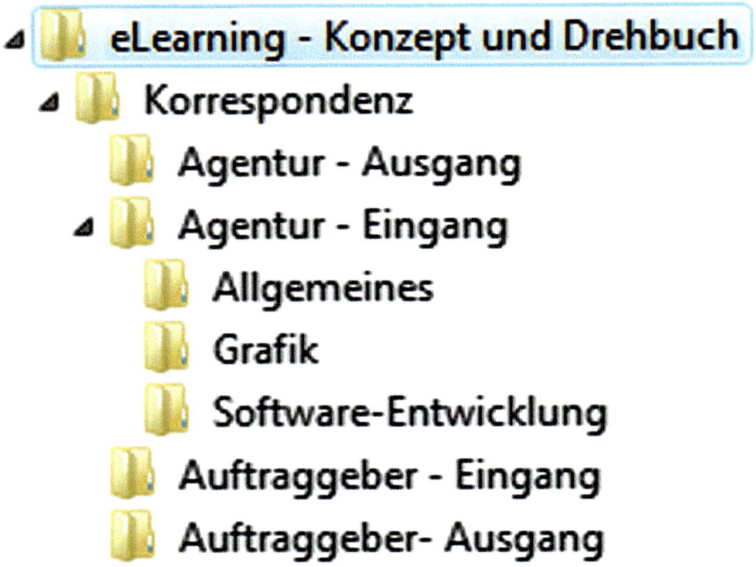

Fig. 7.3 Example of a folder structure on the hard drive for archiving project correspondence

7.3.3 Data Archiving

Computers are devices and therefore prone to technical defects. Windows is particularly known for crashing just when you have written the best five pages of your life. And in the worst case, no "recovery file" appears on the screen after restarting. For the media author, this means: save, save, and save again! During writing, it is a short press on *Ctrl+S*—and the text just created is saved. Every evening, all data must be saved. Two external hard drives are suitable for this, onto which the project folders edited during the day can simply be dragged. The hard drive should have at least 500 GB, as large amounts of data can accumulate due to the images and graphics in eLearning scripts. It is advisable to use both storage media at the end of the office hours, i.e., to perform a *double backup*. It happens again and again that an external hard drive is destroyed by a lightning strike, heat exposure, or simply by movement during operation. After the project is completed, the files should be saved on two separate archive hard drives that are not used for ongoing projects.

7.4 How to Keep Track of Corrections and Versions?

Scripts for eLearning are subject to changes. Some learning content is current and thus loses its validity in a short time. Particularly, clients who are new to eLearning often only realize what they truly want during the course of the project. This is understandable, but it results in numerous changes. As previously described in Sect. 5.1, the history on a script page primarily documents who made what changes, when they were made, and which version it is.

7.4.1 Maintaining an Overview of the Versions

To keep track of the different versions, storage must be consistent according to version numbers, both in the folder structure of the hard drive and in the file folder. The version number appears not only on the script page itself, but the file is also saved under this number in the corresponding folder. For file folders, the version number and the date are clearly visible on the spine, ensuring quick access.

7.4.2 Keeping Track of the Corrections

The corrections, just like the sources, must be carefully indicated. This means that the media author must accurately document the corrections that arise in a script discussion. When incorporating them, he should tick off all completed corrections in color or mark them digitally. This is crucial because he may encounter the correction flags weeks later and no longer remember whether these corrections have already been made. For each additional script discussion, at least the last two corrected scripts must be brought along to precisely trace the history in discussions about the content with the client. This saves the participants a significant amount of search time and also a lot of discussion about who said what at the last script discussion. As soon as the eLearning program is completed and billed, all correction processes can be discarded. It is important to secure the files and archive the final status in paper form.

References

Guderian, Claudia (2008) Arbeitsblockaden erfolgreich überwinden. München: mvg-Verlag.
Hightext Verlag (2015) iBusiness Honorarleitfaden. München: Hightext Verlag.
Weyers, Dorle (2004) Kopfarbeit kalkulieren und verkaufen. Münster: ImPrint Verlag; Bezug via: https://shop.digitalcourage.de/broschuere-kopfarbeit-kalkulieren-verkaufen.html.

How Do I Recognize a Good "Media Author"?

8

Abstract

Chapter 8 presents the skills that a media author should bring to successfully participate in an eLearning production. The rights and obligations of an author around project work are detailed. Finally, the chapter is enriched with information as well as tips and tricks for acquiring new customers for those media authors who operate as freelancers in the eLearning market.

8.1 What Skills Does a Media Author Bring?

> "I expect a media author to bring didactic competence and to understand the offer concept so well that they can present it to the customer independently."—Elke Kast, Senior Project Manager, M.I.T e-Solutions GmbH.

A proficient media author can design a media-didactic concept that adheres to learning psychological principles. They develop the rough concept and elaborate the detailed concept as the foundation of the script. Additionally, a professional media author knows how to develop a specification and is adept at evaluating eLearning programs. They also bring expertise from related professions and are well-versed in copyright and contract law. A freelance media author understands their industry well and knows how to acquire new customers.

A media author constructs a sequence plan, a learning sequence, a game world. However, they always create structures that are closely linked and must follow a logical sequence. In a figurative sense, the media author can be compared to a director who brings all elements of a film together in such a way that they offer an exciting experience for the viewer. They can also be compared to an architect who constructs their

D. Modlinger, *eLearning and Mobile Learning – Concept and Script*,
https://doi.org/10.1007/978-3-658-44695-6_8

houses in such a way that they are stable and ideally also aesthetically pleasing. Each of these professional groups creates something that looks good and simple in the result. The know-how behind it often remains hidden. Precisely because a media author brings such comprehensive knowledge, they need a solid education. So far, media authors are mostly career changers with a humanities university degree: Germanists, educators, psychologists, communication scientists or linguists.

> "Often it is precisely humanities scholars and educators who bring what a media author so urgently needs: empathy, a sense of language and high writing competence."—Thomas Reglin, Scientific Director, Forschungsinstitut betriebliche Bildung (f-bb) gGmbH, Nuremberg.

The concrete practical knowledge is not brought by a media author from their studies. The further education offers of private providers are usually expensive and much too short. For this not so new professional image, there is a lack of university training opportunities, such as those offered by the Stuttgart Media University in their bachelor's degree program "Information Design".

Tip!
Information on the training and further education of media authors and project managers can be found in Sect. 9.4.

The limits of a media author's competences should be drawn at the interface to software development. Software developer is a highly qualified technical profession that requires comprehensive training. Although the media author should be informed about the current developments of eLearning software (for example XML and learning platforms), in project work they should be able to concentrate on the conceptual and content part.

8.1.1 Adjacent Professions

Some professions border directly on the profession of the media author or even form an intersection. The following list shows a selection of possible competences that can reach into the tasks of the media author from these professions:

- Journalists: Research, readable presentation of content, proficiency in many subject areas, knowledge of the effect of text and image on the reader.
- Screenwriters for film and television: Research, visualization power, creating tension (eLearning: motivating the learner to stay on), maintaining the red thread, maintaining the viewer's attention over long distances, fluent dialogue writing, describing film

scenes (important for video scenes in the eLearning script), developing and characterizing characters, clearly defining locations, film language for short and clear description of processes, scribbling scenarios.
- Advertising copywriters: short and concise writing, attracting attention, getting to the point, getting by with little space (important for screen pages), knowledge of the effect of colors and images on the viewer.
- Psychologists: Perception and learning psychology, attention control, motivation of learners, work and organizational psychology (important for the integration of learning programs into existing operational processes), behavioral psychology (helpful for developing and describing scenarios), statistics (useful for example for target group analysis).
- Educators: Basics of education and upbringing, design and evaluation of learning environments, use and evaluation of media in teaching, knowledge management, creation of tasks, teaching design and learning goal development.
- Editors: Research, selection and editing of texts and images, scribbling.
- Information architects: Knowledge management, development of deeply structured navigations and user-friendly design.
- Web designers: Development of a user-friendly user guide, effect of colors and fonts on the web, user-friendly screen design.

Tip!
Media authors are sometimes also called WBT author, scriptwriter for WBT, eLearning author, developer for interactive learning media or courseware designer.

8.2 What About Rights and Obligations?

The obligations of a media author primarily involve understanding copyright and usage rights, as these protect both their own rights and the potential rights of a third party, whose products the media author includes in the eLearning concept. Such products may include text, graphics, audio, and video. A freelance media author seeking a smooth working relationship with a multimedia agency would be well-advised to familiarise themselves with the rights and obligations inherent in work and service contracts. The author should also carefully apply the General Data Protection Regulation (GDPR). As they are engaged on a project basis, their work for a limited period of time is akin to that of an employee. Consequently, there is a legal protection option for this unique professional situation—the artists' social insurance. Furthermore, the media author can join associations to establish a social safety net.

8.2.1 Copyright

The copyright is enshrined in § 11 of the Copyright Act (UrhG): "The copyright protects the author in their intellectual and personal relationships to the work and in the use of the work. It also serves to secure an appropriate remuneration for the use of the work." This means that a work of art or language may not be printed, performed, exhibited, altered, or otherwise used by anyone without the author's permission. Publicists and artists earn a living by granting permissions for the works they have created and demanding a fee for it. Copyright is so significant because "intellectual creations" can be reproduced much faster than, for example, a type of automobile, which is usually also protected by patent law.

Tip!
You can learn more about copyright at the Institute for Copyright and Media Law: http://www.urheberrecht.org.

Example from eLearning practice
The use of photos from a website on the Internet for your own eLearning application can only occur once the rights have been obtained from the operator of the website. If this is not possible, the media author can download the photos, but may only provide them as a template for the graphic designer or photographer who develops a new image based on this.

In Germany, copyright is automatically granted, meaning it does not need to be registered. Legally, the copyright notice ("©") is superfluous in Germany, as there is copyright in Germany. However, the symbol can draw attention to the copyright and is not per se prohibited. The proof of whether a copyright exists must always be provided by the user, not the author.

Tip!
The copyright on a protected work lasts until 70 years after the death of the author (§ 64).

8.2.1.1 Works Protected by Copyright

- Language works (for example, literature, screenplays, utility texts, specialist articles on research results of science),
- Parts of a work (for example, design material, concepts, unfinished works),

- Adaptations of texts (for example, translations),
- Collections of texts (for example, individual compilation of legal texts on the website of a private author),
- Standard works (for example, DIN standards),
- Computer programs, databases, multimedia applications,
- Photographic and film works (for example, photos, films, screenshots),
- Graphics, clipart, logos, virtual characters, screen design (if individually designed),
- Technical plans and drawings, diagrams, tables,
- Maps,
- Musical works (for example, melodies, sound files, MP3 music files),
- Works of visual art (for example, painting, architecture),
- Works of dance art,
- Websites, as well as
- Works on electronic data carriers, such as CD-ROM, DVD and similar.

8.2.1.2 Works Not Protected By Copyright

- General knowledge,
- Ideas for a work,
- Techniques of representation of a work,
- Enumerations of contents,
- Sounds, noises, single tones and single chords,
- Laws, regulations, as well as
- Scientific formulas.

8.2.1.3 Persons/Professional Groups Protected By Copyright

- Authors, for example, screenwriters, composers, directors, journalists, photographers, designers and software developers, as well as
- performing artists, for example, actors or musicians (that is, the distribution of an unauthorized recording of a performance is prohibited).

8.2.1.4 Copyright for Screen Texts of an eLearning Application

Media authors create their concepts and texts either as employees or as self-employed on behalf of a multimedia agency. Usually, the usage rights are transferred to the agency within the framework of the employment, tariff or service contract. This means that the media author remains the author, but no further fee is due for the further marketing of the content they have created (see Sect. 8.2.3).

8.2.2 Right of Use

The creator of a product can grant a third party the right to reproduce, distribute, and publish it, rather than using it themselves. This is known as the right of use or exploitation.

Example of the Right of Use
For the book "eLearning and Mobile Learning—Concept and Script", the author holds the copyright. However, she has transferred the right of use to the publisher through a contract. This entitles the publisher to reproduce and distribute it as stipulated in the mutually agreed publishing contract. Therefore, when drafting the contract, it is crucial to specify exactly which rights of use are transferred from the author to the contract partner, such as the rights to publish the work as a book, in newsletters, on the internet, as a CD-ROM, etc. This also includes agreeing on whether the contract partner may transfer their rights of use to the author's work to third parties. The author then receives a share of the profits from any licenses that arise from this.

Book Tip!
The "Practical Handbook of Multimedia Law" by *Thomas Wüfling & Ulrich Dieckert* covers topics such as copyright, corporate, tax, and labor law.

8.2.3 Exploitation Right

The Exploitation Right is the author's right to reproduce, distribute, and exhibit their products. Collecting societies are private institutions that exercise copyright rights that the individual author could not exercise for practical or legal reasons. The most important collecting societies are:

- *GEMA:* Society for musical performing and mechanical reproduction rights; it represents the copyright of composers, lyricists, and music publishers (http://www.gema.de).
- GVL: Society for the exploitation of performance rights GmbH; it represents the copyright of performing artists and record producers, such as musicians, singers, dancers, actors, as well as record and CD companies and other record producers with their own label (http://www.gvl.de).
- VG WORT: Word Exploitation Society; it represents the copyright of authors and translators of literary, dramatic, and scientific literature as well as of specialist and non-fiction literature; it also represents journalists (http://www.vgwort.de).
- VG Bild-Kunst: Picture Art Exploitation Society; it represents the copyright in the visual field, for example for visual artists, photographers, photojournalists, designers, or film authors (http://www.bildkunst.de).

Users must pay fees to these Collecting Societies. For example, if a piece of music that was not specifically composed for it is to appear in a learning program, you must inquire with GEMA about the cost of the usage rights. The corresponding fee is then paid to GEMA. GEMA, like any other collecting society, regularly pays royalties to the authors registered with it. To be registered in a collecting society, an author must register their works there according to certain guidelines. The collecting society relevant for an author is VG WORT. They report all their publications to it, for example texts in the press (trade journals, reading circles, daily and weekly press, illustrated magazines and the like), in radio and television as well as in non-fiction and specialist books (also new editions).

Tip!
You can directly register self-created texts of any kind with VG WORT online at: http://www.vgwort.de.

VG WORT itself identifies newspaper articles in press reviews, fiction and children's books (borrowing in libraries) as well as the proportion of a text genre in the total volume of photocopies in schools, libraries, etc. It does not grant distributions for PR publications and exclusive publications on CD-ROM or on the Internet. The latter affects the media author, who—unlike, for example, a textbook author—still has no opportunity to declare their "intellectual creations" as an author. The reason is that eLearning is usually produced by companies or public educational institutions for internal use. However, the registration of copyrights via VG Wort refers to publications that are made accessible to the general public. In case of doubt, you can simply ask VG Wort. It is especially important to meet the respective registration deadlines.

8.2.4 GDPR—The General Data Protection Regulation

Since 2018, a common regulation for the protection of personal data has been in place in the European Union. This regulation, known as the General Data Protection Regulation (GDPR), applies in all EU member states and has two objectives. Firstly, it protects personal data generated during processing by private and public entities within the EU. Secondly, it aims to enable free data traffic within the European internal market. The law outlines certain principles and legalities for the protection of personal data during their processing. Freelancers must also adhere to these legal requirements and obtain appropriate written permission for data processing from their customers, network partners, and clients. Below are some notes on the use of the GDPR:

- Detailed information on the GDPR can be found on the website of the Federal Ministry of the Interior for Building and Home Affairs: https://www.bmi.bund.de (search term "GDPR").

- The operators of the following website aim to explain the individual legal points of the GDPR in a simple way: https://eu-datenschutz-grundverordnung.net/eu-dsgvo.
- The website of the Bavarian State Office for Data Protection provides many practical aids and information, for example, a self-assessment in the form of an online test on the way to implementing the GDPR. Also of great use is the formulation aid for a data processing contract under: https://www.lda.bayern.de/media/muster_adv.pdf.

8.2.5 Contract for Work

The contract for work (§§ 631 ff. BGB) is a mutual contractual obligation. A media author who enters into a contract for work with a multimedia agency, for example, is obliged to deliver a complete, error-free script. Conversely, the agency is required to pay the contractually agreed fee once the work (delivered on time) has been received. The media author bears sole responsibility for how they create the work. The multimedia agency, on the other hand, has sole discretion over how it uses the work: produce, archive, discard, or similar.

The delivery of the work is completed when the client (in this case, the multimedia agency) "accepts" the work (in this case, a script). Acceptance can only be refused if the work significantly deviates from the contractual agreements. The more precisely the contents are defined in the contract for work, the less likely there will be discrepancies at the time of acceptance. Since only the ownership is transferred in the contract for work, it is usually combined with a copyright contract.

8.2.5.1 Example Contents of a Contract for Work

- Type, scope, and characteristics of the work, for example, a script for an interactive eLearning application with 100 pages, of which 50 are information pages, 15 are intro and summary pages, and 35 are task pages, with descriptions of the respective visualisations; in addition, fully formulated screen and voice-over texts for each screen page,
- Delivery date,
- Type of delivery (as print by mail, as a file by email, on an electronic data carrier, or similar),
- Fee, value-added tax, travel expenses,
- Payment dates, and
- Acceptance dates.

Multimedia agencies usually enter into "framework contracts" with their media authors, which regulate the basic cooperation; these are then supplemented in individual cases by special, order-related "project contracts".

8.2.6 Service Contract

The service contract (§§ 611 ff. BGB) is a mutual contractual obligation. If a multimedia agency enters into a service contract with a media author, the content is a service to be provided. Unlike a contract for work, the subject of the contract is the mere activity or the pure work performance. For instance, a media author is tasked with writing an eLearning script. He is not obligated to deliver a finished, error-free result as in a contract for work, but only the pure writing performance. The agency, under the service contract, commits to providing the contractually agreed remuneration. The remuneration is due even if the work is not completed. For example, the media author is supposed to finish a script at a certain point in time with the authoring tool provided by the agency. However, if this is not possible because the software is faulty and the deadline cannot be met, the project is frozen. The agency must still pay the media author the remuneration agreed in the service contract, for example, according to the hours spent up to that point.

8.2.6.1 Example Contents of a Service Contract

- The service of the contractor, for example, the media author is tasked with writing a script,
- The scope of the service to be provided, for example, the media author must be available for six hours a day for script writing for a period of four weeks,
- Working hours, for example, weekdays from 10 to 16 o'clock,
- Duration of the contract, for example, the contract begins on 1.5. and ends on 15.6., and
- Notice periods for both contract partners.

Reading Tip!
Further information about the rights of a freelance employee, as well as contract examples, can be found in "Der Freie-Mitarbeiter-Vertrag" by *Christian Ostermaier* or in the "iBusiness-AGB-Leitfaden: allgemeine Geschäftsbedingungen für Agenturen, Dienstleister und Freiberufler" by *Arne Trautmann,* both published by Hightext Verlag.

8.2.7 Artists' Social Security Fund

A freelance media author should check whether they have compulsory insurance in the Artists' Social Security Fund (KSK). Self-employed artists and publicists are largely in an economic and social situation comparable to that of employees. Therefore, they are included as compulsory insured persons in the protection of statutory health and pension insurance and since 1995 also in social long-term care insurance under the Artists' Social Security Act. The KSK registers the insured artists and publicists with the health and long-term care insurance funds and the pension insurance institution and forwards the contributions to them. Benefits from the insurance relationship (pension, sick pay, care allowance etc.) are provided exclusively by the pension insurance institutions and the statutory health and long-term care insurance funds. Those insured in the KSK pay—just like an employee—only half of the social security contributions. The "employer's contribution" is made by the exploiters (for example, multimedia agencies, publishers, broadcasting corporations, film producers, record companies etc.) as a so-called "artists' social contribution", supported by a federal subsidy. From a certain contribution assessment limit, the compulsory insurance in the KSK ceases to apply and there is the possibility to switch to private health insurance as an artist or publicist. However, the following should be considered:

- The older you are when you enter private health insurance, the higher the contributions.
- Women pay significantly higher contributions in private health insurance than men.
- Each family member has to be insured separately.
- There is no guarantee for stable contribution rates.
- The contributions remain unchanged, even if the income decreases, for example due to a lack of orders, a sabbatical year or in retirement.

Tip!
Detailed information about the Artists' Social Security Fund can be found at: http://www.kuenstlersozialkasse.de.

8.2.8 Associations

Associations bolster the individual, particularly when dealing with legal issues. They also offer a platform for the constructive exchange of current market developments and occurrences in the professional lives of colleagues. Freelancers, often isolated in a "closed" office, have the opportunity to connect with like-minded individuals through associations. Frequently, contracts are tendered as part of the association's activities, providing a media author with opportunities to gain new clients. Here is a selection of the most important associations that a media author should be aware of, some of which might be considered for membership:

- BITKOM: The Federal Association for Information Technology, Telecommunications and New Media e.V., primarily represents medium-sized companies and global players in the industry. The association has various working groups, for example, "Learning Solutions". The media author should at least be familiar with the association: http://www.bitkom.org.
- BVDW: The Federal Association of Digital Economy e.V., serves as the interest and professional representation of the digital economy. It acts as a link between the industry and political bodies, such as the Bundestag, ministries, the Federal Chancellery, state parliaments and authorities. The association is politically active and serves as an exchange platform for its members, which include companies, universities and research institutions. For its over 600 members, it develops training and further education models, calculation bases, sample contracts and recommendations for action for new fields of activity: http://www.bvdw.org.
- VDD: The Association of German Screenwriters e.V. represents the interests of screenwriters for film and television. It offers legal advice, know-how, public relations, political representation, further education and a fee mirror. The VDD has about 550 members and could expand its membership spectrum to include media authors on their initiative: http://www.drehbuchautoren.de.
- webgrrls.de e.V.: This is a network for female professionals and executives who work in digital media. It facilitates the active exchange of information, knowledge and opinions via its own communication platform and social media, as well as regional meetings. It also serves job and contract placement and the formation of strategic alliances: http://www.webgrrls.de.
- ver.di: The United Services Union also represents self-employed individuals (as long as they do not employ any employees themselves), such as translators, midwives, web designers, journalists and media authors. The union represents the interests of its members, for example, by concluding collective agreements for freelancers and providing legal aid when a fee claim is not paid by the client. More information can be found at http://www.verdi.de.

8.3 Acquiring New Clients as a Freelance Media Author

eLearning projects usually span a considerable period of time. They typically last no less than a month, and sometimes a media author is involved in a single project for over half a year. This means that they can rarely handle orders in parallel and thus, in principle, only serve one customer at a time. Therefore, they must constantly engage in the acquisition of new orders. Essentially, it applies: Even for the media author, making noise is part of the business! Here are a few tips on how a media author can acquire new clients:

8.3.1 Classic Methods of Acquiring New Customers

- *Owning your own website* significantly aids in cold acquisition, as the media author can refer to it during the initial phone contact. References on the website should be arranged in a manner that allows potential clients to quickly and clearly form an impression. The website should be clear and logically structured. It serves as the best business card, as the customer can infer from it that the media author can also write correspondingly clear and logical concepts and scripts for eLearning.
- *Newsletters* are beneficial for existing customers. The content could relate to the latest developments in information architectures, discuss the world of learning games, or deal with the creation of content. A newsletter not only fosters customer loyalty but also encourages the media author to stay updated on his profession and industry.
- *Visiting trade fairs* and informing yourself about current trends there (see Sect. 9.1.4). It is not advisable to offer your services as a media author directly at the trade fair to multimedia agencies, as they are busy acquiring new customers and have invested a significant amount of money in the stand for this purpose. However, you can use a visit there to have a non-binding conversation with the exhibitors and have the latest developments shown to you. In the end, you can still hand over your business card. This approach is discreet and will be remembered positively.
- *Using job markets* on the internet and registering on *specialist portals* (see Sect. 9.1.1 and 9.5).

Tip!
Section 9.1.3 lists the trade press in which relevant multimedia agencies can be found, as well as specialist portals where a media author should also register.

- *Cold acquisition over the phone:* The media author selects a multimedia agency for which he could work. He should proceed in such a way that he first chooses the agencies located in his area, then those from the region, and finally expands his search to the national territory or even neighbouring countries. He should ask for a project manager and prepare his conversation well. It is best to prepare a list in advance with projects he has worked on so far, with focuses he places in his work and also with the points that particularly interest him about the agency he is calling. The goal of the phone call should be an appointment where he can introduce himself personally and present his previous work.

Literature tip!
If you want to acquire effectively, you should be able to negotiate well. The standard work on this is by *Roger Fisher et al.:* "Getting to Yes", Campus.

8.3.2 Social Media as a Platform for Acquiring New Customers

The triumph of social media applications makes the acquisition of new customers for freelancers easier and more direct. Many commercial providers, who have a web presence on the internet, also use platforms like *Facebook, X, YouTube, Instagram* or *XING* to engage with customers and business partners, present themselves, and communicate directly. Here, one differentiates between platforms like XING, Instagram or Facebook, which allow exchanging messages with selected business partners, friends and other participants, from X and YouTube, where the flow of communication is worldwide and almost unlimited.

Tip!
Visit the website of the business consultant and eLearning professional, *Jochen Robes*. It is an excellent example of how social media can be used for the presentation of a freelancer on the World Wide Web: http://www.weiterbildungsblog.de.

8.3.2.1 Keeping Up with the Times with Facebook

Facebook is still the standard for maintaining an online presence and conducting business over the internet. Students at Harvard University developed Facebook in 2004 to enable their university students to exchange information quickly and easily. Today, the free portal already boasts over two billion users worldwide. As a media author, you can set up your own profile page on Facebook and present your offerings, for example, with articles, text samples, photos, videos or similar. The unique feature of this application, however, lies in the contacts: You list all the contacts that seem important to you on your page. These can then be clicked on by a visitor to your profile; this leads them to their Facebook profile, which in turn lists many contacts. In this way, you will be quickly and easily found by companies looking for a media author.

Tip!
Facebook is ideal for staying connected with your business partners and keeping your offer present on the World Wide Web. However, learning to use it securely is important for a successful internet presence (http://de-de.facebook.com).

8.3.2.2 Connecting with XING

XING, unlike Facebook, is primarily a business platform. XING allows setting up a profile page for free, if you accept advertising. For a small fee, this is omitted and you have further possibilities to connect with other users. The profile displays the address, the company, hobbies, associations, interests and similar. Almost all users of XING regularly update their data. So if you have chosen your business partners as contacts, XING will immediately inform you if an address has changed or a contact has changed their workplace. A separate address book could thus become superfluous. The special advantage of a profile on XING is that you can make many contacts in your work and interest area and these in turn are always kept up to date about your activities. However, it does not offer as many possibilities as Facebook to post photos, videos or comments online in large quantities immediately.

Tip!
With *XING* you can exchange information about work fields, areas of interest and projects, build profitable contacts, manage addresses and coordinate appointments (http://www.xing.com).

8.3.2.3 Staying in Conversation with X

X could be described as the fastest of the platforms in the social web. X was launched in 2006 and now has over 300 million active users worldwide. How does X work in principle? Essentially, it's as if you were wandering from table to table in a crowded café, listening to the conversations for half a minute each, making a brief comment if the topic interests you, or remaining silent and moving on if not. X can be used in two ways: for reading and informing oneself and for communicating and writing.

8.3.2.4 Reading and Informing Yourself

As soon as you visit X, you can constantly read messages (so-called "posts") from users worldwide without interruption. By the way: X has a kind of jargon: As a reader of posts, you are called a "follower". If you enter a topic on X that currently interests you, for example "eLearning App", numerous conversation notes from various users appear. The special thing about X is that the search results are not output according to relevance, as for example by the search engine Google, but purely chronologically according to the time of writing.

8.3.2.5 Writing and Communicating

On X, everyone can freely talk about what is currently moving them—private, political, professional or leisure-related—as long as they do not exceed the number of 280 characters per line of text. Posts can be read by anyone who visits X, worldwide and at any time. The advantage of X: You can quickly and currently configure X to your individual information and contact center.

References

Fisher, Roger et al. (2013): Das Harvard-Konzept, Frankfurt am Main: Campus, 24. edn.

Ostermaier, Christian (2018): der Freie-Mitarbeiter-Vertrag, Regensburg: Walhalla u. Praetoria Verlag.

Trautmann, Arne (2011): iBusiness-AGB-Leitfaden: allgemeine Geschäftsbedingungen für Agenturen, Dienstleister und Freiberufler, München: Hightext Verlag.

Wüfling, Thomas & Ulrich Dieckert (2002) Praxishandbuch Multimediarecht, Heidelberg: Springer-Verlag.

Further Information 9

9.1 Selection of the Producer

Various options are available online and in print for finding and selecting suitable eLearning producers:

9.1.1 Specialist Portals on the Internet

http://www.bildungsserver.de
In the content area "Erwachsenenbildung", the path leads further to "Erwachsenenbildung digital". From there, it goes to the topic "E-Learning" with a sub-point: "Produzenten von E-Learning".

http://www.checkpoint-elearning.de
This is a central specialist portal with constantly up-to-date information on economic and political developments on the topic of eLearning.

http://www.e-learningcentre.co.uk
This English-language portal offers a wealth of information on the topic of eLearning. This includes numerous links and book tips, current articles on the socio-political development of eLearning, and best practice examples.

http://www.seminarmarkt.de
This is a research option for eLearning providers within the framework of general seminar offers.

D. Modlinger, *eLearning and Mobile Learning – Concept and Script*,
https://doi.org/10.1007/978-3-658-44695-6_9

http://www.weiterbildungsblog.de
This is a personal weblog by Jochen Robes, which offers comprehensive information on the topics of eLearning, knowledge management, and corporate learning.

9.1.2 eLearning Courses to Buy and Book

http://www.iwwb.de
The "InfoWeb Continuing Education" of the Leibniz Institute for Research and Information in Education presents this extensive search engine of the German Education Server for continuing education courses.

https://www.ihk-akademie-digital.de
The IHK Akademie Digital der Industrie- und Handelskammern offers numerous online trainings for vocational training and further education on its own learning platform.

http://www.lerneniminternet.de
The portal offers a learning platform with numerous eLearning courses on information technology. All courses have free trial access; in some cases, financial support is possible through the Jobcenter.

http://www.tschlotfeldt.de/elearning-wiki/E-Learning-Anbieter
This is a private wiki of eLearning consultant Tim Schlotfeldt. It contains, among other things, an alphabetical list of well over 100 providers for eLearning applications.

9.1.3 Trade Press

eLearning Journal (http://www.elearning-journal.com)
This is a trade journal with current news specifically on the topics of eLearning, Mobile Learning, digital media and the working world as well as benchmarking. Various additional offers, such as tests of eLearning offers with quality seal and awarding of an annual award by the eLearning Journal, are also available.

managerSeminare (http://www.managerseminare.de)
Continuing Education Magazine for managers, trainers and personnel developers with detailed technical articles, current news and an extensive directory of seminar and continuing education providers.

Economy and Further Education(https://shop.haufe.de/prod/wirtschaft-weiterbildung)
This is a trade journal for training and leadership, personnel development and eLearning; with background reports and eLearningNews, which provide a good overview of eLearning providers; published 10 times a year.

9.1.4 Trade Fairs

DMEXCO—Digital Marketing Expo & Conference
The DMEXCO, hosted by Bundesverband Digitale Wirtschaft e. V. (BVDW), has been held annually in Cologne since 2009. It has been showcasing trends in the internet industry and digital economic sectors for over 20 years.

didacta—the Education Fair
The Education Fair, didacta, takes place annually in various cities, such as Stuttgart or Cologne. The fair targets teachers from all educational sectors in Europe. It includes areas such as vocational training, further education, and teaching and learning with digital media.

Hannover Messe
The Hannover Messe is held every spring in Hannover. It covers topics such as industry-related digital topics, the technology of learning, artificial intelligence, and robotics.

Learntec
Learntec is held annually in January/February in Karlsruhe and is considered a European trade fair and congress for digital education. Topics include learning trends around mobile learning and virtual reality. More than three hundred exhibitors from various countries regularly participate. The target audience includes users of educational technologies, multimedia and eLearning in the education sector, particularly in business, schools, and politics, as well as educational planners, providers, and developers.

Online Educa Berlin
The annual international conference for technology-supported training and further education, which takes place in Berlin, covers topics such as learning in companies, eLearning policy in practice, new roles of teachers and trainers, innovative learning approaches, and future learning technologies.

Worlddidac/Swissdidac
Worlddidac/Swissdidac is held annually in Bern, Switzerland. It is a trade fair for teaching materials and for training and further education. It serves as a meeting point for education officials in schools and training institutions, decision-makers in industry and service companies, and buyers and providers in the fields of training and further education.

Future of Personnel
The Future of Personnel is held annually in Cologne. It is exclusively aimed at HR decision-makers and executives in companies, administrations, and non-profit organizations. It offers a platform for providers from the HR software and HR services industry. At the same time, it informs trade visitors about current trends in HR policy and work. The exhibition focuses on digital learning, the future of work, further education and training, as well as hardware and software for the education sector.

9.2 Selection of Tools

9.2.1 Adobe

Acrobat Reader
This is a program for displaying PDF files.

Captivate
This is a software for creating eLearning applications based on PowerPoint slides.

Creative Cloud
This is a software package for creating and editing interactive multimedia content.

Illustrator
This is a program for creating illustrations and vector graphics.

Photoshop
This is a program for image editing.

Photoshop Elements
This is a program for image editing.

Premiere Pro
This is a program for video editing.

All available at: http://www.adobe.com/de.

9.2.2 Microsoft

Word: This is a text processing program.
PowerPoint: This is a presentation program.
Excel: This is a spreadsheet program.

Project: This is a program for project management.

All available at: http://www.microsoft.com/de-de.

9.2.3 Other Providers

balesio TurboDemo

This is a program for creating simple eLearning courses. http://www.balesio.com.

Camtasia
This is a program for creating Rapid eLearning. https://www.techsmith.de/camtasia.html.

draw.io
This is a program for creating flowcharts. https://www.draw.io.

Edraw Max
This is a program for creating flowcharts. https://www.edrawsoft.com

Final Cut Pro
This is a program for video editing with Mac. https://www.apple.com/de/final-cut-pro.

iMovie
This is a free program for video editing with Mac. https://www.apple.com/de/imovie.

Inspiration
This is a program for brainstorming and creating simple, intuitive flowcharts. http://www.inspiration.com.

Lightworks
This is a free program for video editing: https://www.lwks.com.

Magix Video deluxe
This is a program for video editing: https://www.magix.com.

Paint.net
This is an image editing program. https://www.getpaint.net.

PaintShop Pro X4 Ultimate
This is an image editing program. http://www.paintshoppro.com/de.

MindManager
This is a program for brainstorming and planning. http://www.mindjet.com/de.

Shotcut
This is a free, cross-platform video editor. https://shotcut.org.

Toolbook
This is an authoring tool for creating eLearning programs. http://tb.sumtotalsystems.com.

WBTplus
This is an update program for existing eLearning applications from M.I.T. e-Solutions GmbH. http://www.mit.de.

9.3 Partners and Reference Companies

Versicherungskammer Bayern
Versicherungsanstalt des öffentlichen Rechts
Maximilianstraße 53
80530 Munich
http://www.vkb.de

Beck et al. Services GmbH
Zielstattstr. 42
81379 Munich
https://www.becketal.com

Bildersprache
Kommunikation und Design
Isabellastr. 33
80796 Munich
http://www.bildersprache.de

Bundesministerium für Wirtschaft und Energie BMWi
Referat Soziale Medien, Öffentlichkeitsarbeit
Scharnhorststr. 34–37
10115 Berlin
http://www.bmwi.de

Gemeinnütziges Bildungswerk des Deutschen Gewerkschaftsbundes e.V.
Hans-Böckler-Str. 39
40476 Düsseldorf
https://www.dgb-bildungswerk.de

Forschungsinstitut Betriebliche Bildung (f-bb) gGmbH
Rollnerstraße 14
90408 Nuremberg
http://www.f-bb.de

Microsoft Germany GmbH
Walter-Gropius-Straße 5
80807 Munich
http://www.microsoft.com/de-de

M.I.T e-Solutions GmbH
Am Houiller Platz 4c
61381 Friedrichsdorf
http://www.mit.de

Teleteach GmbH
Jeschkenstr. 49
82538 Geretsried
http://www.teleteach.de

Editorial Office
Barbara Dexheimer
Theresienstr. 10
93128 Regenstauf

9.4 Education and Further Training for Media Authors and Project Managers

Daniela Modlinger, M.A.
Markusplatz 12
96047 Bamberg

This company provides in-house training for media authors, project managers, and technical authors who are interested in "Concept and scriptwriting for eLearning" or who wish to optimize existing projects. The workshops last one to two days, depending on the requirements. Additionally, individual coaching is offered for existing concepts and scripts for eLearning applications.

Fachhochschule Stuttgart
Hochschule der Medien
Nobelstr. 10
70569 Stuttgart
http://www.hdm-stuttgart.de
The University of Media offers numerous courses that focus on the development and management of digital media. These are available as bachelor's or master's degree programs, as well as further education courses.

ILT Solutions GmbH
Clevischer Ring 121 b
51063 Cologne
https://www.ilt-solutions.de
The company offers a six-week further education course for eLearning authors, which also includes learning content for specific eLearning project management. Upon successful completion, participants receive a Cert-EU certificate.

Technische Universität Kaiserslautern
Distance and Independent Studies Center (DISC)
Erwin-Schrödinger-Straße
Building 57
67663 Kaiserslautern

http://www.zfuw.uni-kl.de
The distance learning master's program "Erwachsenenbildung (Adult Education)" lasts four semesters and covers topics of adult education via online learning in didactic, methodological, pedagogical, and conceptual aspects. Admission requirements include a six-semester university degree and one year of relevant professional experience. Alternatively, applicants with many years of relevant professional experience but without a university degree can take an aptitude test to enroll in the course.

Universität Duisburg-Essen
Fachbereich Bildungs- und Sozialwissenschaften
Forsthausweg 2
47057 Duisburg

http://www.uni-due.de
The University of Duisburg-Essen offers the online master's program "Educational Media—Bildung & Medien" as a part-time course. Over four semesters, students learn about media didactics, media technology, educational organization, and project management. The admission requirement is a first professional qualifying university degree with a scope of at least 180 ECTS credits.

9.5 Internet Job Markets

Media authors can utilise internet job markets for customer acquisition:

http://www.bildungsserver.de/jobboerse
The Education Server's job market provides a platform for job searches and offers in the field of pedagogy and educational science. Searches can be conducted in the Economy/ Media industry and by federal state, among other criteria.

https://www.horizontjobs.de
Job Marketof the communication industry provides offers and searches from the areas of marketing, advertising, and media. Search options include activity, industry, type of employment, and federal state.

http://www.ibusiness.de
Under the category "Service/Job Market", there are more than 2500 offers and requests for and from professionals in the multimedia industry.

http://www.monster.de
This job portal is not limited to the IT and multimedia industry. It offers the possibility to publish your resume for free and to use a salary calculator. An email notification informs about the receipt of a job that matches the previously entered search criteria.

https://stellenmarkt.wuv.de
This is the job portal of the magazine "Advertising & Selling". Job seekers must have previously placed a job request in the print edition of Advertising and Selling. Job offers can be researched by fields of activity and postal codes.

http://www.stepstone.de
This career portal specializes in job offers for specialists and executives. The interested party can find more than 80,000 job offers. There is the possibility to publish your resume for free and to use a salary calculator.

http://www.sueddeutsche.de
Job offers can be researched by industry, professional field, position, and region, among other criteria.

Checklists 10

Abstract

Chapter 10 provides you with numerous checklists that were referred to in the book and that will be of practical help in the everyday life of an eLearning production.

10.1 Evaluation of Production Progress

See Table 10.1

10.2 Evaluation of Transfer Performance by the Learning Program

See Table 10.2

10.3 Client Fact Sheet

See Table 10.3

10.4 Questionnaire for the Client

See Table 10.4

D. Modlinger, *eLearning and Mobile Learning – Concept and Script*, https://doi.org/10.1007/978-3-658-44695-6_10

Table 10.1 Evaluation of Production Progress

Project Phase/Project Feature	Good	Less Good	Suggestion for Improvement
Significance of the project request			
Agency's offer in relation to later project progress			
Information about tasks and responsibilities of individual team members			
Preparation by the client			
Preparation by the agency (project manager)			
Preparation by the scriptwriter			
Procedure of author briefing			
Quality of advice by the agency (project manager)			
General: Procedure of project meetings			
General: Quality of moderation and leadership of project meetings by the project manager			
Quality of advice by the scriptwriter			
Quality of research for content, data and facts			
Budgeting during project progress			
Satisfaction with chosen learning system (technology)			
Satisfaction with navigation through the learning program			
Understandability of the rough concept			
Quality of learning objectives in the detailed concept			
Readability of the scripts			
Usability of the authoring tool by the scriptwriter			
Adherence to delivery dates by the client (content, matters to be clarified, etc.)			
Adherence to delivery dates by the agency (rough and detailed concept, script, corrections, protocols, prototype, etc.)			
Adherence to delivery dates by the scriptwriter (including rough and detailed concept, script, corrections, research, etc.)			
Clarity of statements in the protocols			
Consistency of the specification sheet			
Quality of script approval meetings			
Execution of corrections			
General communication			

(continued)

Table 10.1 (continued)

Project Phase/Project Feature	Good	Less Good	Suggestion for Improvement
Communication from the client regarding content and learning objectives			
Communication from the client regarding dates and costs			
Communication from the client regarding corrections			
Communication from the agency/project manager regarding dates and costs			
Communication from the agency/project manager regarding the feasibility of wishes, ideas, and suggestions			
Communication from the agency/project manager regarding corrections and their costs			
Communication from the scriptwriter regarding corrections (feasibility, meaningfulness)			

10.5 Preparation for the Briefing by the Client

See Table 10.5

10.6 Teamwork in Briefings

See Table 10.6

10.7 Types and Techniques of Questions

See Table 10.7

Further Recommendations

- Ask only one question at a time.
- Be concise.
- Ask important questions.
- Choose clear formulations.
- Avoid double negatives.
- Attentive and vigilant listening can eliminate the need for some questions.

Table 10.2 Evaluation of Transfer Performance by the Learning Program

Evaluation Criterion	Good	Less Good	Suggestion for Improvement
Quality of the program's introduction			
User-friendliness of the program			
Navigation guidance through the program			
Didactic organization of learning content into modules (chapters)			
Readability and learnability of the screen texts			
Clarity of the illustrations			
Relevance of the chosen visualizations to the content			
Memorability of the graphic design			
Layout's ease of perception on screen pages			
Clarity of the audio texts			
Pleasantness of additional soundtracks (sounds, music)			
Encouragement of motivation to continue learning			
Alignment of task difficulty level with previously conveyed learning content			
Clarity of the task types			
Evaluation level of the task assignments			
Feedback on the tasks			
Applicability of the conveyed learning content in daily professional practice			
Currency of the learning content			
Accuracy and reliability of the learning content			
Support for practical application (such as through real-world examples, opportunities to ask questions, etc.)			
Fulfillment of the requirement to bridge knowledge gaps			
Technical functionality			
Storage capability for learner data			
Suitability of the chosen learning medium for the content to be conveyed			
Evaluation of the learning level (difficulty level)			
Consideration of different learning styles			

- For alternative questions: clarify all alternatives or ask open questions.
- For sensitive questions: avoid trigger words.
- Vary question formulations to avoid creating an interrogation-like atmosphere.

Table 10.3 Client Fact Sheet

Data and facts about the client	Result
Company name, legal form, address, URL of the company website	
Members of the project team with names, positions, and contact details (ask the client's project manager)	
Check website: is it strict and information-heavy (conservative) or playful (youthful)?	
Social media habits (which channels are used? Customer approach: casual/conservative? What visual language is used in the videos/images?)	
Company philosophy (trendy company, conservative values, ecological or social responsibility, etc.)?	
Current developments of the company that are documented in the trade press	
Size of the company: number of employees, annual turnover, branches (possibly global)	
Which industry is the company active in?	
What collaborations has the company entered into?	

Table 10.4 Questionnaire for the Client

Questionnaire for the Client	Remark
Why do you want to create an eLearning application?	
Do you already have digital learning applications in your company? What experiences have you had with them?	
What do you expect from this eLearning application?	
How have you provided for training and further education so far?	
Where did you encounter the most trouble? What problem areas arose?	
What basic text is available?	
What image material is available?	
What statement/design is desired for the illustrations (colors, objects, situations)?	
What type of illustration do you prefer (drawing, illustration, photo, video)?	
Is there already a specification sheet?	
Can the specification sheet be viewed?	
How do you feel about a leading figure?	
What tonality is desired? Should the target group be addressed casually or rather formally?	

10.8 Technical Facilities and Specifications

See Table 10.8

Table 10.5 Preparation for the Briefing by the Client

Briefing Element	To be clarified: Date? With whom?	Done? Who?	Remark
1. Initial Situation and Problem Statement			
How would you briefly describe the company you work for in relation to the project?			
What was the initial situation or problem that led to the decision to develop an interactive learning application?			
Is the problem truly based on educational deficits? (Problems in technology or management cannot be solved with an interactive learning application.)			
What future company developments are on the horizon? How will they influence the eLearning production (for example, collaborations, new infrastructure, international orientation)?			
What internal and external communication strategies does your company employ?			
What life cycles are planned for the eLearning to be produced (for example, are updates required)?			
Is the eLearning production integrated into an existing educational concept? If yes: How should the new educational measure "eLearning" be integrated into it?			
What synergies with other projects in the company can be identified?			
What design guidelines does the company provide (for example, specifications, corporate identity)?			
Why was this particular agency chosen (core competence, special orientation)?			
What questions do you have for the agency and the media author that you would like to clarify in the briefing (for example, regarding technology, learning concept, navigation, screen design)?			
2. Requirement Profile andTarget Objective			
Possible areas where a specific educational need exists: for certain tasks, positive financial balance, occupational safety, smooth work processes, as part of or data supplier for a company training measure.			

(continued)

Table 10.5 (continued)

Briefing Element	To be clarified: Date? With whom?	Done? Who?	Remark
What type of educational need is present: normative, subjective, demonstrated, future or event-oriented (see Table 3.1)?			
What is the overarching learning objective (formulated sentence) that guides the interactive learning application? (This results from the compilation of the requirement profile.)			
3. Describe Target Group			
What are the characteristics of the target group (for example, education, age, position)?			
What specific requests regarding content, design etc. have been brought to your attention by the employees?			
4. Analyze and Bundle Technical Content			
What skills and knowledge do we aim to build and how?			
What content do we aim to convey and how?			
What materials are available for this (basic material)?			
Is the basic material complete and up-to-date (numbers, laws, content, etc.)?			
Can we send parts of the basic material to the multimedia agency/media author in advance?			
Can the basic text be prioritized according to broad learning objectives?			
Do you expect the service provider to conduct research on the topic? If yes, what kind?			
5. Compile resources/Organizational matters			
Team Which colleagues will be involved in the project (names, contact details, positions, and responsibilities)?			
Deadline specifications What deadlines does the eLearning training measure have (fixed start or end date, times of tight personnel resources)? What milestones are planned for the production? What times are scheduled in the company for checking the scripts and prototypes (for example, 1 day a week or 1 hour daily)? Consider vacation planning and downtime!			

(continued)

Table 10.5 (continued)

Briefing Element	To be clarified: Date? With whom?	Done? Who?	Remark
Information exchange How do we want to check the concepts and scripts for approval (digitally or as a printout)? What formats are available for data exchange (for example, DOC, PDF, XLS, PPT, etc.)? Are there any restrictions on sending emails?			
Place of use Where does the target group learn (for example, at the workplace, at home, or on the go)? What technology is available at the learning places (for example, internet access or multimedia equipment)?			
Budget What budget do we have available? Can it be distributed to small work packages?			

Table 10.6 Teamwork in briefings

Briefing Element	Good	Less Good	Suggestion for Improvement
Work atmosphere (openness, equal speaking time, willingness to discuss, etc.)			
Clarification of roles and responsibilities of team members			
Communication within the team (open communication flow, managing tensions, avoiding insistence on being right, promoting loyalty)			
Willingness to engage in discussion in case of differing opinions			
Willingness to collaborate on problem-solving			
Willingness of team members to immediately start with the tasks defined in the briefing			
Overall quality of the briefing			

10.9 Selecting eLearning

See Table 10.9

Table 10.7 Types and techniques of questions. (Source: Patzak and Rattay 2017, p. 355 f.)

Types of Questions	Description and Examples	Application Situations and Advantages
Open Questions	Introduced by "Who? Where? What?" Examples: "What do you think of…? How do you see…? What must this solution offer? What does it not need to offer? Who can help with this?"	Useful for starting a conversation, leaving many possibilities open to the sender, gathering information, creating a good conversation atmosphere, and learning more about what is important to the customer - not just what you think is important to them.
Choice Questions	At least two options are presented. The result is almost always a decision.	Useful for further specification, identifying and finding solutions, and narrowing down the variants.
Closed Questions	Introduced by verbs or auxiliary verbs. Answer options: Yes or No, numbers and facts. Examples: "How many computers do you need? Who will be the project leader? When do you start? Do you already have a network?"	Useful for simple questions, summarizing and securing the understood, sealing of agreements made. Attention: Many closed questions can give the impression of an interrogation.

10.10 Script Approval

See Table 10.10

10.11 Change Request Form

See Table 10.11

10.12 Standards for eLearning

See Table 10.12

Table 10.8 Technical Facilities and Specifications

Requirement	Comment/To-do
How is the eLearning application viewed (for example, on a computer or laptop screen, projector presentation, or smartphone)?	
What operating system is installed on the end device (for example, Microsoft Windows, Linux, Android, iOS, or Mac OS)?	
What software is installed on the end device (for example, Microsoft Word or company-specific software that should be integrated into the eLearning application)?	
What plug-ins are available (for example, Acrobat Reader, streaming video and audio formats, or applets)?	
Which plug-ins need to be added for the eLearning application?	
Is access to the internet secured at a sufficient speed?	
Which internet browsers are installed and what versions are they (for example, Internet Explorer, Mozilla Firefox, Opera, Chrome, or other browsers)?	
What is the processor performance?	
What is the clock frequency?	
How large is the cache?	
How large is the RAM?	
How much free hard disk space is available?	
What is the storage capacity of the graphics card?	
Are sound cards and speakers available on all learning computers?	
What is the working capacity of the sound card?	
What data transmission media are available (for example, ISDN, xDSL, 5G)?	
What screen resolution do the monitors have (for example, 1280 × 800 for laptops, 1024 × 768, 1920 × 1080 or 1280 × 1024)?	
What distribution options are available to the customer for the learning program (for example, online learning platform, CD delivery, FTP server, online app)?	

Table 10.9 Selecting eLearning. (Source: edited after Brönner 2003, p. 143)

Selection question	Yes	No	Comment
Do the participants have enough time to use the eLearning application?			
Does the eLearning variant provide content that meets the participants' expectations?			
Does the type of eLearning application meet the learning objectives and expectations of the participants?			
Can the elements of eLearning promote the desired behaviour? (There is a difference between merely conveying knowledge and applying it.)			
Is orientation knowledge necessary for processing the content, or should it be conveyed by the eLearning course?			
Is the course aimed at beginners or advanced learners?			
Do the elements of the chosen eLearning application match the level of experience with self-directed learning that the majority of participants have?			
Do the elements of the chosen eLearning application match the learning style (receptive or exploratory) of the participants?			
Can the participants intuitively handle the individual elements of the chosen eLearning application?			

Table 10.10 Script Approval

Review criteria	Comment	Yes: fulfilled	No: What is missing?
1. Formalities The document contains the following information: Title of the learning program, Module title, Numbering for integration in the overall text and as a basis for later version indication, Author, Date, Table of contents, Page numbers, and realistic time estimates for the duration of processing individual chapters			
2. General The script provides an intuitive preview of the presentation in the later eLearning application. The screen pages are clearly designed. The ratio between visualization and text is balanced. The screen layout is consistent, according to the respective learning page type, such as task, information, or example (recognition effect). The transitions between the learning pages are coherent (for example, the introductory or announcing audio text matches the next learning content). The principle "1 screen page = 1 thought" is followed.			
3. Learning Content All learning content specified in the briefing is depicted, as controlled based on the briefing protocol. The learning content is oriented towards the learning objectives, meaning it can be queried according to these objectives. The learning content, tonality, and structure are appropriate for the target group. The respective learning objectives are mentioned at the beginning of an eLearning application and at the start of each module. At the end of an eLearning application or a module, a summary of the learned content is provided. The learning content forms a meaningful unit. Numbers, facts, and statistics are up-to-date. The learning content is technically correct. The learning content is structured in an action-oriented manner. The learning content encourages the user to question and deeply understand what has been learned. The learning content addresses task assignments and problems from the users' practice.			

(continued)

Table 10.10 (continued)

Review criteria	Comment	Yes: fulfilled	No: What is missing?
4. Language and Text Abbreviations are meaningful, simple, and explained. Technical terms are meaningful, expressive, and explained. Key terms are highlighted. The spelling is correct, including orthography, grammar, style, and punctuation. Rules for screen texts are followed: short, simple, and logical sentences, minimal use of adjectives, three to a maximum of seven text blocks per screen page, and three to a maximum of seven sentences per text block.			
5. Audio Numbers are always represented as digits. Instructions for specific pronunciation appear in brackets before the entire take. Emphasized places are underlined or bold. Correct spelling includes orthography, grammar, style, and punctuation. Audio texts must be checked separately for the entire eLearning application to avoid duplicate texts and ensure logical speaker guidance. Instructions for emotional colorings or pitches are clear. The audio texts are divided into the smallest possible sequences for better updatability at a later date. The audio texts are consistent: Important terms are always pronounced the same and are identical to the screen text. The audio texts follow a chosen designation; synonyms occur sparingly. The contents of the audio texts appear as a summary on the screen. Audio texts with information important for the further learning process are accompanied by screen texts to account for the transience of the heard. The audio texts are easy to speak when read aloud and sound catchy to the ear. In the audio sentences, the verb is at the front of the sentence, and sentence brackets do not appear. Each audio sentence only transports one new piece of information. The audio texts are written in an action-oriented manner; therefore, they contain many verbs and few nominal constructions. The audio texts use adjectives sparingly. The characters of different speaker types in an eLearning application are consistent and memorable. Dialogues are designed in an action-oriented manner and establish a relationship between the speaker types. For related learning pages: The transitions of the audios match the contents of the following page.			

(continued)

Table 10.10 (continued)

Review criteria	Comment	Yes: fulfilled	No: What is missing?
6. Visualization Visualizations fit into the respective context and support the conveyance of the learning content. Graphics, tables, statistics, etc. are self-explanatory or provided with appropriate explanations. Graphics are clear and easy to understand. The visualization does not distract from the content. The user is guided to engage with the visualization. The selection of images, graphics, photos, videos, or similar is varied, but follows a common style. The description of visualizations allows the reader to accurately imagine the same. The visualization is implemented in a way that is appropriate for the target group. The visualization meets the minimum requirements of the target group's technical equipment. Visualizations that do not come from one's own company name a verifiable source.			
7. Examples The examples are relevant to the target group and action-oriented. The examples are practice-oriented and memorable. The examples arouse the participants' curiosity and thus motivate them to engage with the learning program.			
8.Feedback The feedback is suitable for the target group. The feedback is evaluative. The feedback is motivating.			
9. Tasks The tasks correspond to the taxonomy in terms of their level of difficulty. The types of tasks are diverse. The types of tasks align with the learning content to be assessed.			

Table 10.11 Change Request Form

Request for Change		Statements	
Applicant		Agency Project Manager	
Project		Client	
Page/Index/Chapter		Technical Advisor	
Content of the Change		Screenwriter	
Reason for the Change		Software Developer	
Impact on Other Pages/ Chapters		Graphic Designer	
Date		Others (who?)	
Cost			
Change will be executed by			
Priority: high/medium/low			
Request approved: yes/no		Reason	
Date		Signature	

Table 10.12 Standards for eLearning

Designation	Meaning
ADL (Advanced Distributed Learning)	An organization of the American Department of Defense that develops standardization models for eLearning (see SCORM).
API (Application Programming Interface)	A communication interface between LMS (see "LMS") and WBT that allows for data exchange and provides information about the status of the learning content (for example, "is finished").
5G (Fifth Generation)	The international standard for mobile telephony and mobile internet, 5G, builds on the mobile communication standard "Long Term Evolution" (LTE or also "4G"). LTE, in turn, is the successor to the basic scheme "Universal Mobile Telecommunications System" (UMTS or also "3G"). The 5G standard is intended to enable data rates of up to 20 GBit/s and use higher frequency ranges. For digital learning courses in company training and further education, the compatibility of machines and devices with 5G is particularly interesting.
GPRS (General Packet Radio Service)	GPRS is a transmission technique that enables internet access via mobile phone or smartphone. In this case, the mobile network operator also serves as the internet provider, meaning that the internet connection is not based on a dial-up connection, but on a signal technique that enables a permanent internet line.
HTML (Hyper Text Markup Language)	HTML is an open standard for the presentation of multimedia content on the World Wide Web. HTML works with hyperlinks, which lead to a linked document when clicked with the mouse.
IEEE (Institute of Electrical and Electronic Engineers)	The IEEE is an American standardization institute that develops eLearning standards and, unlike other standardization bodies, is also authorized to submit a recommendation to the International Organization for Standardization (ISO).
IMS Global Learning Consortium, Inc.	The IMS Global Learning Consortium is an international consortium of more than 500 educational organizations, public authorities, and eLearning producers and users. The consortium's goal is to develop standards for eLearning to make learning content functional on as many Learning Management Systems (LMS) and on the internet as possible. A specification recommended by IMS, for example, is the "Package Description". This aims to standardize learning objects, for example, for the exchange of learning content between authoring programs and LMS. The Package Description also serves to describe course structures and to record learning success.
LIP (Learner Information Package)	The LIP is a standard that describes the properties and characteristics of the actors involved in the learning process. The standard includes, for example, demographic data, degrees, qualifications, or learning preferences.
LMS (Learning Management System)	An LMS is a learning platform that supports functions such as personalization, recording of user data, and electronic billing. LMS should have standardized interfaces to be able to upload as many different eLearning courses as possible.

(continued)

Table 10.12 (continued)

Designation	Meaning
LOM (Learning Object Metadata)	LOM is a recommendation of the IEEE for the standardization of the description of learning objects (for example, courses, WBTs). It includes information on technical, pedagogical, legal, and relationship-specific properties as well as information on the author, creation date, license, and update. The aim is to facilitate the selection of learning objects, for example, by indicating whether a learning object is suitable for a specific target group.
MPEG-x (Motion Pictures Expert Group)	The Motion Pictures Expert Group was founded in 1989 with the aim of specifying a model for the compression of moving images and soundtracks. The first model specifications were made as early as 1990.
SCORM (Shareable Content Object Reference Model)	SCORM is a recommendation developed by the ADL for the standardization of learning objects that should meet the following requirements: reusability, accessibility, durability, and interoperability (communication and data exchange between different systems). The SCORM specifications are intended to help deploy web-based learning content in different learning environments. Web-based LMS should thus be able to use, process, and exchange learning units independently of the system and platform. The work of IEEE and IMS Global Learning Consortium is incorporated into SCORM, among other things.
SGML (Standard Generalized Markup Language)	SGML is a definition system that is intended to help organize large amounts of documents. To this end, documents are given formatting instructions, which makes them easier to organize, structure, and assign. The structure of the documents is separated from their content appearance. Well-known derivatives of SGML are HTML and XML.
TCP/IP (Transmission Control Protocol/Internet Protocol)	TCP/IP is the basis of the network from which the internet is built. TCP delivers the data on the internet, while IP takes care of the transport.
XML (Extensible Markup Language)	A universal data format that separates formatting information from content, similar to the template system in Microsoft Word. This separation allows for easy content changes. With XML, all documents can be interconnected, making XML a kind of meta-language.
XSL (Extensible Stylesheet Language)	A stylesheet that provides formatting information for XML data (refer to "XML").

10.13 Questionnaire for the Target Group

Dear Colleagues,

You may already be aware that an eLearning program is being developed for the warranty contracts of our department store's electronics department. Our aim is to make the learning units as practical as possible. To achieve this, we need your assistance, specifically from your everyday sales experiences. Please take 10 minutes to answer the following questions briefly.

Thank you in advance!

What arguments do customers most frequently present when they decline a consultation you offer on a warranty contract? If possible, please specify the related product (for example, netbook, mobile phone, tablet PC, smartphone, etc.) in brackets.
Please list as many arguments as possible.

____.

____.

____.

What customer arguments most frequently result in not concluding a warranty contract during the consultation? If possible, please specify the related product in brackets.
Please list as many arguments as possible.

____.

____.

____.

When you realize that a customer might need a warranty contract and you want to convince them of a consultation, what arguments do you most often lack in this situation?

____.

____.

____.

What signals do you recognize that a customer might need a warranty contract (for example, asking about the hotline; it becomes apparent in the conversation that they are not particularly familiar with the product they want to purchase)? How do you proceed in practice?

____.

____.

____.

Is there anything else you would like to add on the topic of "consultation/signal recognition" (good tips for colleagues, obstacles, strategies, etc.)?

____

____

____

Thank you very much for your help! Your answers will be incorporated into the eLearning production.

Best regards,
Your eLearning Project Team

10.14 Target Group Analysis

See Table 10.13

Table 10.13 Target group analysis

Analysis Criteria	Characteristics of the Target Group
Size of the target group (number of end users of the eLearning application)	
Structure of the target group (homogeneous/heterogeneous in terms of age, gender, nationality, etc.)	
Age structure of the target group (for example, 30–40 years, 16–25 years)	
Percentage of women and men	
Occupation	
Position in the company (executives, experts, clerks, trainees, craftsmen, salespeople, etc.)	
Education level (school graduation, vocational training)	
Previous use of electronic learning applications (yes/no)	
Media competence (mastery of handling standard hardware and software as well as competence in dealing with common internet and interaction functions via computer or mobile devices)	
Place of learning (at home/workplace/on the move)	
Learning time (limited/unlimited)	
Integration into the educational concept (self-study or use combined with presence seminar)	
Prior knowledge of the learning content	
Expectations of the eLearning application	
Motivation (approval, rejection of the learning content to be conveyed or the introduction of eLearning; extrinsic/intrinsic)	

10.15 Page Design

Practical tips for screen design (Source: Reglin 2000, p. 103)
Minimise the size of graphic files as much as possible.
Especially on the start page(s), do not use elaborate graphics, Java applets, or animations with long loading times.
Avoid tying the navigation to large image maps.
If you use image maps for navigation, offer text links as an alternative.
If large documents need to be used for content reasons, link a "warning" to the user with the relevant link.
Avoid distracting movement on the screen, such as blinking texts.
Do not use background graphics that distract and make reading difficult.
Do not force the user to scroll horizontally.
Ensure good readability of the text. For example, the column width should be significantly less than the screen width.
Do not use excessively long text paragraphs without subdivision.
Use headings, subheadings, or small graphics to structure text.
Avoid using many different font sizes: This creates a restless image.
Do not use excessively long, confusing documents.

10.16 Rough Concept

See Table 10.14

Table 10.14 Rough Concept

Evaluation Criteria	Comment	Yes: Fulfilled	No: What is Missing?
The target group is precisely described.			
The rough learning objectives are clearly and precisely formulated.			
References to external learning objective catalogues (for example, examination catalogues) are listed.			
The necessary knowledge prerequisites for the learners are indicated.			
The contents were selected based on the learning objectives.			
The learning contents are comprehensively listed.			
The chosen teaching approach is thoroughly described and didactically justified.			
The navigation is visualised and explained.			
The navigation is in a meaningful context with the teaching approach.			
The navigation is intuitively comprehensible.			
The delivery of the content is adapted to the target group.			
The design is suitable for the target group and clear.			
The media to be used are completely listed.			
The leading figure is visualised.			
The functions and tasks of the leading figure are described.			
The character of the leading figure is clear.			
The description of the technical requirements is complete.			

10.17 Detailed Concept

See Table 10.15

Table 10.15 Detailed Concept

Test Criteria	Comment	Yes: Fulfilled	No: What is Missing?
The broad learning objectives are subdivided into detailed learning objectives.			
Taxonomy levels are assigned to the detailed learning objectives.			
The detailed learning objectives are clearly operationalized.			
The types of learning pages are listed in the quantity structure.			
The number of learning pages is determined in the quantity structure.			
The content is divided into lessons, learning units, and learning steps.			
The subdivisions are clearly delimited with a beginning and end.			
References to additional information sources are provided.			
The use of media is comprehensively listed and assigned to the individual learning pages.			

10.18 Image Composition

See Table 10.16

Table 10.16 Image composition. (Source: Edited according to Ballstaedt 1997, p. 267)

Evaluation Criteria	Comment	Yes: Fulfilled	No: What is Missing?
Is the function of the image unmistakably clear through its design?			
Does the perspective of the image correspond to the learning objective and the user's location?			
Are the representation conventions explicitly introduced and consistently used?			
Are the components of a visualization (boxes, bars, columns, arrows, etc.) clearly marked by linguistic or visual markers?			
Is the size of the image functionally appropriate for a global overview or a detailed evaluation?			
Are there no unnecessary or unnecessarily complex details in the image?			
Do the colors used have a didactic function?			
Is attention drawn to the important image details by graphic highlights?			
Is only one means of controlling attention consistently used?			
Are the objects, actions, events, or data arranged so that they are absorbed in the correct or desired order?			
Is there a clear organization of the visual field due to the effect of design factors?			
Are individual components of the image clearly recognizable and distinguishable?			

10.19 Feedback

See Table 10.17

Table 10.17 Feedback

Evaluation Criteria	Comment	Yes: Fulfilled	No: What is Missing?
Can the audio feedback be turned off?			
Does the feedback match the learner's response?			
Does the feedback help further, enabling the learner to shape their learning path accordingly?			
Does the feedback provide repetition recommendations?			
Is the feedback constructive, i.e., does it explain what was done incorrectly?			
Is the feedback differentiated, i.e., does it provide hints and food for thought instead of being stereotypical?			
Is the feedback adaptive, i.e., does it adapt to the learner's level of learning?			
Does the feedback establish a personal connection, for example, through encouragement, personal address, or confirmation?			
Is the feedback's wording positive and encouraging?			
Does the feedback take into account the number of solution attempts?			

10.20 Information Meeting Offer

See Table 10.18

Table 10.18 Information Meeting Offer

Questions for the Multimedia Agency	Notes
What number of learning hours is planned?	
Is there already a quantity structure, with the exact specification of the number and types of screen pages?	
If there is a quantity structure, how many screen pages are estimated per learning hour?	
Should the screen pages be pure information pages, i.e., relatively static?	
Should the screen pages be interactive, i.e., more like a film sequence?	
How many tasks are planned per learning hour?	
Should the tasks include differentiated feedback?	
What should the visualization look like (graphics, photos, animation, hand drawing)?	
Are learning objectives and content already given?	
How many days are estimated for the briefing?	
How many days are estimated for the script acceptance?	
Who will cover the travel expenses?	

References

Ballstaedt, Steffen-Peter (1997) Wissensvermittlung. Die Gestaltung von Lernmaterial. Weinheim: Beltz Verlagsgruppe.

Brönner, Andrea (2003) Planungsperspektive: Reflexionsfragen zur Zusammenstellung geeigneter Grundformen innerhalb eines eLearning-Arrangements. In: vbm – Verband der Bayerischen Metall- und Elektroindustrie (Hrsg.) Leitfaden E-Learning.

Patzak, Gerold & Günter Rattay (2017) Projektmanagement. Wien: Linde Verlag, 7. Auflage.

Reglin, Thomas (2000) Betriebliche Weiterbildung im Internet. Bielefeld: Bertelsmann Verlag.

Acknowledgements

Many people have contributed to shaping the book into the form in which it now lies before you. I have received great support from many sides, for which I would like to express my heartfelt thanks!

I am grateful to Prof. Dr. Frank Thissen from the Stuttgart Media University for the foreword he dedicated to this book.

Elke Kast from M.I.T e-Solutions GmbH in Friedrichsdorf has given the book its final touch through her constructive editing from the perspective of an experienced project manager.

I would like to thank Timo Rettig and Georg Engelhard from the Versicherungskammer Bayern in Munich for their competent input from the perspective of a client on script development.

I would like to thank Thomas Reglin from the Forschungsinstitut Betriebliche Bildung in Nuremberg for his patience and the active contribution of specialist literature.

I would like to thank Markus Millauer from Munich for his legal expertise, which ensured that even the chapters with legal questions could appear in the "right light".

I would like to thank my friends Klaus Kurz from Adobe Systems in Munich and Andrea Päusch from Unterschleißheim for the decisive evening in an Italian restaurant when I presented them with my book concept and they encouraged me to put this project into action. I cherish their encouragement and the good tip with Springer Verlag.

I am particularly grateful to Prof. Willie van Peer from Ludwig-Maximilians-University Munich for giving me the freedom to write my master's thesis in German as a foreign language on this topic, which was not very typical for the field in 1999, thus laying the foundation for my work as a media author many years ago.

Last but not least, I would like to express my deepest thanks to my editor, Mrs. Jutta-Maria Fleschutz from Springer Verlag in Heidelberg, who had the courage to start this project with me as a first-time author.

Working on the third edition of a book in the field of digital media after 16 years is almost comparable to writing a completely new book. Without the support of my wonderful family, this would not have been possible. So I would like to thank my two

D. Modlinger, *eLearning and Mobile Learning – Concept and Script*,
https://doi.org/10.1007/978-3-658-44695-6

daughters Emilia and Luzia, who showed a lot of understanding and patience with their very busy mom. For the active help and support, not least in taking care of the children during this time, I thank my mother Ingeborg Modlinger.

I would like to say a big thank you to Christian Ertl from the agency bildersprache in Munich for his patient moral support while working on the second edition.

I would like to thank Barbara Dexheimer from Regenstauf for her excellent editing, her accurate and fast work.

I would like to thank Sabine Kathke from Springer Vieweg for her almost infinite patience with the constant new delays in submitting the book manuscript and for her persuasive power to want to start the third edition with me.

My special thanks go to all the participants of the workshops over the last 20 years. Their creativity, ideas, and joy in their respective projects have inspired me again and again for the topic of eLearning. Many achievements of these intensive working days have flowed into the third edition of the book.

Glossary

Technical Terms

ADL—Advanced Distributed Learning Organization for the development of eLearning standards, which ensure the compatibility between learning content and learning platforms.

Advance Organizer An Advance Organizer is an element of text design placed before the main text. It provides an overview of the subsequent text content and is intended to make it easier for the reader to grasp and retain the text content. It is used primarily in educational texts, scientific works, andTechnical Documentation.

AICC—Aviation Industry CBT Committee International consortium of experts for the standardization of eLearning. For example, the AICC has made provisions for the exchange of data between WBTs and learning platforms.

Affective Attribution related to a person's emotions, attitudes, and values.

Animation An animation is the simulation of movements that can be created through a series of sequentially timed images, for example, on a color monitor. In computer graphics, animations can be generated in various ways.

App—Applet An applet or simply "App" is a small application program that is transmitted over the internet. A prerequisite for reading an app is a browser that can interpret the underlying Java code (see "Java").

Art Director Senior graphic designer or artistic director in an advertising agency, multimedia agency, film production, or similar media agency.

Authoring tool An authoring tool is a software that can be used to develop interactive multimedia applications (for example, an eLearning application) without needing to have in-depth programming knowledge.

AS—Application Sharing In Application Sharing, users mutually use software, data, or other elements as a joint work project on a single computer.

ASP—Application Service Providing Individual information and communication technology tasks are outsourced to an external service provider.

D. Modlinger, *eLearning and Mobile Learning – Concept and Script*,
https://doi.org/10.1007/978-3-658-44695-6

Basal text The term basal text refers to all teaching materials and texts that are intended to form the basis for eLearning concepts and later eLearning scripts. This could be, for example, a textbook, an information brochure, or a legal text.

Blended Learning Learning in media combination. Combination of online and presence learning phases, where various teaching materials are used, for example WBT (see "WBT"), textbook, flipchart.

Beta version The first operational version of a software that the manufacturer releases for testing purposes to identify possible errors.

User interface User-friendly representation of the essential control elements of system and program functions.

Browser A browser is a software with which one can navigate the World Wide Web. With a browser, HTML-formatted pages can be directly accessed.

Briefing A briefing is an instruction or situation discussion. It is the foundation for the agency's exposé and offer, as well as the further course of the project. Therefore, it should be carefully and thoroughly prepared and conducted.

CBT—Computer Based Training In contrast to WBT (see "WBT"), the training content in CBT is available offline, for example, from a CD-ROM.

CD—Corporate Design Distinctive sign or symbol systems belonging to a company's corporate design with high recognition value, such as trademarks or logos.

Cognitive Refers to the functions of the human brain such as thinking, perceiving, storing, and remembering.

Constructivist Learning Learning occurs by drawing one's own insights from the presentation of complex information and prior knowledge, that is, the learners construct their own knowledge.

CI—Corporate Identity Strategic concept for presenting a unified corporate identity internally and externally.

Cloud Term for a global network of servers, each performing its own function, such as: storing and managing data, running applications, streaming videos, providing web mail or software for office work or social media. All data can be accessed online from any internet-enabled device instead of just from the local or personal computer.

CMS—Content Management System Content is stored in a database and prepared in such a way that websites can be created, maintained, and modified without programming knowledge.

Didactics (greek) Didactics is the art of teaching. It describes the selection of appropriate strategies for conveying learning content.

Download The internet user copies files from a public server to their private hard drive.

Drag-and-drop The user can perform various actions on the virtual surface by moving graphical elements with the mouse or by hand, for example, in an exercise, assigning a selection of labels to the correct elements of a graphic.

Drill-and-Practice "Drill-and-Practice" refers to learning software that can be used to train certain skills through repeated exercises (such as basic arithmetic skills).

Expert system An expert system is a software that makes decisions using artificial intelligence and access to large databases. For example, medicine uses expert systems to make diagnoses.

Flowchart A flowchart is a graphical tool used to illustrate a process, for example, the sequence and affiliation of chapters within an eLearning application.

Flystick A Flystick is an input device for interacting with Virtual Reality (see "VR"). By operating a Flystick, one can navigate with optical systems. Together with intelligent infrared cameras, the user can move freely in VR without wiring.

Frame Technique that divides browser windows into different, independent, and scrollable areas. This is intended to keep even complex website structures (see "Site") clear and save loading times. Since only the content of a frame is exchanged, the result is a faster page construction.

HTML5 (Hypertext Markup Language) HTML is a computer language that is available in its fifth version with HTML5. It allows for the networking of texts and other content. It is primarily used on the Internet.

Hyperlink A hyperlink is a highlighted spot in electronic text (for example, through an icon, an underline, or a color) that is linked to further information (for example, text, graphics) on the World Wide Web. A hyperlink is activated by a mouse click and is comparable to the cross-reference in a lexicon, with the difference that you can jump directly to the linked spot with a click.

Hypermedia Works like hypertext (see "Hypertext"), but hypermedia also includes not only pure text but also tables, graphics, databases, sounds, videos, and the like.

Hypertext The term hypertext was coined by Vannevar Bush in 1945 and refers to an HTML formatted document that contains hyperlinks to other documents. Hypertext, unlike hypermedia, consists predominantly of text and presents non-sequential information.

Icon An icon is a small functional field, usually adorned with a pictogram. It is activated by a mouse click, thereby initiating a new function.

Influencer Individuals who frequently and regularly publish digital content, such as texts, images, audios, or videos, on a particular subject. The publication takes place via social media, such as Facebook, Instagram, YouTube, Snapchat, or X. When a person who is highly active on social media achieves a large reach among other users, they are referred to as an "Influencer".

Interactive Whiteboard Digital wall board in the classroom, which is connected to a computer. Nowadays, this is usually a large wall screen with a touch-sensitive surface (= touchscreen). The user can control the activities with a special pen or with their own fingers. Often, the interactive whiteboard is also referred to as a "Smartboard" (see "Smartboard").

Internet—International Network Worldwide connection of computer networks, such as the World Wide Web.

Intranet Computer network that enables communication for closed user groups.

ITS—Intelligent Tutorial System The computer takes on the role of the tutor and always has the current knowledge level of the student.

Incidental Learning Knowledge acquisition occurs incidentally in incidental learning, that is, during another (learning) process.

Java Java is a programming language that is primarily used for applications on the internet. Its particular advantage lies in its platform independence. A program written in Java can be executed on all computer platforms that have integrated a so-called "Java Virtual Machine".

JSP—Java Server Page JSP is an extension of Java (see "Java"), which allows the presentation and function of a website to be separated from each other.

Layout In the multimedia industry, the layout refers to the static representation of the user interface.

LMS—Learning Management System The LMS is a software that supports administrative functions, such as the registration of learners, the storage of learning progress, as well as the management of WBTs (see "WBT") and learning content (see "Learning platform").

Learning object Files that can be used or reused in technology-supported learning.

Learning platform Program for the management, organization, and retrieval of eLearning applications. A learning platform can also serve as a central interface between training providers and demanders. The terms learning environment or LMS (see "LMS") are often used synonymously.

LOM—Learning Objects Metadata The LOM is a recommendation for the standardization of learning objects (see Sect. 10.12).

Multimedia Multimedia information is available in various media types, such as text, graphics, or video.

Mind-Mapping Associations are written around a centrally arranged topic; all found association terms are connected with lines.

Navigation (lat. "course holding for ships", "steering"). In the multimedia industry, the term describes the concept of the manner of movement through multimedia content.

PHP—Hypertext Preprocessor Programming language that is based on an open-source script. PHP is primarily used on web servers.

Pitching Competitive presentation, to which at least two agencies are invited.

Plug-in An additional element for expanding the functions of a software, for example, the "Acrobat Reader" plug-in is used to be able to read PDF files.

Podcast Audio or video recording that can be provided by any user over the internet and can be played back with an MP3 or MPEG-4 capable media player.

Postproduction Postproduction refers to all the steps that serve the post-processing of film and television sequences, as well as photos and web applications.

Prototype (greek) A preliminary version of a later mass production or large-scale production. It is intended to give the client the opportunity to develop a (visual) idea of the final product or also to allow a testing of its properties.

Psychomotor Link between mental (psychic) and physical (motor) performances.

Pull-down menu A pull-down menu is activated by clicking on a small icon or highlighted short text with the mouse. A text then unfolds, displaying an explanation or offering additional functionalities, which can also be activated by mouse click.

Quantity scaffold A list of all pages that appear in an eLearning application, with details about the number and type of pages, for example, Advance Organizer, learning pages, information pages, interaction pages, exercise pages, summary pages, etc.

RGB Mixing of colors on a color monitor with the light colors red, green, and blue.

SCORM—Shareable Courseware Objects Reference Model eLearning standard that ensures compatibility between learning content and learning platforms (see Sect. 10.12).

Screen Screen or monitor. Often, individual screen pages are also referred to as a screen.

Server Central computer for managing and providing data and storage capacity for the users of a network.

Serif font Type of font that is provided with serifs. A serif is a small finishing stroke at the foot and head of the letters.

Site A site consolidates all the information that can be accessed via a web address. A site is composed of several web pages.

Smartboard (see "Interactive Whiteboard")

Specification Sheet In many large projects, a Specifiation Sheet is used. It describes precisely how and with what the contractor will implement the client's requirements.

Style Guide Design guidelines for the appearance and structure of products or websites, which concern, for example, color design, font type and size, navigation principle, and similar aspects.

Software Program that allows you to run certain applications on a computer, such as word processing, spreadsheet calculation, or image design.

Take A sequence of speech that is recorded in one piece.

Template Templates can be filled with individual content. For example, the document templates in Microsoft Office programs serve as a template.

Testimonial Well-known individuals ("celebrities") appear in the media with the aim of advertising a product. In doing so, they pretend to like using this product and consider it to be good.

Tonality Appropriate quality of word, image, and sound to best appeal to the target audience.

Tutor A tutor is an animated or simply graphically drawn companion who guides the learner through an eLearning application.

VR—Virtual Reality A virtual world or virtual reality is a three-dimensional illusionary reality generated by a computer, which the user can enter using a data suit, glove, or helmet. The data suit, glove, or helmet is electronically networked with the computer. It is worn over the user's body and serves as a haptic interface to the virtual world.

WBT—Web Based Training In WBT, the learning content is available online on the Internet or Intranet. This results in advantages such as worldwide access and easy updating.

Weblog A publicly accessible website, usually by a single author, with diary-like listed posts on various topics. Often, weblogs are good sources of information for finding further links and cross-references on a subject area.

Website See "Site".

Whiteboard The whiteboard is an advancement of the classic school blackboard. It has a smooth surface, usually made of white plastic or white enameled metal sheet, on which one writes with special felt-tip pens (board markers). As with the school blackboard, the writing can be easily wiped off. On metal surfaces, magnets can also be attached.

WWW—World Wide Web The WWW is a worldwide, platform-independent multimedia network, which can be accessed via the Internet (see "Internet") and is based on Hypertext (see "Hypertext"). It has a graphical user interface and multimedia data. It has been publicly available since 1992.

WYSIWYG—what you see is what you get The display between screen view and final product is identical.

Abbreviations of the Multimedia World

Acrobat Reader Free plug-in from Adobe for displaying PDF files (see Sect.9.2.1).

AVI—Audio Video Interleaved Standard format for video playback under Windows.

BMP—Bitmap Standard bitmap graphics format under Windows.

DOC—Document Files of the Microsoft Word text processing program.

GIF—Graphics Interchange Format A graphic format frequently used on the internet so far. GIF files have high quality while simultaneously requiring little storage space.

HTML5 (Eng.: Hypertext Markup Language) HTML is a computer language that is available in its fifth version with HTML5. It allows for the networking of texts and other content. It is mainly used on the Internet.

JPG/JPEG A raster graphics format developed by the Joint Photographic Experts Group. Due to the compression, it requires only a small amount of storage capacity, however, the image loses quality or sharpness. JPG files are particularly suitable for posting photos online.

MPG/MPEG Format developed by the Moving Picture Experts Group for digitally compressed audio and video files.

MP3 Format for digitally compressed audio files developed by the Moving Picture Experts Group Layer 3, which require only a small storage capacity despite high quality. As of 2017, MP3 is available patent-free.

PDF—Portable Document Format File format for displaying images and graphics with the Adobe Acrobat Reader program. PDF presents images and texts in high quality with low storage capacity.

PNG—Portable Networks Graphics Graphic format that compresses data without loss. On the internet, it is the most commonly used graphic format.

PPT—Powerpoint File format of the identically named presentation program by Microsoft.

PSD—Photoshop File File format of the professional image editing software Adobe Photoshop.

RA—Real Audio Audio format from RealMedia, which the program Real Player (see "Realplayer") plays.

Realplayer Program from RealNetworks that plays video and audio files; also referred to as 'media player".

RTF—Rich Text Format Text file that can be exchanged between different programs and operating systems.

SIT—StuffIt Compressed file that can contain various file formats (for example DOC, XLSE, AVI) and is unpacked with the StuffIt program.

TIF/TIFF—Tagged Image File Format Graphic file format with high quality and therefore very large image files.

TXT Abbreviation for "Text": Text files that have little formatting options, but high compatibility. Common file format on the internet, as it is important for the cross-system exchange of data.

WAV WAV files were developed by Microsoft. They contain information about the format of the audio data and the audio data itself. Consequently, WAV files are used for playback and editing of audio material. Accordingly, WAV is a relatively large audio format.

Windows Media Player Standard program in the Windows operating system that plays audio and video files; also referred to as "media player".

XLSX File format of the spreadsheet program MS Excel from Microsoft.

ZIP Compressed file that can contain various file formats (for example DOC, XLSE, AVI) and is unpacked with the WinZip program.

Further Reading

eLearning

Back, Andrea (2001) E-Learning im Unternehmen. Zürich: Orell Füssli Verlag.

Bendel, Oliver & Stefanie Hauske (2004) E-Learning: Das Wörterbuch. Aarau: Sauerländer Verlag.

Ballstaedt, Steffen-Peter (1997) Wissensvermittlung. Weinheim: Beltz Verlag.

Ballstaedt, Steffen-Peter (2012) Visualisieren. Konstanz: UVK Verlagsgesellschaft mbH.

Baumgartner, Peter et al. (2002) Auswahl von Lernplattformen. Innsbruck: StudienVerlag.

Bloom, Benjamin et al. (1976) Taxonomie von Lernzielen im kognitiven Bereich. Weinheim: Beltz Verlag, 5. Auflage.

Bohinc, Tomas (2009) Grundlagen des Projektmanagements: Methoden, Techniken und Tools für Projektleiter. Offenbach: Gabal Verlag.

Brönner, Andrea (2003) Planungsperspektive: Reflexionsfragen zur Zusammenstellung geeigneter Grundformen innerhalb eines eLearning-Arrangements. In: vbm –Verband der Bayerischen Metall- und Elektroindustrie (Hrsg.) Leitfaden E-Learning.

Buzan, Tony (2013) Das Mind-Map-Buch. München: mvg Verlag.

Dittler, Ulrich (2011) E-Learning – Einsatzkonzepte und Erfolgsfaktoren des Lernens mit interaktiven Medien. München: De Gruyter, Oldenbourg Verlag, 3. überarb. und erw. Auflage.

Edwards, Betty (2017) Das neue Garantiert zeichnen lernen. Reinbek: Rowohlt Taschenbuch Verlag, 17. Auflage.

Fietz, Gabriele et al. (2004) eLearning für internationale Märkte. Bielefeld: Bertelsmann Verlag.

Fries, Christian (2016) Grundlagen der Mediengestaltung. München: Hanser Verlag, 5. Auflage, neu bearbeitet.

Häfele, Hartmut & Kornelia Maier-Häfele (2016) 101 e-Learning Seminarmethoden. Methoden und Strategien für die Online-und Blended-Learning Seminarpraxis. Bonn: managerSeminare Verlag, 6. Auflage.

Hasebrook, Joachim (1998) Multimedia-Psychologie. Heidelberg: Spektrum Akademischer Verlag.

Kerres, Michael (1999) Didaktische Konzeption multimedialer und telemedialer Lernumgebungen. In: HMD Praxis der Wirtschaftsinformatik, Heft 205: Multimediale Bildungssysteme, Heidelberg, S. 9–21.

Kerres, Michael (2018) Mediendidaktik: Konzeption und Entwicklung digitaler Lernangebote. München: De Gruyter, Oldenbourg Verlag, 5. vollständig überarbeitete Auflage.

D. Modlinger, *eLearning and Mobile Learning – Concept and Script*,
https://doi.org/10.1007/978-3-658-44695-6

Kerres, Michael et al. (2002) E-Learning. Didaktische Konzepte für erfolgreiches Lernen. In: von Schwuchow, Karlheinz & Joachim Guttmann (Hrsg.) Jahrbuch Personalentwicklung & Weiterbildung 2003. Köln: Luchterhand.

Mandl, Heinz & Katrin Winkler (2001) Online-Studium – Neue Formen des Lehrens und Lernens. In: VdS Bildungsmedien e. V. (Hrsg.) Werkstatt Multimedia, S. 17–23.

Mayer, Horst Otto & Dietmar Treichel (2004) Handlungsorientiertes Lernen und eLearning. München: De Gruyter, Oldenbourg Verlag.

Meyer, Elke & Stefanie Widmann (2014) Flipchart ART, Erlangen: Publicis, 4. Auflage.

Muir, Nancy (2013) Microsoft Project 2013 für Dummies. Weinheim: Wiley-VCH Verlag.

Niegemann, Helmut et al. (2008) Kompendium multimediales Lernen. Heidelberg: Springer.

PAS 1032-1, -2 (2004) Aus- und Weiterbildung unter besonderer Berücksichtigung von e-Learning – Teil 1: Referenzmodell für Qualitätsmanagement und Qualitätssicherung – Planung, Entwicklung, Durchführung und Evaluation von Bildungsprozessen und Bildungsangeboten – Teil 2: Didaktisches Objektmodell; Modellierung und Beschreibung didaktischer Szenarien, siehe:http://www.beuth.de.

Reglin, Thomas (2000) Betriebliche Weiterbildung im Internet. Bielefeld: Bertelsmann Verlag.

Reinmann-Rothmeier, Gabriele & Heinz Mandl (2001) Virtuelle Seminare in Hochschule und Weiterbildung. Drei Beispiele aus der Praxis. Bern: Huber Verlag.

Rey, Günter Daniel (2009) E-Learning. Wien: Hans Huber Verlag.

Rietsch, Petra (1997) Multimedia-Anwendungen. Wien: Wirtschaftsverlag Carl Ueberreuter.

Rinn, Ulrike & Dorothee M. Meister (2004) Didaktik und neue Medien. Münster: Waxmann Verlag.

Riser, Urs et al. (2002) Konzeption und Entwicklung interaktiver Lernprogramme. Berlin: Springer- Verlag.

Schulmeister, Rolf (2005) Lernplattformen für das virtuelle Lernen. München: Oldenbourg Verlag.

Weidenmann, Bernd (1994) Wissenserwerb mit Bildern. Bern: Huber Verlag.

Wurman, Richard Saul (1996) Information Architects. Berkeley, CA/USA: Gingko Press.

Mobile Learning

Aichele, Christian & Marius Schönberger (2016) App-Entwicklung – effizient und erfolgreich. Wiesbaden: Springer Vieweg.

Bachmair, Ben (2009) Medienwissen für Pädagogen. Medienbildung in riskanten Erlebniswelten. Wiesbaden: Verlag für Sozialwissenschaften.

Beranek, Angelika & Simon Zwick (2015) Actionbound – laufend lernen. In: Friedrich, Katja et al. (Hrsg.).: smart und mobil, München: kopaed, S. 217–228.

Buchem, Ilona (2015) Mobiles Lernen und die Ent-/Didaktisierung der Lernräume. In: Friedrich, Katja et al. (Hrsg.): smart und mobil, München: kopaed, S. 43–61.

De Witt, Claudia & Christina Gloerfeld (Hrsg.) Handbuch Mobile Learning, 2018. Heidelberg, Dordrecht, London, New York: Springer.

Dittler, Ullrich (2017) Die 4. Welle des E-Learning: Mobile, smarte und soziale Medien erobern den Alltag und verändern die Lernwelt. In: Dittler, Ullrich (Hrsg.) E-Learning 4.0. Berlin, Boston: Walter de Gruyter Oldenbourg, S. 43–67.

Dittler, Ullrich (Hrsg.) E-Learning 4.0 2017. Berlin, Boston: Walter de Gruyter Oldenbourg.

Fatke, Reinhard & Hans Merkens (Hrsg.) Bildung über die Lebenszeit, 2006. Wiesbaden: Verlag für Sozialwissenschaften.

Friedrich, Katja et al. (Hrsg.) smart und mobil. Digitale Kommunikation als Herausforderung für Bildung, Pädagogik und Politik, 2015. München: kopaed.
Gatterer, Christian (2013) Mobile learning – Smartphones im Unterricht. Saarbrücken: Akademie Verlag (jetzt: Walter de Gruyter, Berlin).
Kerres, Michael & Claudia de Witt (2006) Perspektiven der „Medienbildung". In: Fatke, Reinhard & Hans Merkens (Hrsg.) Bildung über die Lebenszeit, 2006. Wiesbaden: Verlag für Sozialwissenschaften, S. 209–220.
Linnhoff-Popien, Claudia & Stephan Verclas (2012) Mit Business-Apps ins Zeitalter mobiler Geschäftsprozesse. In: Linnhoff-Popien, Claudia & Stephan Verclas (Hrsg.) Smart Mobile Apps. Heidelberg, Dordrecht, London, New York: Springer, S. 3–16.
Linnhoff-Popien, Claudia & Stephan Verclas (Hrsg.) Smart Mobile Apps, 2012. Heidelberg, Dordrecht, London, New York: Springer.
Mitschian, Haymo (2010) m-Learning – die neue Welle? Mobiles Lernen für Deutsch als Fremdsprache. Kassel: university press.
Riesenbeck, Wilke (2017) Betriebliche Aus- und Weiterbildung 4.0. In: Dittler, Ullrich (Hrsg.) E-Learning 4.0. Berlin, Boston: Walter de Gruyter Oldenbourg, S. 172–189.
Roth, Jörg (2005) Mobile Computing. Grundlagen, Technik, Konzepte. Heidelberg: dpunkt.verlag, 2. aktualisierte Auflage.
Tremp, Hansruedi, Tobias Bruderer und Daniel Hess (2017): Mobile und Distributed Computing. Norderstedt: BoD.
Schumacher, Gerd & Bianca Wode (2017) Praxisbeispiel: Deutsche Bahn. In: Dittler, Ullrich (Hrsg.) E-Learning 4.0. Berlin, Boston: Walter de Gruyter Oldenbourg, S. 190–208.

Project Management

Back, Louis & Stefan Beuttler (2006) Handbuch Briefing. Stuttgart: Schäffer-Poeschel Verlag, 2. Auflage.
Fisher, Roger et al. (2013) Das Harvard-Konzept, Frankfurt a. M.: Campus, 24. Auflage.
Kellner, Hedwig (2003) Projektmeetings professionell und effizient. München: Hanser Verlag.
Kellner, Hedwig (2003) Projekt-Mitarbeiter finden und führen. München: Hanser Verlag.
Kellner, Hedwig (2003) Zeitmanagement im Projekt. München: Hanser Verlag.
Malik, Fredmund (2019) Führen, Leisten, Leben: Wirksames Management für eine neue Welt. Frankfurt: Campus Verlag.
Patzak, Gerold & Günter Rattay (2017) Projektmanagement. Wien: Linde Verlag, 7. aktualisierte Auflage.
Tiemeyer, Ernst (2018) Handbuch IT-Projektmanagement. München: Hanser Verlag, 3. überarbeitete Auflage.

Fees and Contracts

Dellingshausen, Christoph von (2004) dmmv-Kalkulationssystematik – Leitfaden zur Kalkulation von Multimedia-Projekten. München: Hightext Verlag.
Hightext Verlag (2015) iBusiness Honorarleitfaden. München: Hightext Verlag.
Ostermaier, Christian (2015) Der Freie-Mitarbeiter-Vertrag. Walhalla u. Praetoria Verlag.

Trautmann, Arne (2011) iBusiness-AGB-Leitfaden: allgemeine Geschäftsbedingungen für Agenturen, Dienstleister und Freiberufler, München: Hightext Verlag.
Weyers, Dorle (2004) Kopfarbeit kalkulieren und verkaufen. Münster: ImPrint Verlag; Bezug via:https://shop.digitalcourage.de/broschuere-kopfarbeit-kalkulieren-verkaufen.html.
Wüfling, Thomas & Ulrich Dieckert (2002) Praxishandbuch Multimediarecht, Heidelberg: Springer-Verlag.

Writing Workshop

Duden (2019) Band 8: Das Synonymwörterbuch. Mannheim: Dudenverlag, 7. aktualisierte und erweiterte Auflage.
Guderian, Claudia (2008) Arbeitsblockaden erfolgreich überwinden. München: mvg Verlag.
Immler, Christian (2016) Das große Computer-Lexikon XXXL. München: Markt+Technik Verlag.
Langer, Inghard & Friedemann Schulz von Thun & Reinhard Tausch (2019) Sich verständlich ausdrücken. München: Reinhardt Verlag, 11. Auflage.
Neumann, Peter (2012) Handbuch der Markt- und Werbepsychologie. Bern: Huber Verlag.
Märtin, Doris (2019) Erfolgreich texten! Frankfurt a. M.: Bramann Verlag.
Schneider, Wolf (2006) Deutsch! Das Handbuch für attraktive Texte. Reinbek: Rowohlt Taschenbuch Verlag.
Schulz von Thun, Friedemann (2019) Miteinander reden 1–4. Reinbek: Rowohlt Taschenbuch Verlag, 1. Auflage, Sonderausgabe.

Printed by Printforce, the Netherlands